scikit-learn Cookbook

Over 80 recipes for machine learning in Python with scikit-learn

John Sukup

‹packt›

scikit-learn Cookbook

Portfolio Director: Sunith Shetty
Relationship Lead: Sanjana Gupta
Project Manager: Shashank Desai
Content Engineer: Nathanya Dias
Technical Editor: Seemanjay Ameriya
Copy Editor: Safis Editing
Indexer: Rekha Nair
Proofreader: Nathanya Dias
Production Designer: Prashant Ghare
Growth Lead: Bhavesh Amin

First published: November 2014
Second edition: November 2017
Third edition: December 2025
Production reference: 1141125

Published by Packt Publishing Ltd.
Grosvenor House
11 St Paul's Square
Birmingham
B3 1RB, UK.

ISBN 978-1-83664-445-3
www.packtpub.com

Contributors

About the author

John Sukup has been a data professional for 18 years. His experience of working with data spans from consumer market research to data science to ML and AI. He has over a decade of experience as an AI/ML cloud engineer and consultant at multiple international organizations, including Levi Strauss, Cisco, Anaconda, and Ipsos. He has acted as the lead professional trainer for Fortune 100 organizations and has been featured in *Forbes*, *Oracle*, and *Data Science Central*. He currently acts as managing director and founder at Expected X, a digital application prototyping and market validation organization, as well as cohost of the Unriveted podcast with his colleague, Martin Miller.

About the reviewers

Oleg Okhun is an experienced data scientist and manager with more than 35 years of professional experience in academia and industry under his belt. He has worked in several countries, including his home country, Belarus, as well as Finland, Sweden, and Germany. His professional focus ranges from bioinformatics and biometrics, online and offline marketing, to microfinance and renewable energy analytics. He also taught at the University of Oulu, Finland, and advised several BSc, MSc, and PhD students in Finland and Germany.

I would like to thank Nathanya Dias from Packt for the fruitful collaboration and opinion exchange during the review process.

I dedicate this work to my son, who just started his studies in one of the oldest Swedish universities.

Sahir Maharaj is a lead data scientist and South Africa's first Kaggle Grandmaster, recognized globally for his expertise. He is a prolific content creator on LinkedIn, where his insights on leadership and personal growth have inspired millions.

Sahir has designed and deployed end-to-end AI solutions at some of the world's leading brands, including BMW, Volkswagen, Audi, Old Mutual, and S2W Media. He is a Microsoft Super User and subject matter expert for Coursera programs on Power BI, Copilot, and generative AI. As a mentor, Sahir has led 900+ sessions on Topmate.io, helping professionals worldwide grow their careers.

He coined and lives by the following quote:

A mind in motion becomes a life in motion.

Special thanks to God, and my mum, dad, and brother.

Table of Contents

1

2

5

Linear Models and Regularization   93

6

Advanced Logistic Regression and Extensions   123

7

Support Vector Machines and Kernel Methods   157

8

Tree-Based Algorithms and Ensemble Methods   187

9

Text Processing and Multiclass Classification   213

10

Clustering Techniques   253

11

Novelty and Outlier Detection   279

13

Deploying scikit-learn Models in Production   331

14

Preface

Although the technology world today is all abuzz about **artificial intelligence** (**AI**) and the **large language models** (**LLMs**) that power them, **machine learning** (**ML**) is still providing value to businesses through predictive modeling and prescriptive analytics. So many systems today are powered by ML on the backend that most people would be surprised to learn how often businesses employ such techniques to refine their marketing strategy, upsell and improve product placement, and customize user experiences, among other applications.

While countless tools and software exist today to enable ML applications, one tool has become the backbone of both hobbyists and enterprises alike: **scikit-learn**. It's hard to believe that scikit-learn v0.1 debuted over 15 years ago in January 2010, yet even after all that time and all the changes and advancements in ML and AI, it still holds its place as one of the foremost Python libraries for both AI/ML.

scikit-learn is a powerful, open source ML library for Python that provides simple and efficient tools for data mining and data analysis, built on top of NumPy, SciPy, and Matplotlib. It offers a versatile, user-friendly framework for implementing a wide range of ML algorithms, enabling efficient development and deployment of predictive models in real-world applications.

This book is devoted to scikit-learn v1.5. It takes you on a journey from understanding the fundamentals of ML and data preprocessing, through implementing advanced algorithms and techniques, to deploying and optimizing ML models in production. Along the way, you will explore practical, step-by-step recipes that cover everything from feature engineering and model selection to hyperparameter tuning and model evaluation, all using scikit-learn 1.5.

Finally, every chapter contains examples designed to give you an opportunity to apply the chapter's learning through coding exercises.

Who this book is for

This book is for data scientists and ML professionals looking to deepen their understanding of advanced ML techniques. Additionally, software engineers and developers who want to implement sophisticated ML models in their applications can benefit equally.

What this book covers

Chapter 1, Common Conventions and API Elements of scikit-learn, covers the standard conventions and core API elements of scikit-learn, including the design principles behind estimators, transformers, and pipelines, as well as common methods such as `fit()`, `predict()`, and `transform()`.

Chapter 2, Pre-Model Workflow and Data Preprocessing, covers preprocessing tools and techniques, including enhanced data transformers and feature engineering methods.

Chapter 3, Dimensionality Reduction Techniques, includes updated approaches for dimensionality reduction with new algorithms and improvements in scikit-learn.

Chapter 4, Building Models with Distance Metrics and Nearest Neighbors, includes updates on the latest developments in distance metric-based models.

Chapter 5, Linear Models and Regularization, covers the linear models and regularization techniques that are now available.

Chapter 6, Advanced Logistic Regression and Extensions, explores the latest advancements in logistic regression and its extensions.

Chapter 7, Support Vector Machines and Kernel Methods, covers features and optimizations in SVMs and kernel methods.

Chapter 8, Tree-Based Algorithms and Ensemble Methods, includes the latest improvements and new ensemble techniques.

Chapter 9, Text Processing and Multiclass Classification, covers new text vectorization methods and multiclass classification strategies.

Chapter 10, Clustering Techniques, explores unsupervised learning techniques for finding naturally occurring groupings of similar data points.

Chapter 11, Novelty and Outlier Detection, covers techniques for finding inlier and outlier data points in training datasets.

Chapter 12, Cross-Validation and Model Evaluation Techniques, covers cross-validation strategies, scoring methods, and model evaluation tools.

Chapter 13, Deploying scikit-learn Models in Production, includes tools and best practices for deploying scikit-learn models in production environments, with a focus on scalability and maintainability.

To get the most out of this book

This book is designed to provide basic examples of the most important features of scikit-learn v1.5. In order to maximize the effectiveness of your learning, in addition to completing the exercises in each chapter, we encourage you to try your own examples and explore additional function arguments beyond those presented. Additionally, combining your learning from different chapters is an effective way to coalesce your scikit-learning understanding holistically.

Software/hardware covered in the book	OS requirements
scikit-learn v1.5 or greater	
Git >=2.46.x	Windows, macOS X, and Linux (any)
Python >=3.9.x	

Each chapter reminds you of the GitHub repository where example code is stored and how to install it locally.

Installing Python libraries in virtual environments with requirements.txt

Installing Python packages from a `requirements.txt` file is a common practice for managing project dependencies. Here's a step-by-step guide:

1. Navigate to your `project` directory.

2. Open your Terminal or Command Prompt and navigate to the root directory of your Python project, where the `requirements.txt` file is located:

   ```
   cd /path/to/your/project
   ```

3. Using a virtual environment isolates your project's dependencies from other Python projects on your system, preventing conflicts. Next, create the virtual environment:

   ```
   python -m venv venv_name
   ```

   (Replace venv_name with your desired name for the virtual environment, e.g., `venv` or `scikitlearncookbook`.)

4. Activate the virtual environment:

   - On macOS/Linux, use the following:

   ```
   source venv_name/bin/activate
   ```

   - On Windows, use this:

   ```
   venv_name\Scripts\activate
   ```

Installing the packages

With your virtual environment activated (if you created one), use `pip` to install the packages listed in `requirements.txt`:

```
pip install -r requirements.txt
```

If you are not using a virtual environment or need to specify a particular Python executable, you might use `pip3` instead of `pip`.

Verifying installation (optional)

You can verify that the packages are installed by running the following:

```
pip list
```

This command will list all the installed packages in your current environment, including those from `requirements.txt`.

When you are finished working on the project, you can deactivate the virtual environment:

```
deactivate
```

If you are using the digital version of this book, we advise you to type the code yourself or access the code via the GitHub repository (link available in the next section). Doing so will help you avoid any potential errors related to the copying and pasting of code.

Download the example code files

The code bundle for the book is hosted on GitHub at `https://github.com/PacktPublishing/scikit-learn-Cookbook-Third-Edition`.

We also have other code bundles from our rich catalog of books and videos available at `https://github.com/PacktPublishing`. Check them out!

Conventions used

There are a number of text conventions used throughout this book.

`CodeInText`: Indicates code words in text, database table names, folder names, filenames, file extensions, pathnames, dummy URLs, user input, and X/Twitter handles. For example: "Load `KNeighborsClassifier` from `sklearn.neighbors`."

A block of code is set as follows:

```
from sklearn.model_selection import learning_curve
from sklearn.metrics import confusion_matrix
import seaborn as sns
```

Bold: Indicates a new term, an important word, or words that you see on the screen. For instance, words in menus or dialog boxes appear in the text like this. For example: "Our single decision tree reported an accuracy of **0.867**, while our random forest's accuracy is **0.911**."

> **Tips or important notes**
> Appear like this.

Get in touch

Feedback from our readers is always welcome.

General feedback: If you have questions about any aspect of this book or have any general feedback, please email us at customercare@packt.com and mention the book's title in the subject of your message.

Errata: Although we have taken every care to ensure the accuracy of our content, mistakes do happen. If you have found a mistake in this book, we would be grateful if you reported this to us. Please visit http://www.packt.com/submit-errata, click **Submit Errata**, and fill in the form.

Piracy: If you come across any illegal copies of our works in any form on the internet, we would be grateful if you would provide us with the location address or website name. Please contact us at copyright@packt.com with a link to the material.

If you are interested in becoming an author: If there is a topic that you have expertise in and you are interested in either writing or contributing to a book, please visit http://authors.packt.com/.

Share Your Thoughts

Once you've read *scikit-learn Cookbook*, we'd love to hear your thoughts! Scan the QR code below to go straight to the Amazon review page for this book and share your feedback.

https://packt.link/r/1-836-64445-0

Your review is important to us and the tech community and will help us make sure we're delivering excellent quality content.

Free Benefits with Your Book

This book comes with free benefits to support your learning. Activate them now for instant access (see the "*How to Unlock*" section for instructions).

Here's a quick overview of what you can instantly unlock with your purchase:

PDF and ePub Copies   **Next-Gen Web-Based Reader**

Free PDF and ePub versions   **Next-Gen Reader**

Access a DRM-free PDF copy of this book to read anywhere, on any device.

Use a DRM-free ePub version with your favorite e-reader.

Multi-device progress sync: Pick up where you left off, on any device.

Highlighting and notetaking: Capture ideas and turn reading into lasting knowledge.

Bookmarking: Save and revisit key sections whenever you need them.

Dark mode: Reduce eye strain by switching to dark or sepia themes

How to Unlock

UNLOCK NOW

Scan the QR code (or go to `packtpub.com/unlock`). Search for this book by name, confirm the edition, and then follow the steps on the page.

Note: Keep your invoice handy. Purchases made directly from Packt don't require an invoice.

1

Common Conventions and API Elements of scikit-learn

It's hard to believe that the scikit-learn project started back in 2007 and officially launched in 2009. Even after so many years, it is hard to deny the impact the Python library has had on the world of data science and **machine learning (ML)**. For many of us, scikit-learn is one of the first libraries we hear about when we begin our journey in ML programming and engineering—and that hasn't changed, with the library being one of the most widely used in research, academia, and production applications at scale in the business world.

This chapter will cover the standard conventions and core API elements of scikit-learn, including the design principles behind estimators, transformers, and pipelines, as well as common methods such as `fit()`, `predict()`, and `transform()`. The exercises provided throughout the rest of this book will involve using these conventions to build and evaluate models, all while focusing on understanding the consistent structure of scikit-learn's API to enhance usability and flexibility in ML projects.

In this chapter, we're going to cover the following recipes:

- Introduction to scikit-learn's design philosophy
- Understanding estimators
- Transformers and the `transform()` method
- Handling custom estimators and transformers
- Pipelines and workflow automation
- Common attributes and methods
- Hyperparameter tuning with search methods
- Working with metadata: Tags and more
- Best practices for API usage

> **Free Benefits with Your Book**
>
> Your purchase includes a free PDF copy of this book along with other exclusive benefits. Check the *Free Benefits with Your Book* section in the Preface to unlock them instantly and maximize your learning experience.

Technical requirements

This chapter does not have any technical requirements. If you're more seasoned in scikit-learn, feel free to jump forward to *Chapter 2* to get started right away.

Introduction to scikit-learn's design philosophy

scikit-learn's design is centered around a few core principles: consistency, simplicity, modularity, and reusability. At its foundation, scikit-learn offers a unified interface for a broad range of ML algorithms, where most models follow a similar pattern: they use `fit()` to train the model, `predict()` to make predictions, and `transform()` to manipulate data. This consistency allows users to easily switch between models, improving productivity and reducing the learning curve.

Additionally, scikit-learn is designed to be modular, meaning individual components such as estimators, transformers, and pipelines can be combined and reused across different tasks. This modularity enables users to build complex workflows by chaining these components together, while maintaining flexibility and readability in their code. It's also a great way to save time as a developer via software reuse!

For example, data preprocessing steps such as scaling and encoding can be integrated directly into the modeling process using scikit-learn's `Pipeline()` class. The ability to encapsulate preprocessing and modeling into a single object makes workflows not only more efficient but also easily reproducible. This is fairly important today, considering the reduced timelines many businesses enforce on their developers' output. Moreover, this design ensures that scikit-learn can be easily extended—advanced users can create custom transformers or estimators that conform to scikit-learn's interface and fit effortlessly into the broader ecosystem of their organization's use cases.

> **Proper capitalization of scikit-learn**
>
> You may have noticed that *scikit-learn* is always lowercase and never capitalized. This is not a mistake and is the intended spelling by the original project authors. The correct pronunciation is *sy-kit*, with *sci* being an abbreviation for the word *science*. So, you can think of the library as a *(data) science kit*.

Understanding estimators

So, what exactly is an **estimator** anyway? The concept of estimators lies at the heart of scikit-learn. Estimators are objects (in the sense of Python's **Object-Oriented Programming** (**OOP**)) that implement algorithms for learning from data and are consistent across the entire library. Every estimator in scikit-learn, whether a model or a transformer, follows a simple and intuitive interface. The two most essential methods of any estimator are `fit()` and `predict()`, both of which were mentioned previously. The `fit()` method trains the model by learning from data, while `predict()` is used to make predictions on new data based on the trained model. This is the raison d'être of ML.

For example, in one of the simplest—yet often most powerful—ML models, `LinearRegression()`, calling `fit()` with training data allows the model to learn the optimal coefficients for predicting outcomes. Afterward, `predict()` can be used on new data to generate predictions:

```
from sklearn.linear_model import LinearRegression
import numpy as np

# Example data
X = np.array([[1], [2], [3], [4], [5]])  # Feature matrix
y = np.array([1, 2, 3, 3.5, 5])  # Target values

# Create and fit the model
model = LinearRegression()
model.fit(X, y)

# Predict values for new data
X_new = np.array([[6], [7]])
predictions = model.predict(X_new)
print(predictions)

# Output:
[5.75, 6.7]
```

The library also provides a nice *shortcut* method, `fit_predict()`, that combines these operations into a single API call—a very useful tool! Now, there is a reason why scikit-learn has both the `fit()` and `predict()` methods separate, as well as `fit_predict()`. Typically, the `fit_predict()` method is applied when you want to obtain predictions within the same dataset the model was trained on. This is often the case in unsupervised learning. An example of this can be seen here regarding KMeans, where our data does not contain a target variable we are trying to predict in the training data. In supervised learning scenarios where we do have a target, the `fit()` method would be applied to the training data, and the `predict()` method would be applied to our holdout dataset.

This is not to say you *can't* use `fit_predict()` in unsupervised learning scenarios. Datasets can still be split into training, validation, and testing sets:

```
# Fit_predict is not used in LinearRegression,
# but as an example for clustering:
from sklearn.cluster import KMeans

# Example data
X = np.array([[1], [2], [3], [4], [5]])

# KMeans Clustering example
kmeans = KMeans(n_clusters=2)
labels = kmeans.fit_predict(X)
print(labels)

# Output:
[0,0,0,1,1]
```

scikit-learn's design ensures that whether you are working with simple linear regression or more complex algorithms such as random forests, the pattern remains the same, promoting consistency and ease of use.

Throughout this book, we will explore various estimators, including `LinearRegression()` (*Chapter 5*), `DecisionTreeClassifier()` (*Chapter 8*), and `KNeighborsClassifier()` (*Chapter 4*), while demonstrating how to use them to train models, evaluate performance, and make predictions, all using the familiar `fit()` and `predict()` structure.

Transformers and the transform() method

In scikit-learn, **transformers** are tools that modify data by applying transformations such as scaling, normalization, or encoding to prepare it for modeling. Each transformer follows a consistent interface, using the `fit()` method to learn any necessary parameters from the data and the `transform()` method to apply those transformations. For instance, `StandardScaler()` calculates the mean and standard deviation during `fit()` and uses those values to transform the data by scaling it (as you may recall from high school statistics, this transformed value is called a z-score).

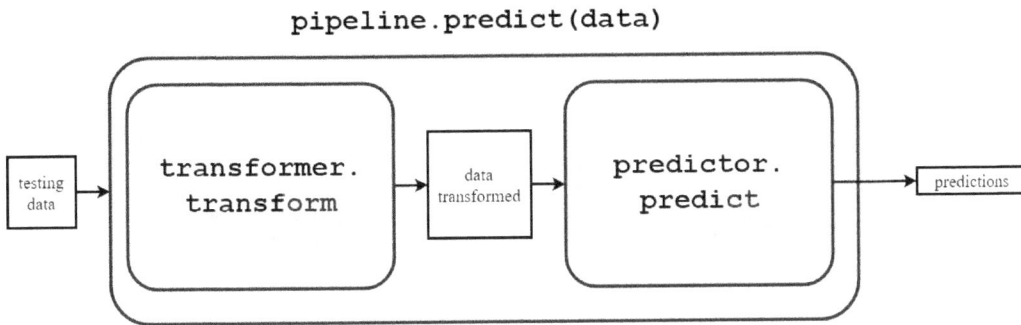

Figure 1.1 – Data transformation in the context of scikit-learn's Pipeline() class

Data transformations provide several benefits when applied to ML scenarios. First, many models presuppose data to be normally distributed, free of outliers, and so on. Second, most real-world datasets do not come in this neat-and-tidy format and require some massaging before modeling occurs:

```
from sklearn.preprocessing import StandardScaler
import numpy as np

# Example data
X = np.array([[1, 2], [3, 4], [5, 6]])

# Create a StandardScaler instance
scaler = StandardScaler()

# Fit the scaler on the data
scaler.fit(X)

# Transform the data
X_scaled = scaler.transform(X)
print(X_scaled)

# Output:
[[-1.22474487 -1.22474487]
 [ 0.          0.         ]
 [ 1.22474487  1.22474487]]
```

Another common shortcut that we saw previously, `fit_transform()`, allows users to perform both steps in one command, making preprocessing workflows more efficient. Again, when to use `fit_transform()` and `fit()` with `transform()` separately depends on the task at hand. Typically, we should apply the `fit_transform()` method to our training data if we want to transform our data immediately based on the calculated transformation, something the `fit()` method can't achieve by itself. However, when applying transformations to our test dataset, we wouldn't want to reapply the `fit()` method; this would impose a potentially different data transformation, as our test data will be slightly different from our training data. Remember, our test dataset is meant to be treated exactly like our training data for model consistency purposes, so implementing a separate `fit()` method on it could potentially alter our test data and make our model predictions unreliable when applied in a real-world scenario:

```
from sklearn.preprocessing import StandardScaler
import numpy as np

# Example data
X = np.array([[1, 2], [3, 4], [5, 6]])

# Create a StandardScaler instance and
# fit_transform the data in one step
scaler = StandardScaler()
X_scaled = scaler.fit_transform(X)
print(X_scaled)

# Output:
[[-1.22474487 -1.22474487]
 [ 0.          0.        ]
 [ 1.22474487  1.22474487]]
```

This consistency across all transformers allows them to be integrated seamlessly into ML pipelines, ensuring that the same transformation is applied to both the training and test data, something that becomes significantly important when implementing production-level models.

We will explore various transformers, including `StandardScaler()`, `MinMaxScaler()`, and `OneHotEncoder()`, in *Chapter 2* to demonstrate how they can be used to prepare data for ML models using the `fit()`, `transform()`, and `fit_transform()` methods. Practical examples will be provided to illustrate how you can integrate transformers into workflows to ensure your data is preprocessed consistently.

Handling custom estimators and transformers

scikit-learn's API is designed to be extensible, allowing developers to create custom estimators and transformers that integrate seamlessly into existing workflows. By subclassing `BaseEstimator()` and **mixin** classes, you can implement custom ML algorithms or data transformations. Each custom estimator should follow the scikit-learn interface by implementing the `fit()` and `transform()` (for transformers) or `fit()` and `predict()` (for models) methods, ensuring compatibility with tools such as `GridSearchCV()` and `Pipeline()`.

> **Mixin classes**
>
> In scikit-learn, a mixin is a way to extend the functionality of classes without using traditional class inheritance found in Python and other OOP languages. Mixins are useful for code reusability, allowing programmers to share functionality between different classes. Instead of repeating the same code, common functionality can be grouped into a mixin and then included in each class that requires it.

We'll cover essential elements such as parameter validation using `check_is_fitted()`, hyperparameter management, and integrating custom objects into pipelines in various chapters throughout this book. You'll also learn how to test and validate your custom objects using scikit-learn's utilities, ensuring they work with cross-validation and preprocessing steps, just like built-in estimators.

These practices will enable you to extend the functionality of scikit-learn while maintaining code that is clear, reusable, and fully compatible with the library's ecosystem. Hopefully, by the end of this book, you'll come to learn that scikit-learn can handle almost any ML task, whether on your laptop or in a full enterprise environment!

Pipelines and workflow automation

ML workflows typically take on a linear progression of sequential steps (although most production applications require several additional steps to create a *cyclical* pattern for the model monitoring, continuous training, and **continuous integration/continuous delivery** or **deployment (CI/CD)** stages found in **machine learning operations (MLOps)**—more on this later in this book). In scikit-learn, pipelines provide a structured way to automate ML workflows by chaining together multiple processing steps, such as data preprocessing, model training, and prediction, into a single, cohesive object. This allows for efficient and consistent execution of complex workflows while ensuring that each step, from transformation to prediction, is executed in the correct sequence.

> **MLOps**
>
> MLOps refers to the practice of integrating ML workflows into the larger life cycle of software development and operations. It focuses on automating the process of developing, testing, deploying, and maintaining ML models, ensuring they are scalable, reliable, and sustainable in production environments. MLOps is essential in a production environment for several reasons:
>
> 1) It bridges the gap between data science, ML engineering, and operational teams so that there is less of a "this is your job, this is our job" mindset between them
>
> 2) It improves collaboration since teams must think holistically about how models are utilized from various vantage points
>
> 3) It speeds up model deployment by creating an ecosystem that automates pipeline tasks and maintains a framework for easy reproducibility across projects
>
> 4) It enhances model performance monitoring, observability, and explainability to address issues such as model drift or technical debt

MLOps is crucial for businesses that rely on ML models to drive decision-making and automation, as it ensures that models are consistently performing at their best even after deployment. It enhances reproducibility and traceability, both of which are key for compliance, auditing, and continuous improvement. By employing MLOps, organizations can build efficient workflows for retraining models, managing datasets, and monitoring real-time model behavior, which minimizes disruptions and reduces risks associated with outdated or underperforming models. Remember, there is "No such thing as a free lunch" and, equally, "There is no such thing as a model that works well forever!"

scikit-learn supports MLOps workflows through tools such as the `Pipeline()` class for automating preprocessing and modeling steps, `GridSearchCV()` for hyperparameter optimization, and model persistence libraries such as `joblib` and `pickle` for saving and deploying models. Additionally, scikit-learn's compatibility with other MLOps platforms ensures that models built with it can be integrated into larger ML life cycle systems such as MLflow or Kubeflow.

In *Chapter 14*, we will demonstrate how to create pipelines that include transformers such as `ColumnTransformer()` and estimators such as `RandomForestClassifier()` to streamline data preprocessing, model selection, and cross-validation into a unified process. By encapsulating this workflow, pipelines help eliminate manual intervention and make your ML process more reproducible. Furthermore, this encapsulation process is tightly bound to the scikit-learn paradigm of modularity, which makes creating a custom library of functions, pipelines, estimators, and transformers easy.

Common attributes and methods

As model complexity grows, it becomes harder and harder to look inside and understand a model's inner workings (especially with artificial neural networks). Thankfully, scikit-learn models share several key attributes and methods that provide valuable insights into how a model has learned from data. For instance, attributes such as `coef_` and `intercept_`, found in linear models specifically, store the learned coefficients and intercepts to help with interpreting model behavior.

Similarly, methods such as `score()` allow users to evaluate model performance, typically returning a default metric such as accuracy for classifiers or R^2 for regressors. These common features ensure consistency across different models and simplify model analysis and interpretation:

```python
from sklearn.linear_model import LinearRegression
import numpy as np

# Example data
X = np.array([[1], [2], [3], [4], [5]])  # Feature matrix
y = np.array([1, 2, 3, 3.5, 5])  # Target values

# Create and fit the model
model = LinearRegression()
model.fit(X, y)

# Access coefficients (slope of the linear model)
print("Coefficients:", model.coef_)

# Access y-intercept
print("Intercept:", model.intercept_)

# Use score() method to evaluate the model (R-squared value)
print("Model R-squared:", model.score(X, y))

# Output:
Coefficients: [0.95]
Intercept: 0.04999999999999938
Model R-squared: 0.9809782608695652
```

> **Note**
>
> R-squared has received criticism in some cases as being misleading as it can be influenced by how *messy* or *organized* your data is. It will also always increase with the addition of more variables in your data. Often, the adjusted R-squared is used to account for the number of variables in your dataset, applying a penalty when many variables are included.)

We will look more closely at these shared attributes and methods across various scikit-learn models throughout this book, with examples on how to access and interpret values such as `coef_` and how to use methods such as `score()` to quickly evaluate performance. Practical examples will be provided to show how these features can be applied in real-world scenarios, such as evaluating model accuracy or interpreting regression coefficients for better model insights.

Hyperparameter tuning with search methods

Hyperparameter tuning is crucial for optimizing candidate ML models, and scikit-learn makes this process easier with a variety of built-in search methods. The library provides two popular methods, `GridSearchCV()` and `RandomizedSearchCV()`, in easy-to-implement APIs, along with their counterpart methods, that implement a successive halving approach to hyperparameter search.

scikit-learn also allows a manual approach to setting hyperparameters if you wish to adjust default values for your own training purposes: the `set_params()` and `get_params()` methods. The `set_params()` method allows users to adjust model hyperparameters programmatically, while `get_params()` retrieves the current hyperparameter settings. This functionality ensures flexibility when experimenting with different model configurations and can be paired with the techniques mentioned earlier for efficient tuning:

```
from sklearn.ensemble import RandomForestClassifier

# Create a RandomForestClassifier model
model = RandomForestClassifier()

# Set hyperparameters prior to training using set_params()
model.set_params(n_estimators=100, max_depth=10, random_state=42)

# Check the updated parameters
print(model.get_params())

# Output:
{'bootstrap': True, 'ccp_alpha': 0.0, 'class_weight': None,
'criterion': 'gini', 'max_depth': 10, 'max_features': 'sqrt', 'max_
leaf_nodes': None, 'max_samples': None, 'min_impurity_decrease': 0.0,
'min_samples_leaf': 1, 'min_samples_split': 2, 'min_weight_fraction_
leaf': 0.0, 'monotonic_cst': None, 'n_estimators': 100, 'n_jobs':
None, 'oob_score': False, 'random_state': 42, 'verbose': 0, 'warm_
start': False}
```

As you can see, scikit-learn provides a detailed output of model hyperparameters that provide the best fit. This is something we can use in our model for training purposes.

Working with metadata: Tags and more

scikit-learn uses metadata, such as estimator tags, to control how models behave in various contexts, including cross-validation and pipeline processing, as well as to control their capabilities, such as supported output types. Additionally, tags can provide information about an estimator, such as whether it can handle multi-output data or missing values, enabling scikit-learn to optimize workflows dynamically.

scikit-learn's metadata captures information related to model inputs and outputs and then typically uses this information to control the flow of data between different tasks in a pipeline. Metadata objects come in two varieties: **routers** and **consumers**. Here, routers move metadata to consumers, and consumers use that metadata in their calculations. This is known as **metadata routing** in scikit-learn.

> ### More on metadata routing
>
> In scikit-learn, metadata routing is a feature that allows users to control how metadata is passed between router and consumer objects in a pipeline or workflow. It enables the dynamic management of metadata such as sample weights, group labels, or fit parameters, allowing models and transformers to access additional information beyond the input data. This makes workflows more flexible and customizable, as metadata can be routed through specific steps or even ignored when not relevant, reducing the need for manual intervention.
>
> For example, in a data science project that involves handling imbalanced datasets, metadata routing can be used to pass sample weights to specific transformers and classifiers in a pipeline. By routing the sample weights through only the required steps—such as oversampling or weighting in the classifier—while ignoring them in others, such as scaling, the workflow ensures proper handling of imbalances without it affecting the preprocessing steps unnecessarily. This leads to more accurate and efficient model training.

We'll explore how to access and modify metadata by covering practical examples of how these tags influence model behavior during cross-validation and pipeline execution later in this book (see *Chapters 12* and *13*). You'll also learn how to create custom tags for your own estimators.

Best practices for API usage

Once you've gotten a feel for the underlying scikit-learn programming paradigm, you'll realize just how powerful it is! When working with scikit-learn's API, following best practices ensures that your code remains clear, modular, and maintainable. This includes leveraging reusable components such as pipelines, adhering to the consistent `fit()`, `predict()`, and `transform()` methods, and making effective use of hyperparameter tuning tools such as `GridSearchCV()`. Keeping models and data processing steps modular allows for easy debugging and scaling of your ML workflows.

Here are a few additional model development best practices and key takeaways related to scikit-learn functionality that you should keep in mind as we move forward and explore some of the concepts laid out in this chapter further, in more granular detail:

- **Uniform API**: All estimators in scikit-learn follow the same basic pattern of `fit()`, `transform()` (for transformers), and `predict()`, making code more readable, maintainable, and easier to develop

- **Data preprocessing**: Always preprocess your data using the appropriate tools from `sklearn.preprocessing`, such as scaling, encoding, or handling missing values, before feeding it to the model

- **Pipelines**: For complex workflows involving multiple transformations and models, use `Pipeline()` to chain operations together, simplifying code and managing hyperparameter tuning

- **Cross-validation**: Evaluate model performance using cross-validation techniques from `sklearn.model_selection` to get a reliable estimate of generalization ability

- **Hyperparameter tuning**: Use tools such as `GridSearchCV()` or `RandomizedSearchCV()` to find optimal hyperparameters for your model

2

Pre-Model Workflow and Data Preprocessing

Without question, the quality of your data is the most important element in achieving successful outcomes from ML models. Unfortunately, many of the training courses and content you find today gloss over this critical aspect since, for lack of a better way of putting it, it can be seen as *dull*, *boring*, or even *tedious* compared to the actual training and deployment of models into production environments. Regardless of your own perceptions, keep in mind that the idiom *garbage in, garbage out* absolutely relates to what will happen to your ML pipeline. Furthermore, as data changes over time, data preprocessing isn't a one-time endeavor but an ongoing task that must be accounted for.

This chapter will help you learn essential data preprocessing techniques, such as handling missing data, scaling, and encoding categorical data, using scikit-learn's transformers and pipelines. The exercises cover preparing datasets for ML models using real-world data examples.

In this chapter, we're going to cover the following recipes:

- The impact of raw data on model performance
- Handling missing data
- Scaling techniques
- Encoding categorical variables
- Introduction to pipelines in scikit-learn
- Feature engineering

Technical requirements

It is advisable to create a Python environment for safely isolating your work from other Python installations/libraries. See the GitHub repository for more details (`https://github.com/PacktPublishing/scikit-learn-Cookbook-Third-Edition`).

- Git >=2.46.x

- Python >=3.9.x

- Cloned GitHub repository and Python environment built from the `requirements.txt` file

The impact of raw data on model performance

ML algorithms are designed to learn patterns from data. However, when the input data is flawed—whether due to missing data, outliers, or irrelevant features—the model's ability to generalize from training data on unseen data diminishes. For instance, a model trained on *noisy* or biased data may yield inaccurate predictions, leading to poor decision-making in real-world applications.

Consider a simple classification task where the dataset contains missing data. If these values are not addressed through appropriate preprocessing techniques, the model may either ignore the affected instances or make erroneous assumptions about the missing data. This can result in a skewed understanding of the underlying patterns, ultimately degrading model performance.

Common data issues

Some of the most common instances of data quality issues in ML model development include the following:

- **Missing data**: Incomplete datasets are common (if not the standard) in real-world scenarios. Missing data can arise from various sources, such as errors in data collection, system failures, or data corruption. scikit-learn provides several strategies for handling missing data, including imputation techniques using `SimpleImputer()` or `KNNImputer()`.

- **Outliers**: Outliers can distort statistical analyses and lead to misleading results. Identifying and treating outliers is vital for maintaining the integrity of your model. Techniques such as Z-score analysis or using scalers such as `RobustScaler()` can help mitigate their impact.

> **Note**
> Outliers, while potentially detrimental to model training data, can also be insightful for data scientists seeking evidence of rarely occurring events in their domain of interest.

- **Categorical variables**: Many ML algorithms require numerical input; thus, categorical variables need to be transformed into a suitable format. scikit-learn offers utilities such as `OneHotEncoder()` and `LabelEncoder()` to facilitate this transformation.

- **Feature scaling**: Features with different scales can negatively affect model convergence and performance, especially for algorithms that rely on distance metrics (e.g., **k-nearest neighbors (KNN)**). Standardization (`StandardScaler()`) and normalization (`MinMaxScaler()`) are common techniques used to scale features appropriately.

- **Data leakage**: This occurs when information from *outside* the training dataset is used to create the model, leading to overly optimistic performance metrics. Careful separation of training and testing datasets during preprocessing is essential to prevent this issue. This is a common challenge for those in the MLOps field, where managing real-time data streams is central to mitigating this occurrence.

Cleaning and preparing data

scikit-learn provides a comprehensive suite of tools for preprocessing data effectively, including, but not limited to, the following:

- `Pipeline()`: Utilizing `Pipeline()` allows users to streamline their preprocessing steps alongside model training, ensuring that all transformations are applied consistently across training and testing datasets.

- `ColumnTransformer()`: For datasets with mixed types of features (numerical and categorical), `ColumnTransformer()` enables users to apply different preprocessing steps to different columns seamlessly.

- `sklearn.feature_selection`: Techniques such as `SelectFromModel()` and **Recursive Feature Elimination (RFE)** help identify and retain only the most relevant features for model training, reducing complexity and improving interpretability. Remember the adage: as model complexity increases, interpretability decreases and vice versa.

Effective data preprocessing is not just a preliminary step; it is an *integral part* of building robust ML models. By understanding common data issues and employing scikit-learn's powerful preprocessing tools, data scientists, ML engineers, and MLOps engineers can enhance their models' performance and reliability significantly.

Handling missing data

Missing data can arise from various sources, including human error, technical failures, or data corruption. It is important to address missing values before training ML models, as most algorithms cannot handle them directly, and most scikit-learn methods won't even execute when they are detected in your training data. Sometimes, with large enough datasets, we can simply drop the records that contain missing values with little impact on the resulting model, but this isn't always viable. Thankfully, scikit-learn provides several strategies for imputing missing values, allowing practitioners to fill in gaps with estimated values based on available data. This recipe introduces three of the most commonly used methods for imputing missing values in a dataset with scikit-learn.

Getting ready

To begin, we will create a toy dataset composed of random, quantitative data, 10 features, and several missing data values randomly spread throughout. We will then store the dataset in a pandas `DataFrame()` object for better readability.

Take the following steps:

1. Load the libraries:

    ```
    import numpy as np
    import pandas as pd
    ```

2. Create a larger sample dataset with missing values:

    ```
    np.random.seed(2024)   # For reproducibility
    n_samples = 20
    n_features = 10
    ```

3. Generate random data:

    ```
    data = {
        f"Feature{i+1}": np.random.uniform(0, 100, n_samples)
        for i in range(n_features)
    }
    ```

4. Convert it to a DataFrame:

    ```
    df = pd.DataFrame(data)
    ```

5. Randomly introduce missing values (approximately 20% of the data):

    ```
    for column in df.columns:
        mask = np.random.random(n_samples) < 0.2
        df.loc[mask, column] = np.nan
    ```

6. Display the DataFrame with missing values:

```
display(df)
```

The first six rows are displayed in the following figure:

	Feature1	Feature2	Feature3	Feature4	Feature5	Feature6	Feature7	Feature8	Feature9	Feature10
0	58.801452	NaN	42.009814	34.680397	49.962259	NaN	NaN	89.954588	41.152421	NaN
1	69.910875	9.554215	6.436369	31.287816	37.966499	NaN	82.005649	NaN	75.797616	91.382492
2	NaN	96.090974	59.643269	84.710402	NaN	84.109027	NaN	70.288128	1.778343	4.117690
3	NaN	25.176729	83.732372	88.023110	16.886931	97.205554	84.696823	NaN	NaN	80.077973
4	20.501895	NaN	89.248639	67.655865	58.635861	78.225721	60.911562	NaN	65.114243	99.119187
5	10.606287	76.825393	20.052744	5.367515	NaN	19.703051	34.423301	93.399494	72.206680	12.640276

Figure 2.1 – DataFrame with missing values

How to do it...

There are a variety of methods for dealing with missing data. scikit-learn contains three approaches: SimpleImputer(), KNNImputer(), and IterativeImputer(). They are outlined next.

Using the SimpleImputer() class

The SimpleImputer() class in scikit-learn is one of the most straightforward methods for handling missing values. It allows users to replace missing entries with a specified statistic such as the mean, median, or most frequent value. This method is particularly useful when dealing with numerical features.

The steps are as follows:

1. Load the libraries:

```
from sklearn.impute import SimpleImputer
```

2. Initialize SimpleImputer and set the strategy to "mean", "median", or "most_ frequent":

```
imputer = SimpleImputer(strategy="mean")
```

3. Fit and transform the data:

```
imputed_data = imputer.fit_transform(df)
imputed_df = pd.DataFrame(imputed_data, columns=df.columns)
imputed_df
```

4. The first six rows of the imputed dataset can be seen in the following figure. You'll notice that the missing data (NaN) from the original dataset has been replaced.

	Feature1	Feature2	Feature3	Feature4	Feature5	Feature6	Feature7	Feature8	Feature9	Feature10
0	58.801452	53.864661	42.009814	34.680397	49.962259	57.822964	51.145011	89.954588	41.152421	48.400044
1	69.910875	9.554215	6.436369	31.287816	37.966499	57.822964	82.005649	50.715003	75.797616	91.382492
2	52.558605	96.090974	59.643269	84.710402	46.055883	84.109027	51.145011	70.288128	1.778343	4.117690
3	52.558605	25.176729	83.732372	88.023110	16.886931	97.205554	84.696823	50.715003	60.616723	80.077973
4	20.501895	53.864661	89.248639	67.655865	58.635861	78.225721	60.911562	50.715003	65.114243	99.119187
5	10.606287	76.825393	20.052744	5.367515	46.055883	19.703051	34.423301	93.399494	72.206680	12.640276

Figure 2.2 – DataFrame with SimpleImputer() applied

After application, we can see the results of `SimpleImputer()`, for example, on `Feature1`. The original dataset had both the second and third records as NaN, but these have been replaced by the calculated mean value (i.e., `52.558605`) for that feature.

Using the KNNImputer() class

For more complex datasets, `KNNImputer()` can be employed. This method uses the KNN algorithm to impute missing values based on the values of neighboring samples. Simply put, `KNNImputer()` takes each missing value and identifies the nearest labeled values in the dataset's feature space (the number of labeled values is determined by the `'n_neighbors'` hyperparameter). Then, based on the majority label appearing among those values, the missing value is assigned the same. This technique can capture more nuanced relationships within the data compared to simpler methods.

The steps are as follows:

1. Load the libraries:

    ```
    from sklearn.impute import KNNImputer
    ```

2. Initialize KNNImputer:

    ```
    knn_imputer = KNNImputer(n_neighbors=2)
    ```

3. Fit and transform the data using the previously defined DataFrame:

    ```
    knn_imputed_data = knn_imputer.fit_transform(df)
    knn_imputed_df = pd.DataFrame(
        knn_imputed_data, columns=df.columns)
    knn_imputed_df
    ```

The results of this imputation are slightly different than our `SimpleImputer()` results. The first six rows of the imputed dataset can be seen in *Figure 2.3*.

	Feature1	Feature2	Feature3	Feature4	Feature5	Feature6	Feature7	Feature8	Feature9	Feature10
0	58.801452	48.954043	42.009814	34.680397	49.962259	93.910386	52.549271	89.954588	41.152421	59.833678
1	69.910875	9.554215	6.436369	31.287816	37.966499	86.793468	82.005649	45.416191	75.797616	91.382492
2	67.752344	96.090974	59.643269	84.710402	73.338309	84.109027	59.012876	70.288128	1.778343	4.117690
3	47.880864	25.176729	83.732372	88.023110	16.886931	97.205554	84.696823	64.510281	39.726833	80.077973
4	20.501895	31.670912	89.248639	67.655865	58.635861	78.225721	60.911562	25.903612	65.114243	99.119187
5	10.606287	76.825393	20.052744	5.367515	59.716773	19.703051	34.423301	93.399494	72.206680	12.640276

Figure 2.3 – DataFrame with KNNImputer() applied

Using the IterativeImputer() class

`IterativeImputer()` offers an advanced approach by modeling each feature with missing values as a function of other features in a round-robin fashion. More explicitly, this method models each feature with missing values as a regression function, where it takes the place of the y value (the output), and all other features (without missing values) take the place of x values (the input). Then the regression model is used to predict the missing values for the feature. This process is repeated for each feature with missing values. This method can provide more accurate imputations by considering multivariate relationships in the dataset.

Take the following steps:

1. Load the libraries:

    ```
    from sklearn.experimental import (
        enable_iterative_imputer
    )# Experimental feature requires loading
    from sklearn.impute import IterativeImputer
    ```

2. Initialize `IterativeImputer`:

    ```
    iterative_imputer = IterativeImputer()
    ```

3. Fit and transform the data using the previously defined DataFrame:

    ```
    iterative_imputed_data = iterative_imputer.fit_transform(df)
    iterative_imputed_df = pd.DataFrame(
        iterative_imputed_data, columns=df.columns)
    iterative_imputed_df
    ```

Here is our output. The first six rows of the imputed dataset can be seen in the following figure.

	Feature1	Feature2	Feature3	Feature4	Feature5	Feature6	Feature7	Feature8	Feature9	Feature10
0	58.801452	54.365008	42.009814	34.680397	49.962259	58.680582	51.178102	89.954588	41.152421	48.292275
1	69.910875	9.554215	6.436369	31.287816	37.966499	60.070634	82.005649	50.710323	75.797616	91.382492
2	52.539676	96.090974	59.643269	84.710402	46.121290	84.109027	51.155371	70.288128	1.778343	4.117690
3	52.630591	25.176729	83.732372	88.023110	16.886931	97.205554	84.696823	50.680265	50.650877	80.077973
4	20.501895	53.198954	89.248639	67.655865	58.635861	78.225721	60.911562	50.691674	65.114243	99.119187
5	10.606287	76.825393	20.052744	5.367515	46.156310	19.703051	34.423301	93.399494	72.206680	12.640276

Figure 2.4 – DataFrame with IterativeImputer() applied

This imputation technique is a bit more computationally complex, but should elicit slightly better predictions for missing values.

There's more...

Selecting the appropriate imputation strategy depends on several factors:

- **Data type**: Numerical features may benefit from mean or median imputation, while categorical features might require mode imputation.

- **Data distribution**: Understanding the distribution of your data can guide you on whether to use the mean, median, or more complex methods such as KNN.

- **Missing data pattern**: Analyzing how data is missing (e.g., completely at random versus not at random) can influence the choice of imputation method.

- **Amount of missing data**: Some imputation methods work better depending on how much of your dataset contains missing values. When >5% of your dataset contains missing values, `SimpleImputer()` is a good candidate since it's computationally lightweight and doesn't introduce much bias. When your dataset contains a moderate level of missing values, say, 5–10%, using `KNNImputer()` is ideal for datasets with all numeric features, while `IterativeImputer()` works with mixed dataset types. For an even sparser dataset with >10% missing values, if missing values reside within a single feature, consider dropping that feature unless it's absolutely necessary to your model. If that's the case, you may need to apply domain-specific approaches that lie outside the scope of this book.

Keep in mind that not all datasets need missing value imputation since some ML algorithms will automatically accommodate features with them. Most notably, decision trees and their related algorithm, Random Forest, do not require data imputation.

Hands-on exercises

To illustrate these techniques, please reference the GitHub repository (`https://github.com/PacktPublishing/scikit-learn-Cookbook-Third-Edition`). You will engage in hands-on exercises using scikit-learn's imputation tools on datasets with missing values. Although we've included the code examples in the repository, we encourage you to explore them on your own and try using these tools with different arguments to see the results. The following steps outline a general workflow:

1. Load your dataset and identify missing values.

2. Choose an appropriate imputation method based on your analysis.

3. Apply the imputer to fill in missing values.

4. Evaluate model performance using cross-validation to assess the impact of different imputation strategies.

Scaling techniques

When working with datasets, features can have vastly different scales. For instance, a feature representing age may range from 0 to 100, while another feature representing income could range from 0 to 100,000. Many ML algorithms, such as KNN and gradient descent-based methods (e.g., linear regression), are sensitive to these differences in scale. Therefore, scaling helps ensure that no single feature dominates the learning process. This recipe covers the three most commonly used scaling techniques in ML.

The following are key concepts. It is worth noting that sometimes these two terms are used interchangeably, but they are *not* the same and should *not* be implemented as such!

- **Standardization (Z-score transformation)** changes the data to have a mean of 0 and a standard deviation of 1

- **Normalization** changes the range of the data distribution so values fall between 0 and 1

Getting ready

We will use the previously defined `iterative_imputed_df` DataFrame from the earlier *Using the IterativeImputer() class* subsection for this recipe, so there is no need to redefine it.

How to do it...

Determining the correct scaling technique depends on several factors, including the model(s) you plan to use during training, the presence of outliers in your data, and the distributions of your features. We will look at three common techniques, utilizing scikit-learn's `StandardScaler()`, `MinMaxScaler()`, and `Normalizer()`.

StandardScaler()

Standardization transforms features to have a mean of 0 and a standard deviation of 1. This method is particularly useful when the data follows a Gaussian (normal) distribution. The formula for standardization is as follows:

$$z = \frac{(x - \mu)}{\sigma}$$

Here, x is the original value, μ is the mean of the feature, and σ is the standard deviation.

Let's load our libraries and apply the scaler:

1. Load the libraries:

    ```
    from sklearn.preprocessing import StandardScaler
    ```

2. Initialize `StandardScaler`:

    ```
    scaler = StandardScaler()
    ```

3. Fit and transform the data using the iterative imputed DataFrame:

    ```
    scaled_data = scaler.fit_transform(iterative_imputed_df)
    scaled_df = pd.DataFrame(
        scaled_data, columns= iterative_imputed_df.columns)
    scaled_df
    ```

    Here is the output table.

	Feature1	Feature2	Feature3	Feature4	Feature5	Feature6	Feature7	Feature8	Feature9	Feature10
0	0.271931	0.019495	-0.373057	-0.894258	0.188761	0.031844	0.001905	1.683800	-0.780898	-0.003574
1	0.756048	-1.874939	-1.592196	-1.043864	-0.391744	0.085949	1.426871	-0.000534	0.652484	1.429056
2	-0.000939	1.783513	0.231259	1.311954	0.002887	1.021588	0.000854	0.839730	-2.409929	-1.472256
3	0.003022	-1.214477	1.056818	1.458037	-1.411839	1.531340	1.551267	-0.001824	-0.387917	1.053212
4	-1.397054	-0.029802	1.245866	0.559887	0.608499	0.792594	0.451822	-0.001334	0.210478	1.686279
5	-1.828276	0.969036	-1.125549	-2.186891	0.004582	-1.485267	-0.772566	1.831653	0.503915	-1.188904

Figure 2.5 – DataFrame with StandardScaler() applied

The result of `StandardScaler()` is a Z-score that centers our feature's values around a mean of 0, meaning some of our scaled values may become negative.

MinMaxScaler()

Min-max scaling rescales features to a fixed range, typically [0, 1]. This technique is useful when you want to preserve the relationships between values while ensuring that all features contribute equally. The formula for min-max scaling is as follows:

$$x' = \frac{x - Xmin}{Xmax - Xmin}$$

Here, x is the original value and *Xmin* and *Xmax* are the minimum and maximum values of the feature, respectively.

The application of this scaler is largely the same as `StandardScaler()`:

1. Load the libraries:

   ```
   from sklearn.preprocessing import MinMaxScaler
   ```

2. Initialize `MinMaxScaler()`:

   ```
   minmax_scaler = MinMaxScaler()
   ```

3. Fit and transform the data using the iterative imputed DataFrame:

   ```
   minmax_scaled_data = minmax_scaler.fit_transform(
       iterative_imputed_df)
   minmax_scaled_df = pd.DataFrame(
       minmax_scaled_data,
       columns=iterative_imputed_df.columns
   )
   minmax_scaled_df
   ```

   Here is the resulting output from `MinMaxScaler()`.

	Feature1	Feature2	Feature3	Feature4	Feature5	Feature6	Feature7	Feature8	Feature9	Feature10
0	0.603506	0.517824	0.380540	0.354639	0.569020	0.555896	0.435006	0.962767	0.402156	0.464988
1	0.721357	0.000000	0.000369	0.313594	0.413077	0.571920	0.833074	0.538604	0.756013	0.918562
2	0.537080	1.000000	0.568987	0.959922	0.519088	0.849027	0.434713	0.750206	0.000000	0.000000
3	0.538045	0.180530	0.826426	1.000000	0.139045	1.000000	0.867825	0.538279	0.499171	0.799569
4	0.197218	0.504349	0.885377	0.753589	0.681776	0.781206	0.560692	0.538402	0.646896	1.000000
5	0.092244	0.777371	0.145886	0.000000	0.519543	0.106575	0.218656	1.000000	0.719336	0.089710

Figure 2.6 – DataFrame with MinMaxScaler() applied

Let's move on to our final scaler, `Normalizer()`.

Normalizer()

Normalization (L1 or L2 normalization) scales individual samples to have the unit norm. This technique is particularly useful when dealing with sparse data or when you want to treat each sample equally regardless of its magnitude. The formulas for L1 and L2 normalization, respectively, are as follows:

$$||x||_1 = \sum_{i=1}^{n} |x|$$

$$||x||_2 = \sqrt{\sum_{i=1}^{n} x_i^2}$$

Here, x is the original value. Let's apply this:

1. Load the libraries:

    ```
    from sklearn.preprocessing import Normalizer
    ```

2. Initialize `Normalizer`:

    ```
    normalizer = Normalizer()
    ```

3. Fit and transform the data using the iterative imputed DataFrame:

    ```
    normalized_data = normalizer.fit_transform(
        iterative_imputed_df)
    normalized_df = pd.DataFrame(
        normalized_data,
        columns=iterative_imputed_df.columns
    )
    normalized_df
    ```

    The resulting output from `Normalizer()` is as follows.

	Feature1	Feature2	Feature3	Feature4	Feature5	Feature6	Feature7	Feature8	Feature9	Feature10
0	0.339168	0.313579	0.242313	0.200037	0.288183	0.338471	0.295196	0.518860	0.237368	0.278551
1	0.376706	0.051482	0.034682	0.168591	0.204578	0.323683	0.441878	0.273247	0.408426	0.492404
2	0.264336	0.483450	0.300075	0.426192	0.232044	0.423166	0.257371	0.353631	0.008947	0.020717
3	0.243762	0.116607	0.387811	0.407684	0.078213	0.450213	0.392278	0.234729	0.234592	0.370886
4	0.095909	0.248868	0.417511	0.316499	0.274302	0.365945	0.284948	0.237139	0.304609	0.463686
5	0.068115	0.493382	0.128781	0.034471	0.296421	0.126535	0.221071	0.599823	0.463720	0.081177

Figure 2.7 – DataFrame with Normalizer() applied

Each technique provides a different approach to data scaling, but keep in mind that just like with missing values, not all data requires data scaling. Again, tree-based methods such as decision trees and Random Forest work using the raw data values for input features, so scaling these before modeling would have a detrimental impact on results.

There's more...

Scaling techniques will impact ML training differently depending on the choice of algorithm:

- **KNN**: Sensitive to distance metrics; performance can vary significantly based on scaling

- **Support vector machines (SVM)**: Also sensitive to feature magnitudes; effective with standardized data

- **Linear regression**: Convergence speed can be improved with standardized features

Hands-on exercises

To illustrate these techniques, please reference the GitHub repository (`https://github.com/PacktPublishing/scikit-learn-Cookbook-Third-Edition`). You will engage in hands-on exercises using scikit-learn's imputation tools on datasets with missing values. Although we've included the code examples in the repository, we encourage you to explore them on your own and try using these tools with different arguments to see the results. The following steps outline a general workflow:

1. Load your dataset and identify features that require scaling.

2. Choose appropriate scaling methods based on the characteristics of your data.

3. Apply each scaling technique to your dataset.

4. Train multiple models using different scaled datasets.

5. Evaluate model performance using metrics such as accuracy, precision, recall, or mean squared error.

Encoding categorical variables

Categorical variables are a common feature in many datasets, representing discrete values such as categories, labels, or groups. However, most ML algorithms (well, computers in general, it should be said) require numerical input, making it essential to convert categorical data into a suitable format.

Categorical variables can be divided into two main types:

- **Nominal variables**: These represent categories without any intrinsic ordering (e.g., color, brand)

- **Ordinal variables**: These have a clear ordering among categories (e.g., ratings from 1 to 5)

Choosing the right encoding method depends on the type of categorical variable and the specific requirements of the ML algorithm being used. These recipes teach us how to convert non-numeric variables into a numeric representation that our training algorithms can utilize appropriately.

Getting ready

To begin, like we did earlier, we will create a toy dataset, only this time, our features will be composed of *qualitative* data:

1. Load the libraries:

    ```
    import numpy as np
    ```

2. Create sample categorical data with 20 records:

    ```
    np.random.seed(2024)   # for reproducibility
    categories = ["A", "B", "C", "D"]
    categorical_data = pd.DataFrame(
        {
            "Department": np.random.choice(
                categories, size=20),
            "Position": np.random.choice(
                ["Junior", "Senior", "Manager"], size=20),
            "Location": np.random.choice(
                ["NY", "SF", "LA", "CHI"], size=20),
        }
    )
    ```

3. Display the DataFrame with categorical values:

    ```
    display(categorical_data)
    ```

    Let's look at the top of our data table.

	Department	Position	Location
0	A	Manager	LA
1	C	Manager	LA
2	A	Junior	NY
3	A	Manager	LA
4	D	Manager	NY
5	A	Senior	LA

    Figure 2.8 – Toy dataset of categorical features

Now, let's transform these into something more *digestible* for our learning algorithms.

How to do it...

As you've seen so far, choosing the appropriate approach to a stage in data preprocessing requires an understanding of not only what you are trying to accomplish with your model but also the implications of the techniques you choose, such as OneHotEncoder(), LabelEncoder(), or ColumnTransformer().

OneHotEncoder()

One-hot encoding is a popular method for converting nominal categorical variables into a numerical format. This technique creates binary columns for each category, allowing the model to treat each category independently. For example, if a feature, *Department*, has four categories (*A*, *B*, *C*, and *D*), one-hot encoding will create four new binary features and populate them with ones and zeros, where a *1* indicates the original category for that particular record.

Take the following steps:

1. Load the libraries:

    ```
    from sklearn.preprocessing import OneHotEncoder
    ```

2. Initialize OneHotEncoder:

    ```
    onehot_encoder = OneHotEncoder(sparse_output=False)
    ```

3. Fit and transform the data:

    ```
    onehot_encoded_data = onehot_encoder.fit_transform(
        categorical_data)
    onehot_encoded_df = pd.DataFrame(
        onehot_encoded_data,
        columns=onehot_encoder.get_feature_names_out()
    )
    onehot_encoded_df
    ```

OneHotEncoder() transforms our dataset of categorical variables into a series of binary features, where each new feature represents one of our original feature's categories, for example, LA for Location.

	Department_A	Department_B	Department_C	Department_D	Position_Junior	Position_Manager	Position_Senior	Location_CHI	Location_LA	Location_NY	Location_SF
0	1.0	0.0	0.0	0.0	0.0	1.0	0.0	0.0	1.0	0.0	0.0
1	0.0	0.0	1.0	0.0	0.0	1.0	0.0	0.0	1.0	0.0	0.0
2	1.0	0.0	0.0	0.0	1.0	0.0	0.0	0.0	0.0	1.0	0.0
3	1.0	0.0	0.0	0.0	0.0	1.0	0.0	0.0	1.0	0.0	0.0
4	0.0	0.0	0.0	1.0	0.0	1.0	0.0	0.0	0.0	1.0	0.0
5	1.0	0.0	0.0	0.0	0.0	0.0	1.0	0.0	1.0	0.0	0.0

Figure 2.9 – DataFrame with OneHotEncoder() applied

Keep in mind that a dataset containing many categorical features and/or numerous categories within features can result in OneHotEncoder() making extremely large, sparse datasets of ones and zeros, which will have negative impacts on many training algorithms.

LabelEncoder()

Label encoding assigns a unique integer to each category in a nominal feature. While this method is straightforward and efficient, it may introduce unintended ordinal relationships between categories. For example, Color may be encoded as follows:

- Red: 0

- Green: 1

- Blue: 2

This could mislead algorithms that interpret these integers as having a ranking, so be sure to utilize it appropriately. Let's now apply LabelEncoder():

1. Load the libraries:

    ```
    from sklearn.preprocessing import LabelEncoder
    ```

2. Initialize LabelEncoder:

    ```
    label_encoder = LabelEncoder()
    ```

3. Create a new DataFrame to store label-encoded values:

    ```
    label_encoded_df = pd.DataFrame()
    ```

4. Fit and transform each categorical column:

    ```
    for column in categorical_data.columns:
        label_encoded_df[f"{column}_encoded"] = (
            label_encoder.fit_transform(
                categorical_data[column]
            )
        )
    label_encoded_df
    ```

Now, each color is assigned a numeric value within its original feature, rather than breaking the feature into separate, binary features, like with `OneHotEncoder()`.

	Department_encoded	Position_encoded	Location_encoded
0	0	1	1
1	2	1	1
2	0	0	2
3	0	1	1
4	3	1	2
5	0	2	1

Figure 2.10 – DataFrame with LabelEncoder() applied

> **Note**
>
> `LabelEncoder()` will assign arbitrary values to categorical features, and these values could be interpreted by ML algorithms as defining some measure of distance when, in fact, they do not. Even though we used this approach on the original dataset from the previous example, you'd want to consider whether a feature was nominal or ordinal prior to using this technique.

ColumnTransformer()

When working with datasets that contain both numerical and categorical features, the `ColumnTransformer` class allows for seamless application of different preprocessing techniques across different columns. This is particularly useful when you want to apply one-hot encoding to categorical features while leaving numerical features unchanged. We will create a new toy dataset that combines both quantitative and qualitative features.

The steps are as follows:

1. Load the libraries:

    ```
    from sklearn.compose import ColumnTransformer
    from sklearn.preprocessing import StandardScaler
    ```

2.   Create sample mixed data with 20 records:

```
np.random.seed(2024)  # for reproducibility
mixed_data = pd.DataFrame(
    {
        "Age": np.random.randint(25, 65, size=20),
        "Salary": np.round(np.random.normal(
            60000, 15000, size=20), 2),
        "Experience": np.random.randint(
            1, 20, size=20),
        "Department": np.random.choice(
            ["IT", "HR", "Sales", "Finance"], size=20),
        "Position": np.random.choice(
            ["Junior", "Senior", "Manager"], size=20),
    }
)
```

3.   Display the DataFrame with mixed data:

```
display(mixed_data)
```

Now we have a dataset with a variety of feature types requiring different transformation techniques.

	Age	Salary	Experience	Department	Position
0	33	59420.36	12	Finance	Manager
1	57	82895.92	17	Sales	Junior
2	25	38165.76	16	Finance	Manager
3	52	38242.36	7	IT	Junior
4	61	55088.65	8	Sales	Manager
5	26	78688.88	9	Sales	Senior

Figure 2.11 – DataFrame featuring different data types

`ColumnTransformer()` will allow us to handle each feature transformation individually.

4.   Initialize `ColumnTransformer()`:

```
column_transformer = ColumnTransformer(
    transformers=[
        ("num", StandardScaler(),
         ["Age", "Salary", "Experience"]),
        ("cat", OneHotEncoder(),
```

```
        ["Department", "Position"]),
    ],
    remainder="passthrough",
)
```

5. Fit and transform the data:

```
transformed_data = column_transformer.fit_transform(mixed_data)
```

6. Get feature names for the transformed columns:

```
numeric_cols = [
    "Age_scaled", "Salary_scaled", "Experience_scaled"
]
categorical_cols = (
    column_transformer
    .named_transformers_ ["cat"]
    .get_feature_names_out(
        ["Department", "Position"]
    )
)
```

7. Create the transformed DataFrame:

```
transformed_df = pd.DataFrame(
    transformed_data,
    columns=numeric_cols + list(categorical_cols)
)
transformed_df
```

Using `ColumnTransformer()`, we can apply multiple techniques to convert our categorical features into numeric ones.

	Age_scaled	Salary_scaled	Experience_scaled	Department_Finance	Department_HR	Department_IT	Department_Sales	Position_Junior	Position_Manager	Position_Senior
0	-1.045349	-0.305043	0.327303	1.0	0.0	0.0	0.0	0.0	1.0	0.0
1	0.727681	1.105091	1.262454	0.0	0.0	0.0	1.0	1.0	0.0	0.0
2	-1.636358	-1.581768	1.075424	1.0	0.0	0.0	0.0	0.0	1.0	0.0
3	0.358300	-1.577167	-0.607848	0.0	0.0	1.0	0.0	1.0	0.0	0.0
4	1.023186	-0.565241	-0.420818	0.0	0.0	0.0	1.0	0.0	1.0	0.0
5	-1.562482	0.852382	-0.233788	0.0	0.0	0.0	1.0	0.0	0.0	1.0

Figure 2.12 – Transformed DataFrame with ColumnTransformer() applied

Let's try these techniques out in the next section.

Hands-on exercises

To illustrate these techniques, please reference the GitHub repository (`https://github.com/PacktPublishing/scikit-learn-Cookbook-Third-Edition`). You will engage in hands-on exercises using scikit-learn's imputation tools on datasets with missing values. Although we've included the code examples in the repository, we encourage you to explore them on your own and try using these tools with different arguments to see the results. The following steps outline a general workflow:

1. Identify categorical features in your dataset that require encoding.

2. Choose the appropriate encoding method based on the type of variable (nominal versus ordinal).

3. Apply the selected encoding technique using scikit-learn's preprocessing tools.

4. Integrate encoded features back into your dataset, ensuring compatibility with numerical features.

5. Evaluate model performance to understand how different encoding methods impact outcomes.

Introduction to pipelines in scikit-learn

In ML, managing the workflow of data preprocessing and model training can become complex, especially when multiple steps are involved (which is almost *always* the case in the real world). The `Pipeline()` class in scikit-learn offers a powerful solution to streamline this process. By allowing users to chain together various preprocessing steps and model training into a single object, pipelines enhance code efficiency and reduce the likelihood of errors. This recipe will introduce you to the concept of pipelines, demonstrating how to create and utilize them effectively for data preprocessing in scikit-learn. We'll be utilizing pipelines throughout the book as we add more steps to our model development workflow.

What is a pipeline?

A pipeline in scikit-learn is essentially a sequence of steps that are executed in order. Each step in the pipeline consists of a name and an associated transformer or estimator (refer to *Chapter 1* if you have forgotten what these are). The primary advantages of using pipelines include the following:

- **Sequential execution:** Each step is performed in the order defined, ensuring that transformations are applied consistently across both training and test datasets.

- **Code simplification:** Pipelines help condense multiple lines of code into a single object, making the code base cleaner and easier to manage.

- **Consistency:** By encapsulating all preprocessing steps into one object, you ensure that the same transformations are applied during both the training and prediction phases, minimizing the risk of data leakage.

- **Easier hyperparameter tuning**: Pipelines integrate seamlessly with scikit-learn's hyperparameter tuning tools, such as GridSearchCV, enabling users to optimize parameters for both preprocessing steps and model training all at once.

- **Modularity**: Pipelines promote modularity by allowing different stages of processing to be encapsulated as reusable components. This makes it easier to experiment with various preprocessing techniques or models without rewriting large portions of code.

Getting ready

The general syntax for defining a pipeline is as follows:

```
pipeline = Pipeline(
    [("name of step", transformer),
     ("name of step", transformer),…,
     ("name of step", estimator]
)
```

It should be noted that the final step in the pipeline, optionally, can be an estimator such as `LogisticRegression()`.

How to do it...

Consider a scenario where you want to preprocess data by handling missing data then scaling features. Here's how you can set up such a pipeline:

1. Load the libraries:

    ```
    from sklearn.pipeline import Pipeline
    from sklearn.impute import SimpleImputer
    from sklearn.preprocessing import StandardScaler
    from sklearn.model_selection import train_test_split
    ```

2. First, separate the features and target (assuming the last column is the target):

    ```
    X = transformed_df.iloc[:, :-1] # all columns except last
    y = transformed_df.iloc[:, -1] # last column
    ```

3. Split the data:

    ```
    X_train, X_test, y_train, y_test = train_test_split(
        X, y, test_size=0.2, random_state=2024
    )
    ```

4. Create a pipeline:

```
pipeline = Pipeline([
    (
        "imputer", SimpleImputer(strategy="mean")
    ),  # handle missing values
    (
        "scaler", StandardScaler()
    ),  # scale the features
])
```

5. Fit and transform the training data:

```
X_train_transformed = pipeline.fit_transform(X_train)
```

6. Transform the test data:

```
X_test_transformed = pipeline.transform(X_test)
```

7. Create DataFrames with the transformed data (to preserve column names):

```
X_train_transformed = pd.DataFrame(
    X_train_transformed,
    columns=X_train.columns,
    index=X_train.index
)
X_test_transformed = pd.DataFrame(
    X_test_transformed,
    columns=X_test.columns,
    index=X_test.index
)
```

You will also notice that prior to applying our pipeline transformations, we added a step to split our dataset into a training and testing dataset using scikit-learn's `train_test_split` function. This may seem trivial at first, but it's important to do this to avoid common pitfalls in ML modeling.

Splitting before data transformations

Applying scikit-learn's `train_test_split` function prior to any transformations is crucial for maintaining the integrity of the ML workflow:

- **Avoids data leakage**: Data leakage occurs when information from the test set inadvertently influences the training process. By splitting the dataset into training and test sets *before* applying any preprocessing techniques, you ensure that the transformations are based solely on the training data. This prevents any information from the test set from leaking into the model during training, which can lead to overly optimistic performance estimates.

- **Realistic model evaluation**: The goal of splitting the data is to evaluate model performance on unseen data. If preprocessing is applied to the entire dataset before splitting, the model may learn patterns that are specific to both the training and test sets, leading to inflated accuracy metrics. By transforming only the training data and then applying those transformations to the test set, you simulate a real-world scenario where new, unseen data is presented to the model.

After fitting a pipeline on the training data, it is essential to use `pipeline.transform()` (or simply `pipeline.predict()`, which includes transformation) on the test dataset rather than reapplying transformations directly:

- **Consistency in transformations**: When you fit a transformation, it calculates parameters (such as the mean and standard deviation for scaling) based solely on the training data. Applying these same parameters to transform the test data ensures that both datasets are treated consistently. This consistency is vital for maintaining model performance and interpretability.

- **Efficiency**: Using a pipeline allows you to streamline your workflow by encapsulating all preprocessing steps and model fitting into one object. Once you fit your pipeline with training data, you can use it directly for predictions on new data without needing to manually apply each transformation step again, reducing code complexity and minimizing errors.

- **Preventing overfitting**: By ensuring that transformations are only based on the training set, you reduce the risk of overfitting your model to specific characteristics of your dataset. This practice helps create models that generalize better to unseen data.

Visualizing pipelines

scikit-learn also allows you to visualize your pipeline using `set_config()` and `display`, which can help in understanding the flow of data through various transformations.

Take the following steps:

1. Load the libraries:

    ```
    from sklearn import set_config
    ```

2. Set the display configuration:

    ```
    set_config(display="diagram")
    ```

3. Display the pipeline:

    ```
    pipeline
    ```

    scikit-learn provides a graph visualization of our simple pipeline structure.

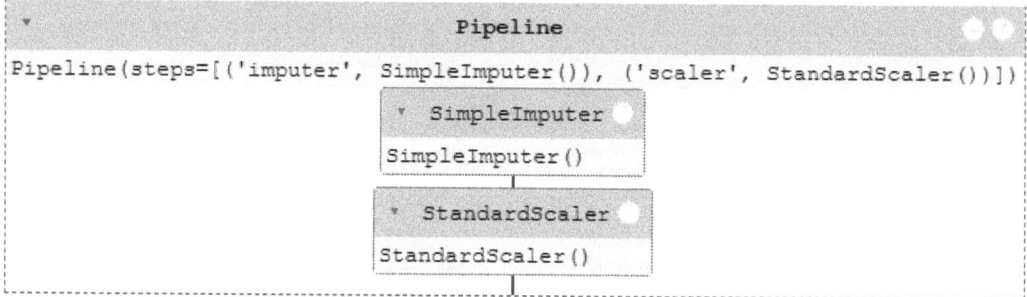

Figure 2.13 – Pipeline graph of simple data transformation workflow

Now, let's apply `Pipeline()` in our hands-on exercises.

Hands-on exercises

To illustrate these techniques, please reference the GitHub repository (`https://github.com/PacktPublishing/scikit-learn-Cookbook-Third-Edition`). You will engage in hands-on exercises using scikit-learn's imputation tools on datasets with missing values. Although we've included the code examples in the repository, we encourage you to explore them on your own and try using these tools with different arguments to see the results. The following steps outline a general workflow:

1. Determine which preprocessing techniques are necessary for your dataset (e.g., scaling, encoding).

2. Choose an appropriate ML algorithm for your task.

3. Use the `Pipeline()` class to chain together preprocessing steps and model training.

4. Train your pipeline on the training data and use it to make predictions on new data.

5. Assess how well your model performs using appropriate metrics.

Feature engineering

Feature engineering is really an umbrella term that generally refers to two main activities: feature extraction and feature selection. Effective feature engineering can significantly enhance model performance by providing algorithms with more informative inputs and reducing or removing *noisy* and/or uninformative ones. These recipes will teach common approaches to feature engineering using existing features to generate new features that may (*"may"* being the keyword) improve model performance.

Understanding feature engineering

Feature engineering encompasses two main activities:

1. **Creating new features (feature extraction)**: This involves transforming existing data into new variables that may capture important patterns or relationships. For example, you might derive a *total spending* feature by combining *price* and *quantity* features.

2. **Selecting relevant features (feature selection)**: This process identifies and retains the most informative features while discarding those that do not contribute meaningfully to the model's predictive power.

Effective feature engineering can lead to simpler models that generalize better to unseen data, ultimately improving accuracy and reducing overfitting.

Getting ready

We will use the previously defined `X_train_transformed` DataFrame from the *What is a pipeline?* subsection for this recipe, so there is no need to redefine it.

How to do it...

Feature engineering methods are generally categorized into three different approaches: filter methods, wrapper methods, and hybrid methods. Filter methods select features based on the statistical/mathematical characteristics of a feature, while wrapper methods evaluate subsets of features by building models with them and then evaluating which features elicit the best performance. Hybrid methods combine elements of both filter and wrapper methods. We will look at some of these methods next.

Common mathematical transformations

You can create new features by applying mathematical transformations to existing ones. Let's look at the common techniques in the next subsection.

PolynomialFeatures()

Let's generate polynomial and interaction features from existing numerical features:

1. Load the libraries:

```
from sklearn.preprocessing import PolynomialFeatures
```

2. Initialize `PolynomialFeatures()`:

```
poly = PolynomialFeatures(degree=2)
```

3. Fit and transform the `X_train_transformed` data. The output only shows a subset of the final result:

```
poly_features = poly.fit_transform(X_train_transformed)
poly_features_df = pd.DataFrame(
    poly_features,
    columns = poly.get_feature_names_out(
        X_train_transformed.columns
    )
)
poly_features_df
```

The resulting transformation is shown in the following figure.

	1	Age_scaled	Salary_scaled	Experience_scaled	Department_Finance	Department_HR	Department_IT	Department_Sales
0	1.0	0.834298	-0.867451	-1.559779	-0.577350	-0.480384	2.081666	-0.774597
1	1.0	-0.689202	1.282818	-0.150946	-0.577350	2.081666	-0.480384	-0.774597
2	1.0	0.544107	-1.173357	-1.761041	-0.577350	-0.480384	2.081666	-0.774597
3	1.0	-1.342131	0.821525	-0.150946	-0.577350	-0.480384	-0.480384	1.290994
4	1.0	1.414679	0.611115	0.654101	-0.577350	-0.480384	-0.480384	1.290994
5	1.0	-1.414679	-1.479801	1.257887	1.732051	-0.480384	-0.480384	-0.774597

Figure 2.14 – Polynomial features output

Now, let's proceed to our next feature engineering technique.

KBinsDiscretizer()

This algorithm works by converting continuous variables into categorical ones by binning them into discrete intervals. Think of it like creating buckets (the number of which is defined by the n_bins= argument) and filling each bucket with a continuous variable based on some defining criteria (based on the `strategy=` argument, where `uniform` means all buckets have the same size boundaries, such as 1-3, 4-6, and so on; `quantile`, where each bucket must have the same number of records assigned to it; or `kmeans`, which assigns each bucket a center value and all assigned records must be a certain distance from it).

Take the following steps:

1. Load the libraries:

```
from sklearn.preprocessing import KBinsDiscretizer
```

2. Initialize `KBinsDiscretizer`:

```
kbins = KBinsDiscretizer(
    n_bins=3, encode="ordinal", strategy="uniform")
```

3. Fit and transform the X_train_transformed data:

```
binned_data = kbins.fit_transform(X_train_transformed)
binned_df = pd.DataFrame(
    binned_data, columns=X_train_transformed.columns)
binned_df
```

Here is our transformed output.

	Age_scaled	Salary_scaled	Experience_scaled	Department_Finance	Department_HR	Department_IT	Department_Sales	Position_Junior	Position_Manager
0	2.0	0.0	0.0	0.0	0.0	2.0	0.0	0.0	0.0
1	0.0	2.0	1.0	0.0	2.0	0.0	0.0	0.0	2.0
2	2.0	0.0	0.0	0.0	0.0	2.0	0.0	0.0	2.0
3	0.0	2.0	1.0	0.0	0.0	0.0	2.0	0.0	0.0
4	2.0	1.0	2.0	0.0	0.0	0.0	2.0	0.0	2.0
5	0.0	0.0	2.0	2.0	0.0	0.0	0.0	0.0	2.0

Figure 2.15 – KBinsDiscretizer output

Now that we have a few techniques in our tool chest for creating new features prior to training, let's take a look at some techniques for automatically removing features that are not valuable to our model.

Techniques for selecting relevant features

Ideally, the optimal ML model is that one that performs the best with the fewest number of necessary features. Simplicity is always favored over complexity, so we should explore techniques for identifying features in our dataset that might not be helpful to model training so they can be removed.

RFE is a powerful technique that recursively removes the least important features based on a specified estimator's importance ranking. At first, our model uses all of the features it's given using a training algorithm that provides some details about feature importance, such as Random Forest, for example. The least important features are removed, or *pruned* in ML parlance, and the model is retrained. There is also an RFECV() method in scikit-learn that adds cross-validation to the approach, furthering the optimization.

Take the following steps:

1. Load the libraries:

```
from sklearn.feature_selection import RFE
from sklearn.linear_model import LinearRegression
```

2. Initialize the RFE:

```
rfe = RFE(
    estimator=LinearRegression(),
    n_features_to_select=1
)
```

3. Fit the RFE:

```
rfe.fit(X_train_transformed, y_train)
```

4. Get the ranking of features:

```
rfe.ranking_
# Output:
array([5, 4, 8, 6, 9, 3, 7, 2, 1])
```

Now, let's try the SelectFromModel() technique, which is a similar approach.

SelectFromModel()

SelectFromModel() allows users to select features based on their importance weights derived from a given model. This method is particularly useful when working with tree-based models such as Random Forest or gradient boosting.

The steps are as follows:

1. Load the libraries:

```
from sklearn.feature_selection import SelectFromModel
from sklearn.linear_model import LinearRegression
```

2. Initialize SelectFromModel with LinearRegression:

```
selector = SelectFromModel(
    estimator=LinearRegression(),
    prefit=False,
    # Use mean of feature importances as threshold:
    threshold='mean'
)
```

3. Fit the selector:

```
selector.fit(X_train_transformed, y_train)
```

4. Get the selected features:

```
selected_features_mask = selector.get_support()
```

5. Get the feature names that were selected:

```
selected_features = X_train_transformed.columns[
    selected_features_mask
].tolist()
```

6. Print feature importance scores and selection status:

```
feature_importance = pd.DataFrame({
    'Feature': X_train_transformed.columns,
    'Importance': selector.estimator_.coef_,
    'Selected': selected_features_mask
})
feature_importance.sort_values(
    'Importance', key=abs, ascending=False)
```

The following table displays both the importance score as well as whether the algorithm selected the feature for training. These parameters can always be adjusted in the model's arguments.

	Feature	Importance	Selected
8	Position_Manager	-5.000000e-01	True
7	Position_Junior	-4.330127e-01	True
2	Experience_scaled	-1.103284e-15	False
1	Salary_scaled	1.054712e-15	False
4	Department_HR	-4.649059e-16	False
3	Department_Finance	4.614364e-16	False
6	Department_Sales	-2.810252e-16	False
0	Age_scaled	2.078464e-16	False
5	Department_IT	-2.046974e-16	False

Figure 2.16 – Feature importances and model selection from SelectFromModel()

Now, let's test your understanding with some exercises.

Hands-on exercises

To illustrate these techniques, please reference the GitHub repository (`https://github.com/PacktPublishing/scikit-learn-Cookbook-Third-Edition`). You will engage in hands-on exercises using scikit-learn's imputation tools on datasets with missing values. Although we've included the code examples in the repository, we encourage you to explore them on your own and try using these tools with different arguments to see what results.

The following steps outline a general workflow:

Understand the characteristics of your dataset and identify potential areas for feature creation.

1. Use mathematical transformations or domain knowledge to derive new variables.

2. Apply techniques such as `RFE()` or `SelectFromModel()` to retain the most informative features.

3. Train models with both original and engineered datasets to compare performance metrics.

Practical exercises on data preprocessing

In this chapter, we've covered several methods commonly applied to data preprocessing. Now it's time to put it all together! Can you guess what tool might be helpful for this exercise? You got it: the `Pipeline()` class!

How to do it...

For these exercises, we will use a publicly available dataset, California Housing, which is included in the scikit-learn library. The dataset contains 20,640 records and 9 features, where the target value (what we are trying to predict with our model) is the average home price per 100,000 homes.

You are tasked with building a comprehensive data pipeline composed of steps you learned in this chapter. In the Jupyter notebook for *Chapter 2*, you will find an incomplete code block at the end called *Comprehensive Pipeline*, where you should add your code to complete the following steps:

1. Load the California Housing dataset.

2. Split the data.

3. Create a comprehensive pipeline with at least three steps, including an estimator (i.e., model) as the final step for predicting the target value.

4. Fit the pipeline to the dataset.

5. Evaluate the pipeline's performance on the test data (this was not covered explicitly in this chapter, so you'll have to research how on your own).

The solution is included in the notebook suffixed with (`Solution`). Keep in mind that your solution may use different transformers and/or estimators.

One topic we covered in *Chapter 1* was feature engineering. In *Chapter 2*, we will explore a related topic, dimensionality reduction, where we use statistical techniques to reduce our dataset's number of features while still retaining maximal information. Here is a diagram you can use to quickly determine the data transformation steps you should take based on characteristics of your data and any special considerations.

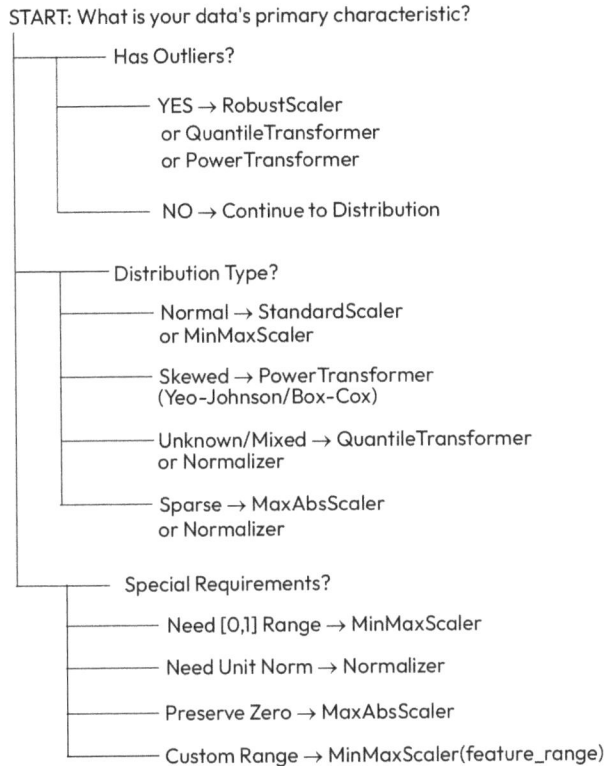

START: What is your data's primary characteristic?

- Has Outliers?
  - YES → RobustScaler
    or QuantileTransformer
    or PowerTransformer
  - NO → Continue to Distribution

- Distribution Type?
  - Normal → StandardScaler
    or MinMaxScaler
  - Skewed → PowerTransformer
    (Yeo-Johnson/Box-Cox)
  - Unknown/Mixed → QuantileTransformer
    or Normalizer
  - Sparse → MaxAbsScaler
    or Normalizer

- Special Requirements?
  - Need [0,1] Range → MinMaxScaler
  - Need Unit Norm → Normalizer
  - Preserve Zero → MaxAbsScaler
  - Custom Range → MinMaxScaler(feature_range)

Figure 2.17 – Decision guide for selecting the appropriate data transformation technique

Get This Book's PDF Version and Exclusive Extras

UNLOCK NOW

Scan the QR code (or go to `packtpub.com/unlock`). Search for this book by name, confirm the edition, and then follow the steps on the page.

Note: Keep your invoice handy. Purchases made directly from Packt don't require an invoice.

3

Dimensionality Reduction Techniques

Imagine you are making soup from scratch in your home's kitchen. This is the first time you've prepared this type of soup, so you decide to follow a recipe from a cookbook you have on hand. However, your ego gets the best of you, and you decide you can make the soup better by adding a few more ingredients and reducing a few. After heating up your new concoction, which, at this point, has strayed far from the original recipe, the taste test reveals…you've ruined the soup!

While we don't often get *recipes* for building ML models (although this book is full of them!), the analogy holds: the right combination of ingredients – or in the case of ML, training features – plays a significant part in model training and model performance.

This chapter is all about *finding the right ingredients* using **dimensionality reduction**. We will explore methods such as **Principal Component Analysis (PCA)**, **Linear Discriminant Analysis (LDA)**, and **t-Distributed Stochastic Neighbor Embedding** (**t-SNE**), focusing on when and how to apply them for data visualization and model efficiency. Coding exercises use datasets to practice reducing dimensions while retaining important features.

In this chapter, we're going to cover the following recipes:

- Introduction to dimensionality reduction
- Transforming datasets with PCA
- Maximizing class separability with LDA
- t-SNE and data visualization
- Selecting the right technique
- Impact on model performance

Technical requirements

It is advisable to create a Python environment for safely isolating your work from other Python installations/libraries. See the GitHub repository for more details (`https://github.com/PacktPublishing/scikit-learn-Cookbook-Third-Edition`).

- Git >=2.46.x

- Python >=3.9.x

- A cloned GitHub repository and Python environment built from the `requirements.txt` file

Introduction to dimensionality reduction

Dimensionality reduction is fundamental in developing robust ML pipelines on par with data preprocessing, explored in *Chapter 2*. It involves reducing the number of features (or dimensions) in a dataset while retaining as much relevant information as possible. There are several reasons for performing this task, including simplifying data, reducing computational costs, and enhancing model performance. Early in many data scientists' careers, they are keen to throw as much data as available into model training, but even though more data is better in some regards, if that data isn't related to our problem domain or doesn't improve our model, we are simply adding in *garbage* (remember, *garbage in, garbage out*)! So, why is dimensionality reduction one of the most important tasks in data preprocessing? Let's look more closely.

Why dimensionality reduction is essential

We often think that more data is always a good thing in ML training, but distilling our data down to a more manageable representation (while simultaneously avoiding information loss) is more important than data quantity.

- **Simplifying data**: High-dimensional datasets can be complex and challenging to visualize. By reducing the number of features, it becomes easier to interpret and analyze the data, allowing for clearer insights and better decision-making.

- **Reducing computational costs**: Fewer features mean reduced computational requirements for training ML models. This can lead to faster training times and lower resource consumption, making it feasible to work with larger datasets or more complex models.

- **Improving model performance**: High-dimensional data can lead to overfitting, where a model learns *noise* rather than the underlying patterns in the data. Dimensionality reduction helps mitigate this risk by eliminating irrelevant or redundant features, leading to models that generalize better on unseen data.

- **Enhancing visualization**: Many visualization techniques are limited to two or three dimensions (sure, you can have a visualization with a fourth dimension showing data evolving over time, but can you really imagine a *fifth dimension*?). Dimensionality reduction allows for the projection of high-dimensional data into lower dimensions, making it possible to visualize complex datasets effectively.

Theoretical foundations of dimensionality reduction

Dimensionality reduction techniques can be broadly categorized into two types. Let's explore them briefly.

Feature selection

Feature selection involves selecting a subset of relevant features from the original dataset without transforming them. This process can be based on statistical tests, model-based importance scores, or domain knowledge. Common methods include the following:

- **Filter methods**: These assess the relevance of features based on their statistical properties (e.g., correlation with the target variable)

- **Wrapper methods**: These evaluate subsets of features by training a model and assessing its performance (e.g., recursive feature elimination)

- **Embedded methods**: These perform feature selection as part of the model training process (e.g., Lasso regression)

There are also *hybrid* methods that combine multiple techniques, but we won't spend much time on those – just be aware that they exist.

Feature extraction

Feature extraction transforms the original features into a new space with fewer dimensions while retaining essential information. This approach includes techniques such as the following:

- **PCA**: PCA identifies the directions (principal components) in which the variance of the data is maximized, projecting the data onto these axes

- **LDA**: LDA is used for supervised dimensionality reduction by maximizing class separability

- **t-SNE**: t-SNE is particularly useful for visualizing high-dimensional data in two or three dimensions by preserving local structures

To effectively implement dimensionality reduction techniques in your ML projects, follow these steps:

1. Assess the dimensionality of your dataset and identify potential issues related to high dimensionality.

2. Depending on your goals – whether you need feature selection or feature extraction – select a suitable dimensionality reduction method.

3.   Use scikit-learn's tools to apply your chosen method to your dataset.

4.   Train models using both original and reduced datasets to compare performance metrics.

Transforming datasets with PCA

PCA is one of the most widely used techniques for dimensionality reduction in ML and data analysis. It helps simplify datasets by transforming them into a new coordinate system, where the greatest variance in the data is captured by the first few dimensions, called *principal components*. In this recipe, you will learn how to implement PCA using scikit-learn, interpret the results, and apply PCA to various datasets to effectively reduce feature dimensionality.

Getting ready

To begin, we will load our toy dataset from scikit-learn. Version 1.5 of scikit-learn contains 6 datasets that are commonly used to illustrate various ML steps and features in the library. In this case, we will be using the Wine dataset.

1.   Load the libraries. We will also load the `warnings` library to suppress warning messages that could clutter up our notebook.

```
import numpy as np
import pandas as pd
from sklearn.datasets import load_wine
import warnings
```

2.   Set random seed for reproducibility and suppress warning. This is just used in case we rely on any random number generation, so your result will be the same as ours.

```
np.random.seed(2024)
warnings.simplefilter(
    action='ignore', category=FutureWarning)
```

3.   Load the dataset. The first 6 rows and columns are displayed here. Before applying PCA, data should always be standardized. This also includes separating the target variable from the dataset if the modeling goal is a supervised learning task. You do not want this value included in the PCA.

```
wine = load_wine()
df_wine = pd.DataFrame(
    data=wine.data, columns=wine.feature_names)
target_wine = wine.target
display(df_wine.head(10))
```

Executing the preceding code will produce a table like the following one, visualizing a subset of our data (note: this figure only shows the first 6 rows, while the executed code will show the first 10).

	alcohol	malic_acid	ash	alcalinity_of_ash	magnesium	total_phenols
0	14.23	1.71	2.43	15.6	127.0	2.80
1	13.20	1.78	2.14	11.2	100.0	2.65
2	13.16	2.36	2.67	18.6	101.0	2.80
3	14.37	1.95	2.50	16.8	113.0	3.85
4	13.24	2.59	2.87	21.0	118.0	2.80
5	14.20	1.76	2.45	15.2	112.0	3.27

Figure 3.1 – Sample of the wine dataset

Now, with our dataset loaded, let's apply PCA.

How to do it...

We will load some additional libraries from scikit-learn, as well as Matplotlib, which is a commonly used Python library for data visualization. You'll also notice that we are using the Pipeline() class to string together the data scaling preprocessing step with PCA. This will be a regular convention in this book, so it's best to get comfortable with it!

1. Load the libraries:

```
from sklearn.preprocessing import StandardScaler
from sklearn.decomposition import PCA
from sklearn.pipeline import Pipeline
import matplotlib.pyplot as plt
```

2. Create a pipeline for PCA:

```
pca_pipeline = Pipeline([
    (
        'scaler', StandardScaler()
    ), # Always scale before PCA
    (
        'pca', PCA(n_components=2)
    ) # Reduce to 2 dimensions
])
```

3. Fit and transform the data:

```
X_pca = pca_pipeline.fit_transform(df_wine)
```

4. Visualize the transformed data:

```
plt.figure(figsize=(10, 8))
shapes = ['o', '^', 'D']
colors = ['r', 'g', 'b']
```

5. Plot the scatter points:

```
for i, (shape, color) in enumerate(zip(shapes, colors)):
    plt.scatter(
        X_pca[target_wine == i, 0],
        X_pca[target_wine == i, 1],
        c=color, marker=shape,
        label=wine.target_names[i]
    )
```

6. Get the PCA components and plot as vectors:

```
pca = pca_pipeline.named_steps['pca']
origin = np.zeros(2)   # Origin point for vectors
arrow_colors = ['black', 'orange']
```

7. Scale the components by their explained variance ratio for better visualization:

```
scaling = 3
for i, (component, ratio) in enumerate(zip(
    pca.components_, pca.explained_variance_ratio_)
):
    plt.arrow(
        origin[0], origin[1],
        component[0] * scaling,
        component[1] * scaling,
        color=arrow_colors[i],
        width=0.02,
        head_width=0.2, head_length=0.2,
        label=f'PC{i+1} ({ratio:.1%} variance)'
    )

plt.xlabel('First Principal Component')
plt.ylabel('Second Principal Component')
plt.title('Wine Dataset - First Two Principal Components')
plt.legend(title="Classes")
plt.grid(True, alpha=0.3)
plt.show()
```

The scatterplot visualizes the application of PCA by first color-coding our data points by class, then plotting them according to their first two derived principal components. The vectors indicate the direction of each component and the proportion of variance described by each.

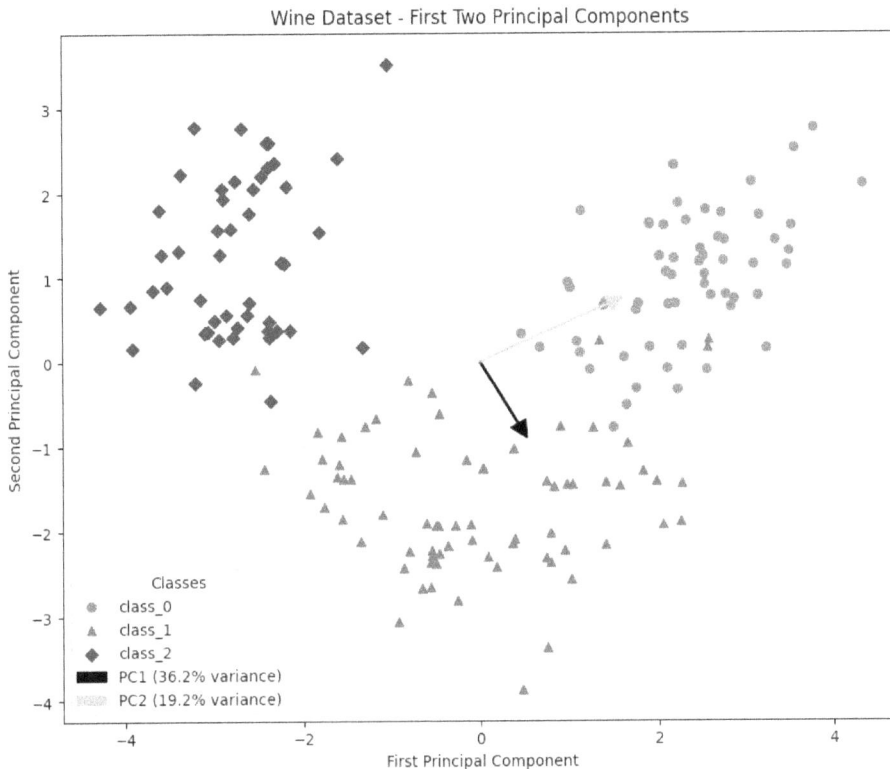

Figure 3.2 – PCA applied to the wine dataset

Even from a cursory inspection of this data, it's easy to see the separation of classes just by looking at the principal components alone. LDA, which is better suited for class separation, will be discussed shortly.

How it works...

PCA works by identifying the directions (principal components) in which the data varies the most. These components are linear combinations of the original features and are orthogonal (i.e., at right angles) to each other. The key steps involved in PCA are as follows:

1. **Standardization**: Since PCA is sensitive to the variances of the original variables, it is essential to standardize the data (mean = 0, variance = 1) before applying PCA.

2. **Covariance matrix computation**: The covariance matrix captures how much the dimensions vary from the mean with respect to each other.

3. **Eigenvalue and eigenvector calculation**: Eigenvalues indicate the amount of variance captured by each principal component, while eigenvectors represent the direction of these components.

4. **Selecting principal components**: By choosing a subset of principal components (based on their eigenvalues), we can reduce the dimensionality of the dataset while retaining most of its variance. In most cases, the first two principal components capture the most variation.

5. **Transforming data**: Finally, we project the original data onto the selected principal components to obtain a reduced representation.

Let's create a quick visualization to illustrate how PCA works.

1. Get the explained variance ratio:

```
pca = pca_pipeline.named_steps['pca']
explained_variance_ratio = pca.explained_variance_ratio_
```

2. Calculate cumulative variance:

```
cumulative_variance = np.sum(explained_variance_ratio)
```

3. Plot a bar chart:

```
fig, ax = plt.subplots()

x = np.arange(1, len(explained_variance_ratio) + 1)
y = explained_variance_ratio
bars = ax.bar(x, y)
```

4. Add percentage labels on the bars:

```
for bar in bars:
    height = bar.get_height()
    ax.text(
        bar.get_x() + bar.get_width()/2.,
        height, f'{height:.2%}',
        ha='center', va='bottom'
    )
```

5. Add cumulative variance text at the upper right:

```
ax.text(
    0.95, 0.95,
    f'Total Variance\nExplained: {cumulative_variance:.2%}',
    transform=ax.transAxes,
    ha='right', va='top',
    bbox=dict(
```

```
                    facecolor='white', alpha=0.8, edgecolor='none'
        )
    )
```

6. Set custom *x*-axis labels for the two principal components:

```
ax.set_xticks(x)
ax.set_xticklabels(['PC1', 'PC2'])

ax.set_xlabel('Principal Component')
ax.set_ylabel('Explained Variance Ratio')
ax.set_title('Explained Variance Ratio by Principal Component')
plt.show()
```

Here, we can see that more than half the total variance in our dataset is represented (i.e., *explained*) by the first two principal components. This information is also shown in *Figure 3.3*.

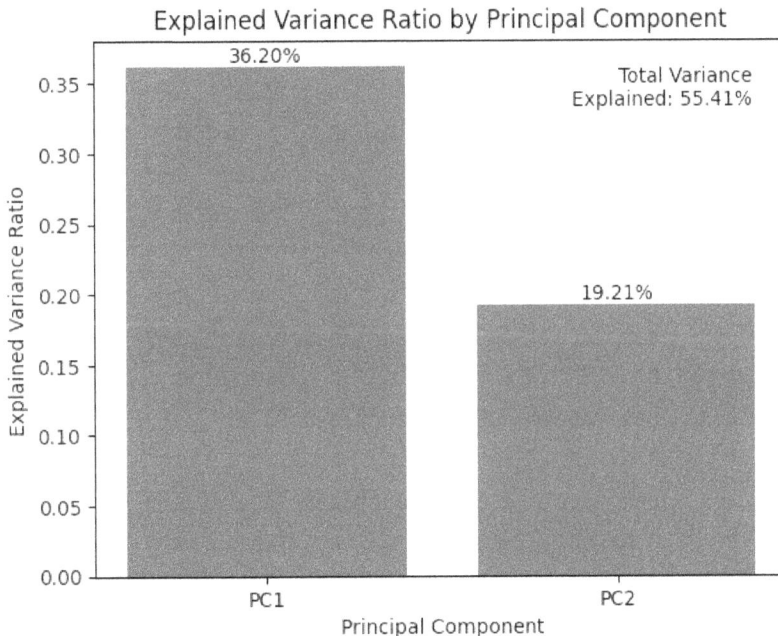

Figure 3.3 – Total variance explained by first two principal components: 55.41%

Remember that PCA is typically applied to high-dimensional data (i.e., data that contains many features) since it's hard to visualize data beyond three dimensions. *Figure 3.2* took into account all the features of the wine dataset when applying PCA, but we can also simplify things from the start by just showing two (standardized) features, both before and after PCA is applied. Code for this visualization is located in the Jupyter notebook and not here, for brevity.

Here, we've applied PCA to different combinations of individual features from our training data.

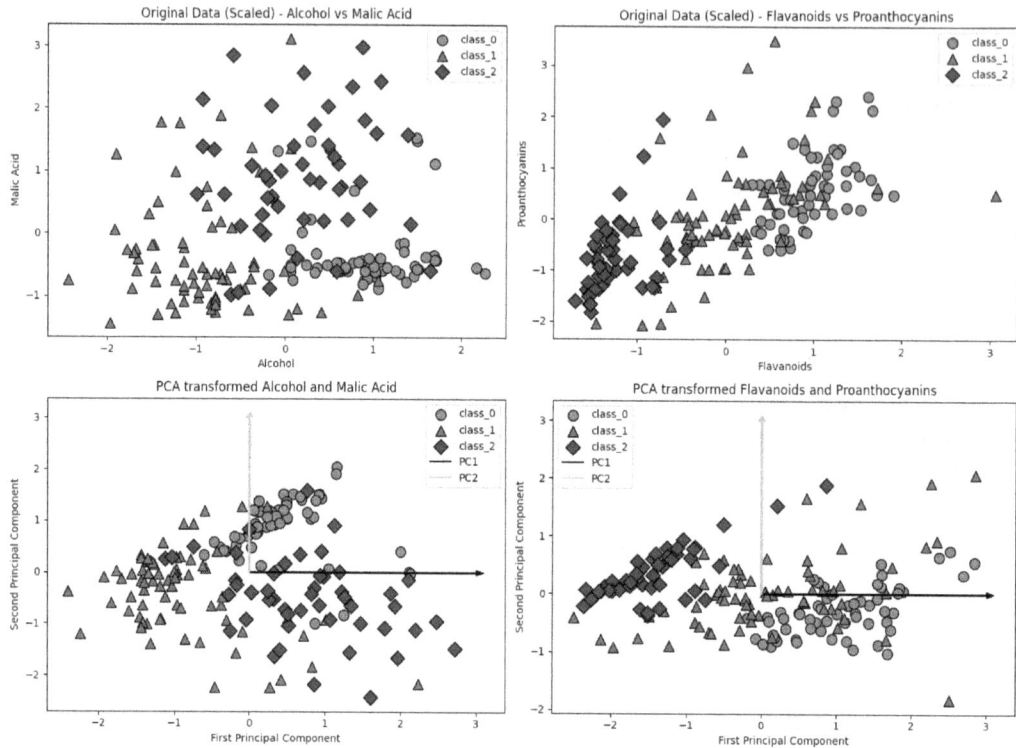

Figure 3.4 – Example of PCA applied to two features in the wine dataset

Figure 3.4 gives us a before-and-after visualization of PCA's application.

1. **Top row: original standardized features**: The first two scatter plots display pairs of original standardized features before PCA: **Alcohol vs Malic Acid** on the left and **Flavanoids vs Proanthocyanins** on the right. Each data point is color-coded by wine class (**class_0**, **class_1**, **class_2**), with distinct markers for each class. The distribution shows overlap and separation among classes in the raw feature space.

2. **Bottom row: PCA-transformed features**: The bottom row shows the same features transformed using PCA, where data is reoriented along the first two principal components (**PC1** and **PC2**). The arrows indicate the directions of PC1 and PC2, which capture the maximum variance in the data. PCA helps to better separate the wine classes by projecting the features into a lower-dimensional space with improved class distinction.

Hands-on exercises

To illustrate these techniques, please reference the GitHub repository (`https://github.com/PacktPublishing/scikit-learn-Cookbook-Third-Edition`). You will engage in hands-on exercises using scikit-learn's `PCA()` class. Although we've included the preceding code examples, we encourage you to explore on your own and try using these tools with different arguments to see what results:

1. Understand your dataset's dimensionality and identify potential issues related to high dimensionality.

2. Ensure that all features are on a similar scale before applying PCA.

3. Use scikit-learn's PCA class to reduce dimensionality while retaining important information.

4. Examine explained variance ratios and visualize transformed data to assess how well PCA has performed.

5. Use reduced features in subsequent modeling tasks for improved performance and efficiency.

Maximizing class separability with LDA

LDA is a powerful dimensionality reduction technique that is particularly useful for supervised learning tasks, especially in classification problems. Unlike PCA, which focuses on maximizing *variance* across all data points without considering class labels, LDA aims to maximize *class separability*.

Getting ready

We will use the same wine dataset used previously, so we do not have to load it again.

How to do it...

As we saw with PCA, LDA only requires loading a single scikit-learn class to perform it on your dataset. We will also be using the `Pipeline()` class to string together our scaling prior to applying LDA.

1. Load the libraries:

```
from sklearn.discriminant_analysis import
LinearDiscriminantAnalysis
```

2. Split the wine dataset by features and target:

```
X_wine, y_wine = wine.data, wine.target
```

3. Create an LDA pipeline for the wine dataset:

```
lda_pipeline_wine = Pipeline([
    ('scaler', StandardScaler()),
    ('lda', LinearDiscriminantAnalysis(n_components=2))
    # min(n_features, n_classes - 1) for wine dataset is 2
])
```

4. Fit and transform the wine data:

```
X_lda_wine = lda_pipeline_wine.fit_transform(
    X_wine, y_wine
)
```

5. Visualize LDA transformation for the wine dataset:

```
plt.figure(figsize=(10, 8))
```

6. Define markers and colors for each class:

```
shapes = ['o', '^', 'D']
colors = ['r', 'g', 'b']
```

7. Plot each class with a different marker and color:

```
for i, (shape, color) in enumerate(zip(shapes, colors)):
    mask = y_wine == i
    plt.scatter(
        X_lda_wine[mask, 0], X_lda_wine[mask, 1],
        c=color, marker=shape, edgecolor='black',
        label=wine.target_names[i]
    )

plt.xlabel('First LDA Component')
plt.ylabel('Second LDA Component')
plt.title('Wine Dataset - LDA Components')
plt.legend()
plt.show()
```

LDA, while similar to PCA, is designed for aiding in class separability, which becomes apparent in the following visualization.

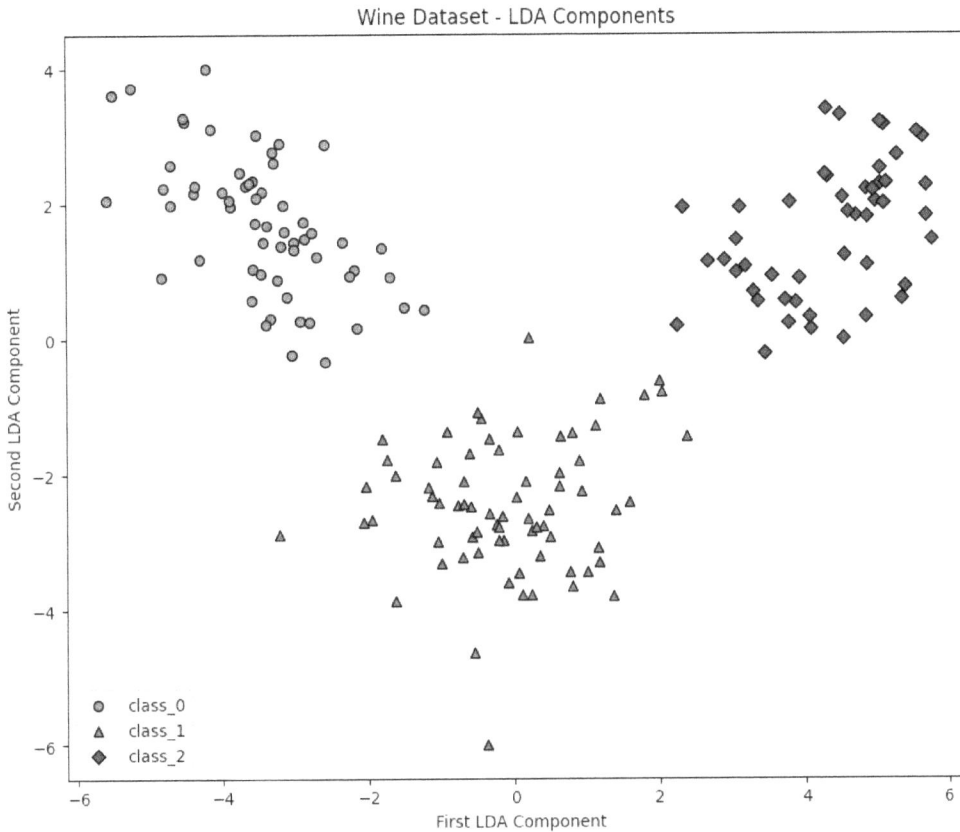

Figure 3.5 – LDA is designed to maximize the separation of clusters

Figure 3.5 shows that, after applying LDA, we can easily see natural groupings of the three classes in our wine dataset.

How it works...

LDA is a supervised technique that seeks to find a linear combination of features that best separates two or more classes. The primary goals of LDA are as follows:

- **Maximize class separability**: LDA identifies the axes that maximize the distance between different classes while minimizing the variance within each class. This helps in enhancing the discriminative power of the features.

- **Dimensionality reduction**: By projecting the data onto a lower-dimensional space defined by the linear discriminants, LDA reduces the complexity of the dataset while retaining information important for classification.

- **Assumptions**: LDA assumes that the data for each class follows a Gaussian (normal) distribution with a common covariance matrix, which, in simple terms, means each feature has a similar variance (this is why we apply standardization). This assumption allows LDA to perform effectively when the classes are well-separated.

Differences between PCA and LDA

While both PCA and LDA are used for dimensionality reduction, they have distinct objectives and methodologies:

- **Supervised versus unsupervised**: PCA is an *unsupervised* method that focuses on *maximizing variance* without considering class labels, while LDA is *supervised* and seeks to *maximize class separability* using labeled data.

- **Objective**: PCA aims to retain as much variance as possible across all data points, whereas LDA aims to maximize the separation between different classes.

- **Output**: PCA generates principal components that capture maximum variance; these components are orthogonal. In contrast, LDA produces linear discriminants that are specifically designed to enhance class separability.

- **Use cases**: PCA is often used for exploratory data analysis and feature extraction when class labels are not available. In contrast, LDA is primarily used for classification tasks where distinguishing between classes is essential.

When visualized, both PCA and LDA can be similar in appearance, depending on the dataset they're applied to.

1. Create side-by-side plots:

```
plt.figure(figsize=(14, 6))

plt.subplot(121)
shapes = ['o', '^', 'D']
colors = ['r', 'g', 'b']

for i, (shape, color) in enumerate(zip(shapes, colors)):
    mask = y_wine == i
    plt.scatter(
        X_pca[mask, 0], X_pca[mask, 1],
        c=color, marker=shape, edgecolor='black',
        label=wine.target_names[i]
    )

plt.xlabel('First Principal Component')
plt.ylabel('Second Principal Component')
```

```
plt.title('Wine Dataset - PCA Components')
plt.legend()

plt.subplot(122)
for i, (shape, color) in enumerate(zip(shapes, colors)):
    mask = y_wine == i
    plt.scatter(
        X_lda_wine[mask, 0], X_lda_wine[mask, 1],
        c=color, marker=shape, edgecolor='black',
        label=wine.target_names[i]
    )

plt.xlabel('First LDA Component')
plt.ylabel('Second LDA Component')
plt.title('Wine Dataset - LDA Components')
plt.legend()
plt.tight_layout()
plt.show()
```

Here, we see PCA and LDA compared side by side.

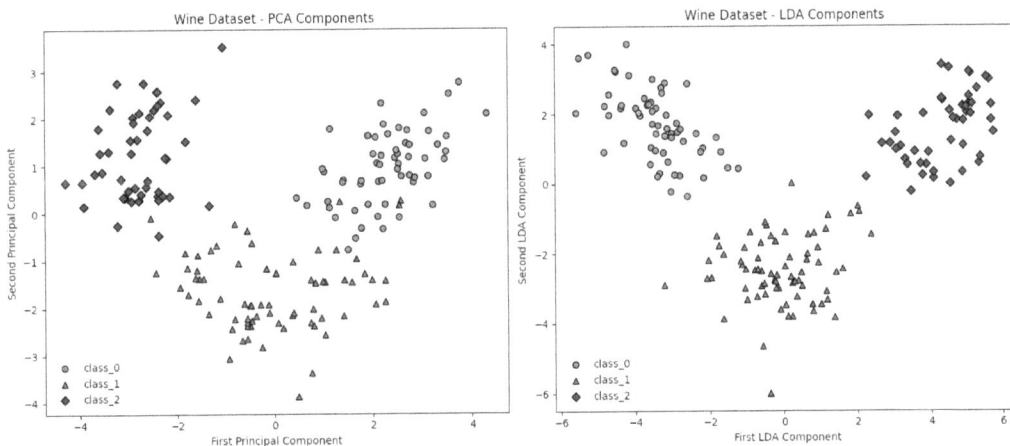

Figure 3.6 – PCA and LDA comparison

Class separation is a little more striking with LDA but this can be attributed, in part, to being a supervised learning method where class labels are known, and utilized, during application.

Hands-on exercises

To illustrate these techniques, please refer to the following GitHub repository (`https://github.com/PacktPublishing/scikit-learn-Cookbook-Third-Edition`). You will engage in hands-on exercises using scikit-learn's `LinearDiscriminantAnalysis()` class. Although we've included the preceding code examples, we encourage you to explore on your own and try using these tools with different arguments to see what results:

1. Ensure you have labeled data suitable for classification tasks.

2. Standardization helps ensure all features contribute equally.

3. Use scikit-learn's LDA class to reduce dimensionality while maximizing class separation.

4. Examine how well different classes are separated in the reduced space.

5. Use reduced features in subsequent modeling tasks for improved performance.

t-SNE and data visualization

t-SNE is a technique for visualizing high-dimensional data by mapping it into a lower-dimensional space, typically two or three dimensions. This method is particularly effective for revealing the underlying structure of complex datasets, making it easier to interpret and analyze patterns, clusters, and relationships within the data.

Getting ready

For our t-SNE demonstration, we'll be using a different dataset: another *famous* machine learning dataset called **MNIST**, which consists of images of handwritten digits 0-9. This is from the UCI Machine Learning Repository: *We used preprocessing programs made available by NIST to extract normalized bitmaps of handwritten digits from a preprinted form. From a total of 43 people, 30 contributed to the training set and different 13 to the test set. 32x32 bitmaps are divided into nonoverlapping blocks of 4x4 and the number [sic] of on pixels are counted in each block. This generates an input matrix of 8x8 where each element is an integer in the range 0..16. This reduces dimensionality and gives invariance to small distortions.*

1. Load the libraries:

```
from sklearn.datasets import load_digits
```

2. Load the dataset:

```
digits = load_digits()
```

This dataset is fairly quick to load and only requires two lines of code.

How to do it...

Again, we will use the `Pipeline()` class to sequentially apply data scaling prior to t-SNE.

1. Load the libraries:

```
from sklearn.manifold import TSNE
```

2. Create a t-SNE pipeline:

```
tsne_pipeline = Pipeline([
    ('scaler', StandardScaler()),
    ('tsne', TSNE(n_components=2, random_state=2024))
])
```

3. Fit and transform the digits data:

```
X_tsne = tsne_pipeline.fit_transform(digits.data)
```

4. Visualize the t-SNE results:

```
plt.figure(figsize=(10, 8))
scatter = plt.scatter(
    X_tsne[:, 0], X_tsne[:, 1],
    c=digits.target, cmap='Paired',
    label=digits.target
)
plt.xlabel('t-SNE Component 1')
plt.ylabel('t-SNE Component 2')
plt.title('Digits Dataset - t-SNE Visualization')
```

5. Create a legend:

```
legend_elements = [
    plt.Line2D(
        [0], [0], marker='o', color='w',
        markerfacecolor=plt.cm.Paired(i/9),
        label=str(i), markersize=10
    )
    for i in range(10)
]
plt.legend(
    handles=legend_elements,
    title='Digit', loc='center left',
    bbox_to_anchor=(1, 0.5)
)
```

```
plt.tight_layout()
plt.show()
```

Similar to LDA, t-SNE excels at class separation, even when the number of classes and underlying dimensions in our data grows, in this case to 10 classes.

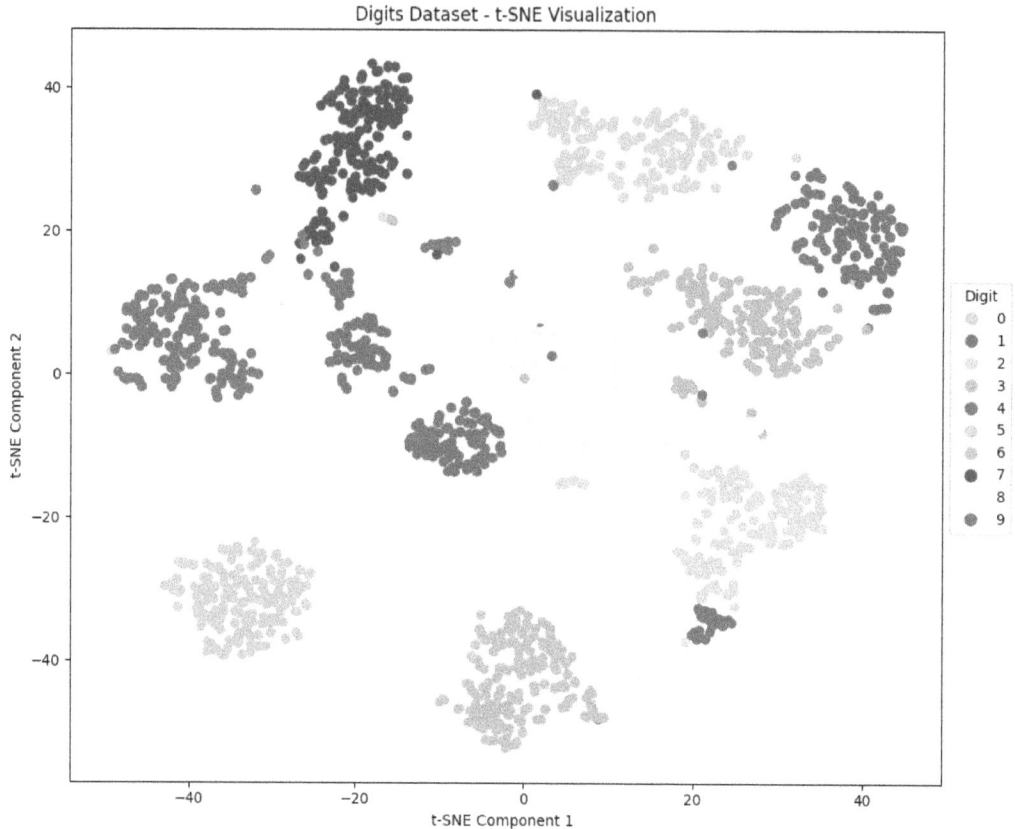

Figure 3.7 – t-SNE can effectively visualize multi-class datasets

Figure 3.7 gives us some insight into the structure of our handwritten digits that, if you think about it, makes sense logically. For instance, we see a lot of "9s" close to the "7s" and "4s," which, when you think about it, makes sense since both "9" and "4," and to some degree "7," are written similarly (depending on how good/bad your handwriting is! We also notice that "0" is clustered and isolated in the bottom-left corner since it resembles no other digit closely (at least in our opinion).

How it works...

t-SNE is a non-linear dimensionality reduction technique that excels in visualizing high-dimensional data. It works by converting high-dimensional, Euclidean distances between points into conditional probabilities that represent similarities. The key stages of t-SNE are as follows:

1. **Pairwise similarities**: t-SNE first calculates pairwise similarities between high-dimensional data points, assigning higher probabilities to similar points and lower probabilities to dissimilar ones.

2. **Low-dimensional mapping**: It then attempts to find a low-dimensional representation (2D or 3D) of the data that preserves these similarities as closely as possible.

3. **Cluster formation**: The result is a visualization where similar data points are grouped closely together, while dissimilar points are spaced further apart, effectively revealing clusters within the data.

Hands-on exercises

To illustrate these techniques, please refer to the GitHub repository (`https://github.com/PacktPublishing/scikit-learn-Cookbook-Third-Edition`). You will engage in hands-on exercises using scikit-learn's `TSNE()` class. Although we've included the preceding code examples, we encourage you to explore on your own and try using these tools with different arguments to see what results:

1. Understand the characteristics of your dataset and identify which features are relevant for visualization.

2. Ensure all features are on a similar scale before applying t-SNE.

3. Use scikit-learn's `TSNE` class to reduce dimensionality while preserving meaningful relationships.

4. Create scatter plots to visualize how well t-SNE has captured the structure of your data.

5. Analyze the resulting clusters to gain insights into patterns and relationships within your dataset.

There's more...

Choosing the appropriate dimensionality reduction technique is essential for effectively managing high-dimensional datasets and enhancing model performance. As we've seen, different techniques serve different purposes and are suited to various types of data and analytical goals. However, keep in mind that sometimes these techniques can be used together in certain instances.

The following flowchart summarizes how to decide between common dimensionality reduction techniques:

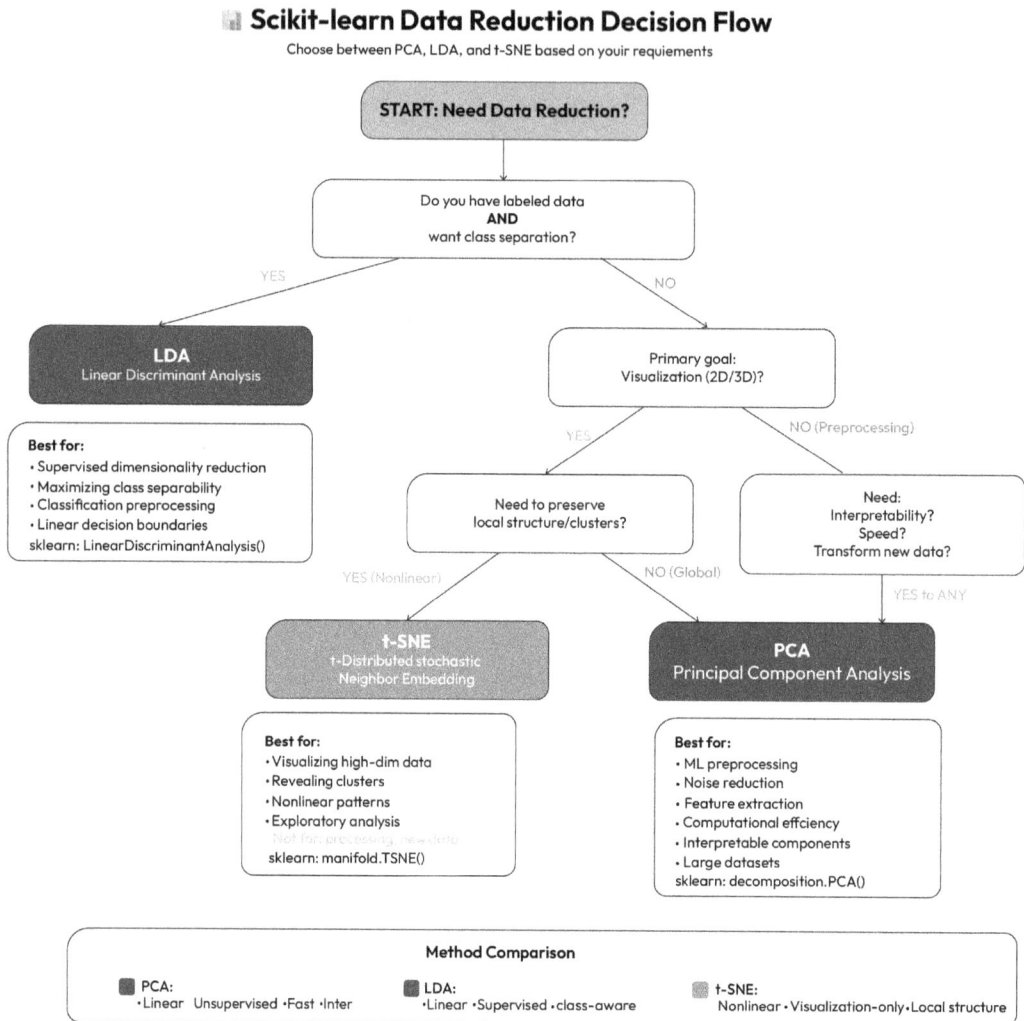

Scikit-learn Data Reduction Decision Flow

Choose between PCA, LDA, and t-SNE based on youir requiements

START: Need Data Reduction?

Do you have labeled data
AND
want class separation?

YES

NO

LDA
Linear Discriminant Analysis

Primary goal:
Visualization (2D/3D)?

YES

NO (Preprocessing)

Best for:
• Supervised dimensionality reduction
• Maximizing class separability
• Classification preprocessing
• Linear decision boundaries
sklearn: LinearDiscriminantAnalysis()

Need to preserve
local structure/clusters?

Need:
Interpretability?
Speed?
Transform new data?

YES (Nonlinear)

NO (Global)

YES to ANY

t-SNE
t-Distributed stochastic
Neighbor Embedding

PCA
Principal Component Analysis

Best for:
• Visualizing high-dim data
• Revealing clusters
• Nonlinear patterns
• Exploratory analysis
Not for preprocessing new data
sklearn: manifold.TSNE()

Best for:
• ML preprocessing
• Noise reduction
• Feature extraction
• Computational effciency
• Interpretable components
• Large datasets
sklearn: decomposition.PCA()

Method Comparison

PCA:
•Linear Unsupervised •Fast •Inter

LDA:
•Linear •Supervised •class-aware

t-SNE:
Nonlinear • Visualization-only• Local structure

Figure 3.8 – Selecting the right dimensionality reduction technique

Guidelines for selecting dimensionality reduction techniques

When deciding which dimensionality reduction technique to use, consider the following factors:

- **Supervised versus unsupervised**: What is the nature of your data? If you have labeled data and are interested in maximizing class separability, LDA is a suitable choice. For unlabeled data where you want to capture variance without considering class labels, PCA is more appropriate. t-SNE can be used for visualization purposes regardless of whether the data is labeled.

- **Variance versus class separability**: What objective are you trying to solve? If your goal is to retain as much variance as possible in the dataset, PCA is ideal. If your focus is on enhancing class separability for classification tasks, LDA should be your choice. For visualizing complex relationships and clusters in high-dimensional data, t-SNE excels.

- **Feature extraction versus visualization**: PCA and LDA are primarily used for feature extraction to improve model performance by reducing dimensionality while retaining essential information. In contrast, t-SNE is specifically designed for visualization, helping to reveal patterns and structures in high-dimensional data.

- **Efficiency**: How computationally complex is your problem space? PCA is generally computationally efficient and can handle large datasets effectively. LDA requires the computation of class means and covariance matrices, which may be less efficient with very high-dimensional data or when the number of classes is large. t-SNE can be computationally intensive, especially with large datasets, due to its iterative optimization process.

- **Understanding results**: Does interpretability play a starring role in your rationale for utilizing one of these techniques? PCA provides principal components that are linear combinations of original features, which can sometimes be difficult to interpret. LDA produces linear discriminants that are more interpretable in terms of class separation. t-SNE results are primarily visual and may not provide direct interpretability regarding feature contributions.

We will compare PCA, LDA, and t-SNE in a tabular format as follows:

Technique	Type	Purpose	Key Features	Best Use Cases
PCA	Unsupervised	Dimensionality Reduction	Maximizes variance; linear combinations of features	Exploratory data analysis, noise reduction, feature extraction
LDA	Supervised	Dimensionality Reduction	Maximizes class separability; linear discriminants	Classification tasks where class separation is important
t-SNE	Unsupervised	Visualization	Non-linear mapping; reveals clusters; preserves local structure	Visualizing high-dimensional data; exploratory analysis

Table 3.1 – Comparison of dimensionality reduction techniques

There are certain instances where the application of one method of dimensionality reduction is better than another. Often, this is dictated by the data itself.

Practical steps for selection

Here's how to select the right dimensionality reduction technique for your specific dataset and problem:

1. Clearly outline what you aim to achieve with dimensionality reduction – whether it's improving model performance or visualizing complex relationships.

2. Understand the nature of your data (labeled versus unlabeled) and its dimensionality characteristics.

3. Assess the size of your dataset and available computational resources, as some techniques may require more processing power than others.

4. If unsure which method works best, consider applying multiple techniques (e.g., PCA followed by t-SNE) to see which provides better insights or model performance.

5. After applying a dimensionality reduction technique, evaluate its effectiveness based on model performance metrics or visualization clarity.

Impact on model performance

Dimensionality reduction can significantly influence model performance. While reducing the number of features can lead to simpler models, faster training times, and reduced risk of overfitting, it can also impact the accuracy and effectiveness of the model.

Understanding the trade-offs

When applying dimensionality reduction techniques, several trade-offs must be considered:

- **Model complexity versus interpretability**:

  - *Reduced complexity*: Fewer features often lead to simpler models that are easier to interpret and understand. This can enhance the ability to communicate findings and insights derived from the model.

  - *Loss of information*: However, reducing dimensions may result in the loss of important information that could be critical for accurate predictions. Striking a balance between complexity and interpretability is vital.

- **Training time versus accuracy**:

  - *Faster training*: Models trained on lower-dimensional datasets typically require less computational time and resources. This can be particularly advantageous when working with large datasets.

  - *Potential accuracy loss*: If important features are discarded during dimensionality reduction, the model's accuracy may suffer. It is crucial to evaluate how much accuracy is sacrificed relative to the gains in efficiency.

- **Overfitting versus generalization**:

  - *Reduced overfitting*: Dimensionality reduction can help mitigate overfitting by eliminating noise and irrelevant features from the dataset. This often leads to better generalization on unseen data.

  - *Risk of underfitting*: Conversely, if too many dimensions are removed, the model may become too simplistic (underfitting), failing to capture essential patterns in the data.

Practical exercises in dimensionality reduction

Wrapping up the chapter, you will engage in practical exercises that involve applying PCA, LDA, and t-SNE to various datasets. These hands-on activities will reinforce the understanding of when and how to use each dimensionality reduction technique to enhance model efficiency and effectiveness.

Example 1: PCA with logistic regression

In this example, we will analyze how applying PCA before training a logistic regression model affects performance on the Iris dataset. We realize we haven't covered logistic regression, so this will be an exercise in pushing your boundaries!

Here are the implementation steps:

1. Load the libraries.
2. Split the data.
3. Create a pipeline without PCA.
4. Create a pipeline with PCA.
5. Fit and evaluate both pipelines.
6. Print the results.

Example 2: t-SNE for visualization

In this example, we will use t-SNE for visualizing high-dimensional data from a more complex dataset (e.g., MNIST) while analyzing how it impacts subsequent classification tasks.

Here are the implementation steps:

1. Load the libraries.
2. Apply K-means clustering.
3. Create side-by-side plots.
4. Plot using true labels.
5. Plot using cluster labels.

Dimensionality reduction techniques can have a profound impact on ML model performance by simplifying datasets and improving interpretability, while potentially sacrificing some accuracy. Understanding these trade-offs is essential for making informed decisions about when and how to apply dimensionality reduction in practice.

Now we are ready to move forward with the core task of ML pipeline development: model training! In the next chapter, we will discuss some of the more fundamental models in the ML ecosystem before moving towards more and more complex models.

Get This Book's PDF Version and Exclusive Extras

UNLOCK NOW

Scan the QR code (or go to `packtpub.com/unlock`). Search for this book by name, confirm the edition, and then follow the steps on the page.

Note: Keep your invoice handy. Purchases made directly from Packt don't require an invoice.

## 4

Building Models with Distance Metrics and Nearest Neighbors

As human beings, it's relatively easy for us to distinguish between objects that are both similar and dissimilar to one another. For example, even a young child could tell you that a Toyota and say, a cheetah are not the same thing… not even close (although they might both be capable of moving fast!). However, a cheetah and a puma *do* share many common characteristics, with both being quadrupedal animals with tails, claws, and so on. So, if shown an image of a Toyota and asked whether it was a car or a cat, our same young child would probably have no problem categorizing it as a car. This type of comparison forms the basis of some of the simplest methods for classification in **machine learning (ML)** and allows us to classify new objects based on their similarity to known objects already classified.

This chapter discusses models based on distance metrics, such as **k-nearest neighbors (KNN)**, covering theory, implementation, and optimization. Exercises include building KNN models on different datasets and tuning parameters for optimal performance. By the end of this chapter, you should feel comfortable understanding the concept of **distance** in ML, as well as how to apply this concept in KNN.

In this chapter, we're going to cover the following recipes:

- Introduction to distance metrics
- Understanding KNNs
- Distance metrics overview
- Model implementation in scikit-learn
- Hyperparameter tuning in KNN
- Evaluating KNN performance

Technical requirements

It is advisable to create a Python environment for safely isolating your work from other Python installations/libraries. See the GitHub repository for more details (`https://github.com/PacktPublishing/scikit-learn-Cookbook-Third-Edition`). You will need the following for this chapter:

- Git >=2.46.x

- Python >=3.9.x

- A cloned GitHub repository and Python environment built from the `requirements.txt` file

Introduction to distance metrics

Distance metrics are fundamental components in many ML algorithms, particularly those that rely on the concept of similarity or dissimilarity between data points. Understanding how to measure the distance between points in a feature space is central for tasks such as clustering, classification, and regression. In this chapter, we will explore various distance metrics, including **Euclidean**, **Manhattan**, and **Minkowski distances**. We will also provide hands-on examples of calculating these metrics using scikit-learn, along with the algorithms that utilize them.

What is "distance" in ML?

In ML, we are often interested in understanding how similar (or dissimilar) different data points are in our dataset. This is especially true in classification problems where we may make the assumption that if it looks like a duck, walks like a duck, and quacks like a duck, well, then it's probably a duck… and not, say, a bear!

Euclidean, Manhattan, and Minkowski distances are three different ways of measuring the distance between points (often vectors) in a space:

- **Euclidean distance**: This is the standard straight-line (some say *as the crow flies*) distance in n-dimensional space. So, if you have a simple chart with an *x* and a *y* axis, the direct measurement between those two points using that coordinate system would be the Euclidean distance.

- **Manhattan distance**: Think of it like navigating a city laid out in a rectangular grid (such as Manhattan in New York City). You can only move along orthogonal (horizontal and vertical) directions, not diagonally. In some ML contexts where *absolute* differences are more meaningful or robust to outliers than *squared* differences, this would be a better metric.

- **Minkowski distance**: The Minkowski distance is really just the generalization of both Euclidean and Manhattan distances, where we adjust a parameter, p, to determine how we aggregate distances into a single metric.

For most use cases, Euclidean distance will be the default choice, but it's good to understand each.

Understanding KNNs

The KNN algorithm is a fundamental supervised learning technique used for both classification and regression tasks. The idea is simple: if we take our collection of existing data points and plot them in feature space before we are given a new data point, can we estimate the characteristics of that new data point based on the existing ones *nearest* to it using a distance metric? When we qualify and/or quantify the characteristics of something (such as the car or cheetah in our introductory example), we can use a variety of measurements to describe it. For example, things such as color and shape would be **qualitative** measurements, while length, width, and height would be **quantitative**. In combination, these types of measurements can be used to form comparisons when introducing a new *something* so that we can make logical guesses regarding how it should be included in the existing set of *somethings* we already have. This next recipe will teach you the basic application of KNN, but it will be expanded in further detail as we progress.

Getting ready

To begin, we will load another toy dataset from scikit-learn and split it into our training and testing datasets. The Iris dataset is yet another commonly used dataset for demonstrating ML concepts:

1. Load the libraries:

    ```
    from sklearn.datasets import load_iris
    from sklearn.model_selection import train_test_split
    ```

2. Load the `iris` dataset. Using the `.data()` and `.target()` methods allows us to easily separate the target feature from the rest of the dataset:

    ```
    iris = load_iris()
    X = iris.data
    y = iris.target
    ```

3. Split the data:

    ```
    X_train, X_test, y_train, y_test = train_test_split(
        X, y, test_size=0.2, random_state=2024
    )
    ```

By now, this step in the workflow – splitting our dataset – should be routine!

How to do it...

scikit-learn makes KNN extremely easy to implement (although the same could be said about most other implementations within the library):

1. Load the libraries:

    ```
    from sklearn.neighbors import KNeighborsClassifier
    from sklearn.metrics import accuracy_score
    ```

2. Create and train a basic KNN model:

    ```
    knn = KNeighborsClassifier(n_neighbors=3)
    knn.fit(X_train, y_train)
    ```

3. Make predictions:

    ```
    y_pred = knn.predict(X_test)
    print("Accuracy:", accuracy_score(y_test, y_pred))
    # Output:
    Accuracy: 0.9333333333333333
    ```

So, after training just using the default arguments of our KNN model, we're able to achieve 93% accuracy, which isn't a bad start.

How it works...

KNN operates on a straightforward principle: it classifies a new data point (the *something* mentioned at the beginning of this recipe) based on the majority label of its KNN in the training dataset. The algorithm follows these steps:

*   **Choosing k**: The k parameter represents the number of nearest neighbors to consider when making predictions. A smaller k value can make the model sensitive to noise in the data, while a larger k value can smooth out predictions but may overlook local patterns.

*   **Calculating distances**: To determine which neighbors are closest to a given point, KNN uses distance metrics such as Euclidean distance, Manhattan distance, or some other implementation of Minkowski distance. The choice of distance metric can significantly affect classification outcomes.

*   **Voting mechanism**: For classification tasks, KNN assigns a label to a new point based on majority voting among its *k* nearest neighbors – if there are more instances of, say, class *A* than class *B* nearest to the new point, we'd predict its class as *A*. In regression tasks, it computes the average of the values of these neighbors.

Visualizing how KNN classifies points can provide insights into its functionality. By plotting data points along with decision boundaries formed by different values of k, you can observe how varying k values affect classification results.

There's more...

Selecting an optimal value for k is crucial for achieving good performance with KNN. Common strategies include the following:

- **Cross-validation**: Use cross-validation techniques to evaluate model performance across different values of k and select one that minimizes error.

- **Elbow method**: Plotting accuracy against different values of k can help identify an *elbow point*, where increasing k yields diminishing returns in performance. This *elbow* is in reference to the visualization used to identify this point.

Distance metrics variations

While Euclidean distance is commonly used, experimenting with other distance metrics (e.g., Hamming for categorical data) can yield better results, depending on the nature of your dataset. We'll talk about these in the next section.

To help you decide which distance metric best suits your dataset, the following diagram outlines a simple decision process:

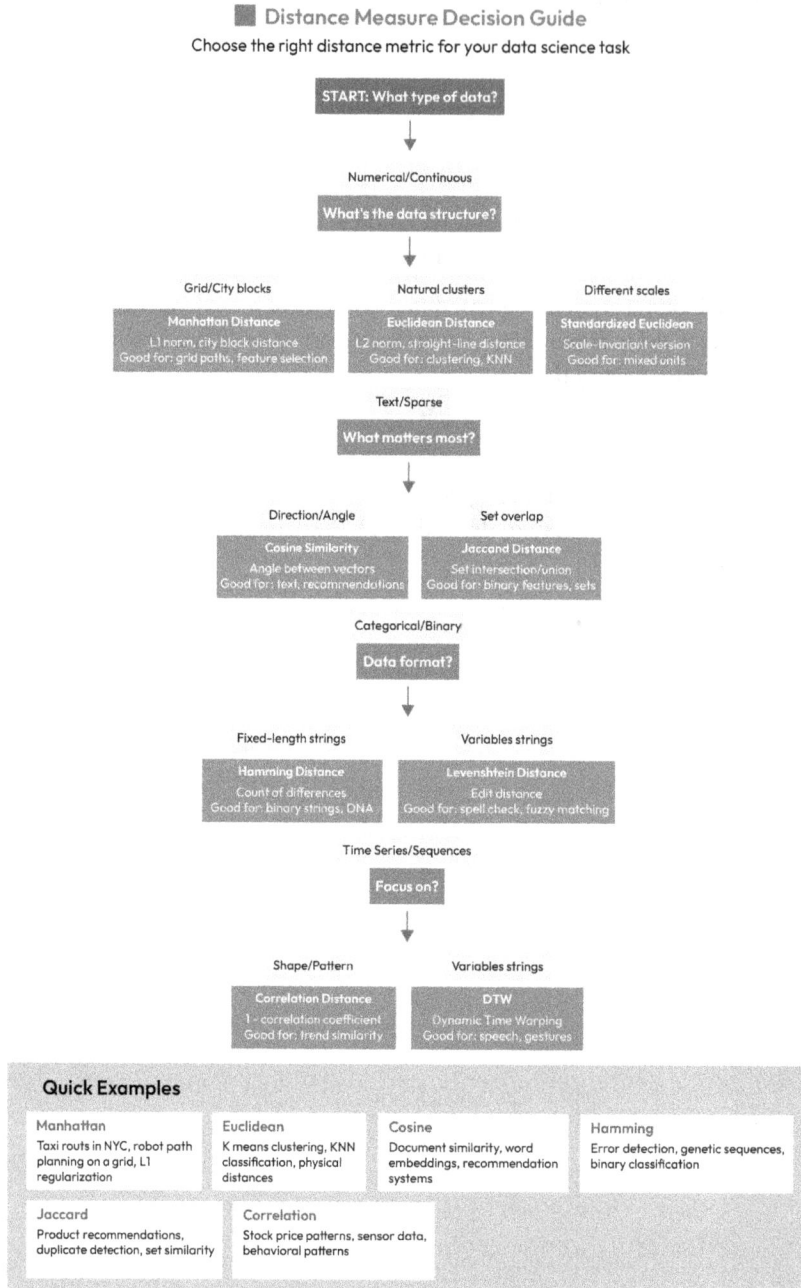

Figure 4.1 – Choosing the right distance metric based on data characteristics and structure

Hands-on exercises

To illustrate these techniques, please reference the GitHub repository (`https://github.com/PacktPublishing/scikit-learn-Cookbook-Third-Edition`). You will engage in hands-on exercises using scikit-learn's KNN algorithm. Although we've included the previous code examples, we encourage you to explore on your own and try using these tools with different arguments to see what results. The following steps outline a general workflow:

1. Load `KNeighborsClassifier` from `sklearn.neighbors`.
2. Choose different values for `k` and observe how it affects classification performance.
3. Use the accuracy score or confusion matrix to assess how well your model performs on unseen data.
4. Experiment with different distance metrics to see their impact on results.
5. Create plots to visualize decision boundaries and highlight correctly classified versus misclassified points.

Distance metrics overview

Distance metrics are essential for measuring the similarity or dissimilarity between data points in various ML algorithms, including KNN. The choice of distance metric can significantly influence model performance, affecting how data points are classified and how clusters are formed, so it's best to get comfortable with more than the standard Euclidean distance most early data science practitioners default to. This recipe will give you an opportunity to see how different distance metrics compare when datasets contain different properties.

Getting ready

We'll create two new datasets for illustrating the differences between distance metrics using scikit-learn's built-in `make_circles()` function:

1. Load the libraries:

```
import matplotlib.pyplot as plt
import numpy as np
from sklearn.datasets import make_circles
from sklearn.model_selection import train_test_split
```

2. Create two synthetic datasets that highlight metric differences:

```
n_samples = 300
```

3. This is the circular dataset with high noise (Euclidean distance should work better):

```
X_circles, y_circles = make_circles(
    n_samples=n_samples,
    noise=0.3, factor=0.3
)
X_circles_train, X_circles_test, \
    y_circles_train, y_circles_test = train_test_split(
        X_circles, y_circles,
        test_size=0.2, random_state=2024
)
```

4. This is the checkerboard pattern dataset (Manhattan distance should work better):

```
x = np.linspace(0, 4, int(np.sqrt(n_samples)))
y = np.linspace(0, 4, int(np.sqrt(n_samples)))
xx, yy = np.meshgrid(x, y)
X_moons = np.column_stack((xx.ravel(), yy.ravel()))
y_moons = np.mod(np.floor(xx.ravel()) + np.floor(yy.ravel()), 2)
X_moons_train, X_moons_test, \
    y_moons_train, y_moons_test = train_test_split(
        X_moons, y_moons,
        test_size=0.2, random_state=2024
)
```

We've now created two different datasets to illustrate how the choice of distance metric can impact the performance of KNN. Keep in mind that these datasets are *illustrative* and you probably won't find a dataset exactly like these in real-world applications!

How to do it...

To compare various distance metrics, we'll cycle through each one and build two KNN classifiers with it on our datasets, then visualize the dataset along with the performance metric, which is accuracy:

1. Compare different distance metrics on both datasets:

```
metrics = ['euclidean', 'manhattan', 'minkowski']
results = {'circles': {}, 'moons': {}}
for metric in metrics:
    # Test on circles dataset
    knn_circles = KNeighborsClassifier(n_neighbors=3,
                                       metric=metric)
    knn_circles.fit(X_circles_train, y_circles_train)
    y_pred_circles = knn_circles.predict(X_circles_test)
    results['circles'][metric] = accuracy_score(
```

```
        y_circles_test, y_pred_circles)
    # Test on moons dataset
    knn_moons = KNeighborsClassifier(n_neighbors=3,
                            metric=metric)
    knn_moons.fit(X_moons_train, y_moons_train)
    y_pred_moons = knn_moons.predict(X_moons_test)
    results['moons'][metric] = accuracy_score(y_moons_test,
                            y_pred_moons)
```

2. Set up plot specs:

```
fig, (ax1, ax2) = plt.subplots(1, 2, figsize=(15, 5))
```

3. Plot the `circles` dataset (the name `circles` is arbitrary):

```
scatter1_train = ax1.scatter(
    X_circles_train[:, 0], X_circles_train[:, 1],
    c=y_circles_train, cmap='viridis',
    alpha=0.6, label='Training Points'
)
scatter1_test = ax1.scatter(
    X_circles_test[:, 0], X_circles_test[:, 1],
    color='red', marker='x', s=50,
    label='Test Points'
)
ax1.set_title('Noisy Circles Dataset')
```

4. Create dummy lines for the legend (this is simply to help with visualization):

```
lines1 = [plt.Line2D([0], [0], color='white')
            for _ in metrics]
legend_text1 = [
    f"Euclidean: {results['circles']['euclidean']:.3f}",
    f"Manhattan: {results['circles']['manhattan']:.3f}",
    f"Minkowski: {results['circles']['minkowski']:.3f}"
]
ax1.legend(
    lines1 + [scatter1_train, scatter1_test],
    legend_text1 + ['Training Points', 'Test Points'],
    title='Accuracy by Metric',
    bbox_to_anchor=(1.05, 1),
    loc='upper left'
)
```

5. Plot moons dataset (the name moons is arbitrary in this case since we are transforming the
    dataset to illustrate Manhattan distance):

```
scatter2_train = ax2.scatter(
    X_moons_train[:, 0], X_moons_train[:, 1],
    c=y_moons_train, cmap='viridis',
    alpha=0.6, label='Training Points'
)
scatter2_test = ax2.scatter(
    X_moons_test[:, 0], X_moons_test[:, 1],
    color='red', marker='x', s=50,
    label='Test Points'
)
ax2.set_title('Checkerboard Dataset')
```

6. Create dummy lines for the legend (this is simply to help with visualization):

```
lines2 = [plt.Line2D([0], [0], color='white')
          for _ in metrics]
legend_text2 = [
    f"Euclidean: {results['moons']['euclidean']:.3f}",
    f"Manhattan: {results['moons']['manhattan']:.3f}",
    f"Minkowski: {results['moons']['minkowski']:.3f}"
]
ax2.legend(
    lines2 + [scatter2_train, scatter2_test],
    legend_text2 + ['Training Points', 'Test Points'],
    title='Accuracy by Metric',
    bbox_to_anchor=(1.05, 1),
    loc='upper left'
)
plt.tight_layout()
plt.show()
```

Let's take a look at the result of our distance metrics on these two, vastly different datasets.

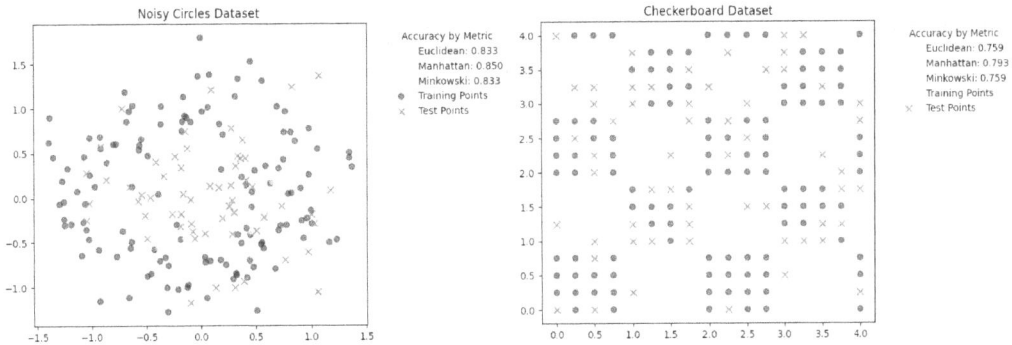

Figure 4.2 – Comparison of three common distance metrics on two differently structured datasets

Although possibly simply by luck in our `Noisy Circles` dataset, the Manhattan distance seems to provide the best estimation. We'd expect this behavior in the `Checkerboard` dataset, given that our data points are neatly arranged in a grid pattern.

How it works...

Distance metrics serve a variety of purposes and should be applied in specific situations rather than simply using the same one for every occasion. Distance metrics (although here, only shown in the context of KNN) serve a broad spectrum of uses in the ML world. The three most common distance metrics are as follows:

- **Euclidean distance**: The most common metric used in KNN. It calculates the straight-line distance between two points in Euclidean space. It is sensitive to outliers and works best when features are scaled similarly.

- **Manhattan distance**: Also known as L1 distance or city block distance. It measures the sum of absolute differences between coordinates. This metric is less sensitive to outliers compared to Euclidean distance.

- **Minkowski distance**: A generalization of both Euclidean and Manhattan distances. By adjusting the p parameter, you can switch between these two metrics (with p=1 for Manhattan and p=2 for Euclidean). This flexibility allows for customization based on specific dataset characteristics.

Impact on model performance

The choice of distance metric can lead to varying model performances due to how each metric interprets distances between points:

- **Sensitivity to scale**: Metrics such as Euclidean distance can be heavily influenced by feature scaling; thus, it is crucial to standardize or normalize features before applying KNN.

- **Dimensionality effects**: In high-dimensional spaces, distances can become less meaningful due to the *curse of dimensionality*. Some metrics may perform better than others depending on the feature space's characteristics.

There's more...

When selecting a distance metric for KNN or other algorithms, do the following:

- Consider the nature of your data (e.g., continuous versus categorical)

- Experiment with multiple metrics to determine which yields the best performance for your specific task

- Use cross-validation techniques to evaluate model performance across different metrics systematically

Hands-on exercises

To illustrate these techniques, please reference the GitHub repository (`https://github.com/PacktPublishing/scikit-learn-Cookbook-Third-Edition`). You will engage in hands-on exercises using scikit-learn to illustrate different distance metrics. Although we've included the previous code examples, we encourage you to explore on your own and try using these tools with different arguments to see what results. The following steps outline a general workflow:

1. Load `KNeighborsClassifier` from `sklearn.neighbors`.

2. Experiment with various distance metrics by setting the metric parameter (e.g., `euclidean`, `manhattan`, `minkowski`, or `cosine`).

3. Use the accuracy score or confusion matrix to assess how well your model performs with each metric.

4. Compare results across different metrics to determine which one yields better accuracy for your dataset.

5. Visualize the results. Create plots to visualize decision boundaries for different metrics and highlight correctly classified versus misclassified points.

Hyperparameter tuning in KNN

Hyperparameter tuning is a critical step in optimizing the performance of ML models, including KNN, but what exactly is a **hyperparameter** anyway? Well, when we think about training an ML model, we can think of that model as a mathematical equation where we provide some input data and output data (in the case of supervised learning) and train our model to determine the best set of **parameters** in the equation to generally match our inputs to our outputs.

For example, if you remember the equation for a linear regression model, $y = mx + b$, x is our input data, y is our output data, and m and b are the slope and y-intercept of our line, respectively. These values are the parameters learned during training. So, while parameters are something our model learns during training, hyperparameters, in essence, tell our model *how* to learn. In this recipe, we'll learn how to apply two different search techniques for finding the optimal mode hyperparameters to achieve maximum performance with our model.

Getting ready

We will use our original dataset, the Iris dataset, and tune the number of neighbors, whether or not to weight our training data by distance from our test data, and the choice of distance metric.

How to do it...

To perform hyperparameter tuning for KNN, we will use the grid search approach. Grid search is a hyperparameter technique that tests an exhaustive number of combinations of model hyperparameters – all combinations are tested, with the resulting combination returned to us as the optimal set. Additionally, cross-validation is used to add an element of randomization that aids in making sure our model is robust when used in the real world. More on that next:

1. Load the libraries:

```
from sklearn.model_selection import GridSearchCV
from sklearn.neighbors import KNeighborsClassifier
```

2. Create a KNN classifier:

```
knn = KNeighborsClassifier()
```

3. Define a hyperparameter grid:

```
param_grid = {
    'n_neighbors': [3, 5, 7, 9, 11],
    'weights': ['uniform', 'distance'],
    'metric': ['euclidean', 'manhattan']
}
```

4. Create a grid search:

```
grid_search = GridSearchCV(
    knn, param_grid, cv=5, scoring='accuracy'
)
```

5. Fit the grid search:

```
grid_search.fit(X_train, y_train)
```

6. Print the best parameters and score:

```
print("Best parameters:", grid_search.best_params_)
print("Best cross-validation score:", grid_search.best_score_)

# Output:
Best parameters: {'metric': 'euclidean', 'n_neighbors': 9,
'weights': 'uniform'}
Best cross-validation score: 0.9916666666666668
```

When we execute the preceding code, scikit-learn's grid search approach determines which set of hyperparameters achieves the best performance, utilizing cross-validation, and prints them out.

How it works...

Hyperparameter optimization is a necessary step in nearly every ML pipeline, including those that contain KNN:

- **Grid search**: This technique exhaustively searches through a specified parameter grid to find the best combination of hyperparameters based on model performance.

- **Cross-validation**: By using cross-validation during grid search (e.g., *k*-fold – again, *k* is a stand-in for a number), you ensure that your model is evaluated on different subsets of data, which helps prevent overfitting and provides a more reliable estimate of model performance.

Evaluating model performance

Once you have identified the best hyperparameters using grid search, you can do the following:

- **Test set evaluation**: Use the best parameters to fit a final model on the training set and evaluate its performance on a separate test set

- **Performance metrics**: Depending on your task (classification or regression), use appropriate metrics such as accuracy score for classifiers or **mean squared error** (**MSE**) for regressors to assess how well your tuned model performs

There's more…

Grid search is just one common approach for hyperparameter optimization. Let's look at another.

Randomized search

In addition to grid search, consider using `RandomizedSearchCV()` for hyperparameter tuning when dealing with large parameter spaces. This method randomly samples from specified distributions of parameters rather than exhaustively searching all combinations, which can save time while still yielding good results.

Hands-on exercises

To illustrate these techniques, please reference the GitHub repository (`https://github.com/PacktPublishing/scikit-learn-Cookbook-Third-Edition`). You will engage in hands-on exercises to optimize hyperparameters for KNN models. Although we've included the previous code examples, we encourage you to explore on your own and try using these tools with different arguments to see what results. The following steps outline a general workflow:

1. Load `KNeighborsClassifier` from `sklearn.neighbors`.

2. Create a dictionary specifying values for `n_neighbors` (e.g., range from 1 to 20) and any distance metrics you want to test (e.g., `euclidean`, `manhattan`, etc.).

3. Load `GridSearchCV` from `sklearn.model_selection` and fit it using your KNN model and parameter grid.

4. Access and print out the best parameters found by grid search, along with their corresponding accuracy scores or other relevant metrics.

Evaluating KNN performance

Evaluating the performance of KNN models is essential for understanding how well the model makes predictions and where it may need improvement. This recipe will cover various techniques for assessing KNN performance, including confusion matrices, precision, recall, and F1-scores.

Getting ready

Again, we will use our toy dataset from before, the Iris dataset, and import a few new functions to help us evaluate our model. We'll evaluate our model using cross-validation scores, learning curves, and a confusion matrix.

Load the libraries:

```
from sklearn.model_selection import learning_curve
from sklearn.metrics import confusion_matrix
import seaborn as sns
```

Next, we'll train our model using the hyperparameters that we found performed the best.

How to do it...

To evaluate the performance of the KNN model, we'll use three different approaches:

1. Get cross-validation scores. These will be from the model trained earlier with the best hyperparameters chosen by grid search:

    ```
    cv_scores = cross_val_score(
        grid_search.best_estimator_,
        X_train, y_train, cv=5
    )
    print("Cross-validation scores:", cv_scores)
    print("Mean CV score:", cv_scores.mean())
    print("Standard deviation:", cv_scores.std())
    ```

2. Generate learning curves:

    ```
    train_sizes, train_scores, test_scores = learning_curve(
        grid_search.best_estimator_,
        X_train, y_train,
        train_sizes=np.linspace(0.1, 1.0, 10),
        cv=5
    )
    ```

3. Plot learning curves:

    ```
    plt.figure(figsize=(10, 6))
    plt.plot(
        train_sizes,
        np.mean(train_scores, axis=1),
        label='Training score'
    )
    plt.plot(
        train_sizes,
        np.mean(test_scores, axis=1),
        label='Cross-validation score'
    )
    plt.xlabel('Training examples')
    ```

```
plt.ylabel('Score')
plt.legend(loc='best')
plt.title('Learning Curves')
plt.show()
```

Figure 4.3 shows the learning curves for the KNN model:

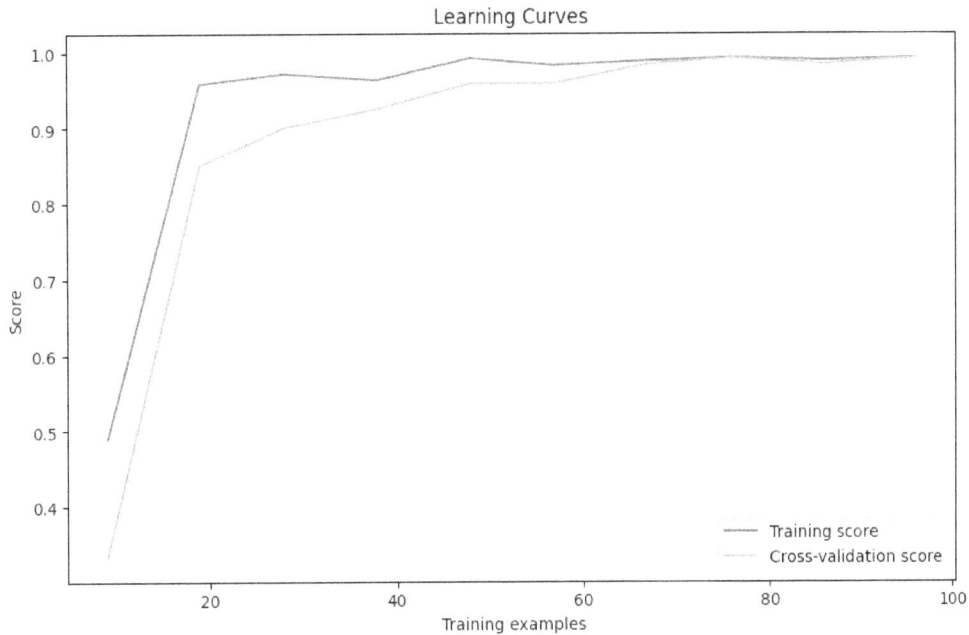

Figure 4.3 – Learning curves

4. Make predictions on the test set:

```
y_pred = grid_search.best_estimator_.predict(X_test)
```

5. Get class names from the iris dataset:

```
class_names = iris.target_names
```

6. Generate and plot a confusion matrix:

```
cm = confusion_matrix(y_test, y_pred)
plt.figure(figsize=(8, 6))
sns.heatmap(
    cm, annot=True, fmt='d', cmap='Blues',
    xticklabels=class_names,
    yticklabels=class_names,
```

```
        cbar_kws={'label': 'Number of Samples'}
    )
plt.xlabel('Predicted')
plt.ylabel('True')
plt.title('Confusion Matrix')
plt.show()
```

Insights from the confusion matrix indicate that our model is making more correct predictions than incorrect ones based on the values along the diagonal.

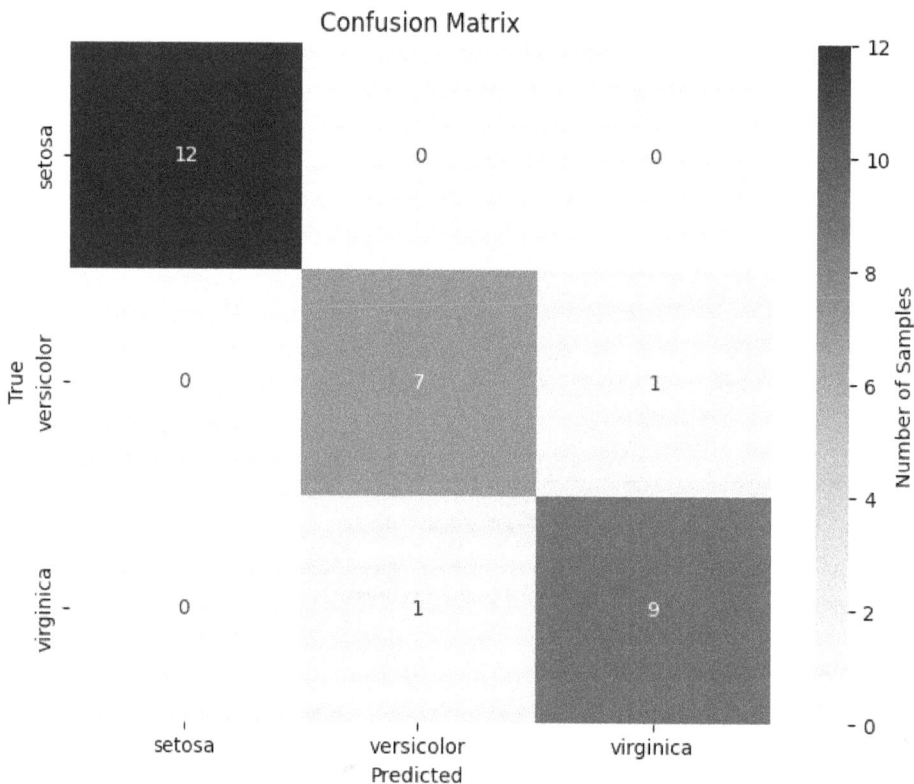

Figure 4.4 – Confusion matrix

7. Get a classification report as a dictionary:

```
report_dict = classification_report(
    y_test, y_pred,
    target_names=class_names,
    output_dict=True
)
```

8. Create a DataFrame for better visualization:

```
report_df = pd.DataFrame(report_dict).transpose()
```

9. Style the DataFrame:

```
styled_df = (report_df
    .style
    .background_gradient(
        cmap='Blues', subset=['precision',
        'recall', 'f1-score']
    )
    .format({
        'precision': '{:.3f}',
        'recall': '{:.3f}',
        'f1-score': '{:.3f}',
        'support': '{:.0f}'
    })
)
print("\nClassification Report:")
display(styled_df)
```

Figure 4.5 depicts the classification report where we can review the performance of our model across several different metrics and even broken down by each label (or iris) in this case.

> **Note**
>
> Normally, we'd be suspicious of 100% precision, recall, and F1-score in the case of the `setosa` label, but this toy dataset is fairly easy for even the simplest of classification models to perform well on!

Classification Report:

	precision	recall	f1-score	support
setosa	1.000	1.000	1.000	12
versicolor	0.875	0.875	0.875	8
virginica	0.900	0.900	0.900	10
accuracy	0.933	0.933	0.933	1
macro avg	0.925	0.925	0.925	30
weighted avg	0.933	0.933	0.933	30

Figure 4.5 – Classification report

On a side note, even though the performance of this model is very good, in the real world, we don't necessarily know what *very good* performance scores without a thorough understanding of the business problem we're trying to model. Just keep this in mind!

Understanding evaluation metrics

There are a variety of methods to evaluate the performance of classification models, and scikit-learn provides several options for utilizing the most common ones:

1. **Learning curves**: These are visual representations that plot the model's performance (accuracy is used by default for KNN) against the size of the training dataset, showing how well the model learns as it is exposed to more training examples, allowing analysts to identify potential issues such as underfitting or overfitting based on the curve's shape. It also allows us insight into when we aren't benefiting from additional training, which can reduce costly compute needs.

2. **Confusion matrix**: A confusion matrix delivers a visual summary of predictions made by a classification model. It shows the counts of **true positives (TPs)**, **true negatives (TNs)**, **false positives (FPs)**, and **false negatives (FNs)**. This matrix helps visualize how well the model is performing across different classes.

3. **Classification report**: The classification report is a scikit-learn function that combines several metrics into a single, easy-to-read table, including the following:

    *   **Precision**: Precision measures the accuracy of positive predictions. It is calculated as $Precision = TP + FP/TP$

    *   **Recall**: Recall (also known as sensitivity) measures the ability of a model to identify all relevant instances. It is calculated as $Recall = TP + FN/TP$.

    *   **F1-score**: The F1-score is the harmonic mean of precision and recall, providing a single metric that balances both concerns. It is particularly useful when dealing with imbalanced datasets. It is calculated as $F1 = 2 \times Precision + Recall/Precision \times Recall$.

    *   **Accuracy**: Accuracy measures the ratio of total correct predictions out of all predictions made. It is calculated as $Accuracy = TP + TN/(TP + FP + TN + FN)$.

    *   **Macro Avg**: This is the average of metrics across all labels.

    *   **Weighted Avg**: This is the average of metrics across all labels weighted by the number of examples per label.

There's more...

Another consideration to take into account is how to evaluate classification models when the dataset contains an imbalanced distribution of classes.

Handling imbalanced datasets

When dealing with imbalanced datasets where one class significantly outnumbers another, you need to consider the following:

- Use metrics such as precision-recall curves or ROC-AUC scores instead of accuracy alone
- Techniques such as resampling (oversampling minority classes or undersampling majority classes) can help balance the dataset before training

Hands-on exercises

To illustrate these techniques, please reference the GitHub repository (`https://github.com/PacktPublishing/scikit-learn-Cookbook-Third-Edition`). You will engage in hands-on exercises for evaluating the performance of KNN models, including confusion matrices, precision, recall, and F1-scores. Although we've included the previous code examples, we encourage you to explore on your own and try using these tools with different arguments to see what results. The following steps outline a general workflow:

1. Load `KNeighborsClassifier` from `sklearn.neighbors`.
2. Split your data into training and testing sets using `train_test_split`.
3. Fit your model on the training data using the `fit` method.
4. Use the `predict` method on your test data to generate predictions.
5. Generate a confusion matrix using `confusion_matrix`.
6. Calculate precision, recall, and F1-score using their respective functions from `sklearn.metrics`.
7. Plot the confusion matrix using libraries such as Matplotlib or Seaborn for better interpretation.

Practical exercises with KNN models

In this final recipe, you will engage in practical exercises that involve building, tuning, and evaluating KNN models on real-world datasets. These exercises are designed to reinforce the concepts learned throughout the chapter and demonstrate how to effectively apply KNN in various scenarios. By the end of these exercises, you will have hands-on experience that you can leverage in your own ML projects.

Exercise 1: Building a KNN classifier

In this example, you'll build a simple KNN classifier using a dataset of your choice. It's encouraged that you use a dataset that requires some upfront data preprocessing, so you can link together what you've already learned from the previous chapters, but this is not required.

These are the implementation steps for *Exercise 1*:

1. Load the libraries.
2. Load the dataset.
3. Preprocess the data.
4. Create and train the KNN classifier.
5. Make predictions.
6. Evaluate performance.

Exercise 2: Tuning hyperparameters with grid search

These are the implementation steps for *Exercise 2*:

1. Load the libraries.
2. Load a different dataset.
3. Preprocess the data.
4. Set up a grid search.
5. Fit the grid search.
6. Evaluate the best model.

Exercise 3: Evaluating a KNN classifier

These are the implementation steps for *Exercise 3*:

1. Load the libraries.
2. Load the dataset.
3. Preprocess the data.
4. Create and train the KNN classifier.
5. Make predictions.
6. Evaluate performance.

There's more...

After mastering the basic implementation techniques, you can do the following:

- Experiment with using distance metrics for other ML tasks, such as clustering and regression

- Consider exploring advanced techniques such as DBSCAN, mean shift, spectral clustering, kernel density, and radius neighbors classifier – all available in scikit-learn

Get This Book's PDF Version and Exclusive Extras

Scan the QR code (or go to `packtpub.com/unlock`). Search for this book by name, confirm the edition, and then follow the steps on the page.

Note: Keep your invoice handy. Purchases made directly from Packt don't require an invoice.

5

Linear Models and Regularization

In *Chapter 4*, we briefly spoke about linear regression in the context of hyperparameter optimization, but now we will take a closer look at it and some of its derivatives. Linear regression is probably one of the first data models we encounter in our formal school days. You may not have realized it at the time (and I won't hold it against you, depending on how long ago you were in high school!), but linear regression is really a type of simple ML model that attempts to find a mathematical relationship between data points that can be represented by the equation for a line. The most straightforward (pun somewhat intended) approach is a straight line like that in **Ordinary Least Squares (OLS)** regression, but as we move along in the chapter, we'll begin to see that there are a variety of methods for *fitting* a line to represent a relationship between data. By the end, you'll have a better idea of the variety of applications regression analysis can be applied to.

In this chapter, we're going to cover the following recipes:

- Introduction to linear models
- Ridge and Lasso regression
- ElasticNet and regularization
- Regularization theory and practice
- Regression and regularization

Technical requirements

It is advisable to create a Python environment for safely isolating your work from other Python installations/libraries. See the GitHub repository for more details (`https://github.com/PacktPublishing/scikit-learn-Cookbook-Third-Edition`).

- Git >=2.46.x

- Python >=3.9.x

- Cloned GitHub repository and Python environment built from the `requirements.txt` file

Introduction to linear models

Linear models serve as the backbone for many predictive modeling techniques, offering an upfront approach to understanding relationships between variables. This recipe provides a foundation for understanding more complex linear techniques and their importance in predictive modeling, setting the stage for advanced topics such as regularized regression and logistic regression.

Getting ready

To get started, you'll notice that we're taking a similar approach to that used in *Chapter 4* by creating a synthetic dataset to demonstrate the concepts of linear models and regularization. scikit-learn provides a function called `make_regression()` that creates a synthetic regression dataset, which we can further refine to create a more interesting dataset that includes some *noise* to make it more challenging.

1. Load the following libraries:

    ```
    import numpy as np
    import pandas as pd
    import matplotlib.pyplot as plt
    from sklearn.datasets import make_regression
    ```

2. Create a synthetic regression dataset with high multicollinearity and more features:

    ```
    X, y = make_regression(n_samples=1000,
                           n_features=100,
                           n_informative=10,
                           noise=20,
                           random_state=123)
    ```

3. Add multicollinearity by creating correlated features:

```
for i in range(50, 100): # Make half the features correlated
    X[:, i] = X[:, i-50] + np.random.normal(0, 0.1, size=1000)
```

4. Create feature names:

```
feature_names = [f'feature_{i}' for i in range(100)]
```

5. Take just the first feature for visualization:

```
X_plot = X[:, 0].reshape(-1, 1)
```

6. Add some non-linearity and make coefficients vary widely in magnitude:

```
y = y * 1000   # Scale up the target
y = (y + np.sin(X_plot.ravel()) * 150
        + np.exp(X_plot.ravel()/10))
```

7. Convert data arrays to a pandas DataFrame with feature names:

```
df = pd.DataFrame(X, columns=feature_names)
df['target'] = y
df_plot = pd.DataFrame({
    'feature_0': X_plot.ravel(), 'target': y
})
```

8. Create a quick visualization of the data:

```
plt.figure(figsize=(10, 6))
plt.scatter(X_plot, y, alpha=0.5)
plt.xlabel('feature_0')
plt.ylabel('target')
plt.title('Synthetic Regression Dataset')
plt.show()
```

Running the code block produces the following scatterplot, where we can see that our data is very random, but mostly normally distributed. Keep in mind that for 2D visualization purposes, we are only showing a single feature from the dataset rather than all 100 that we created.

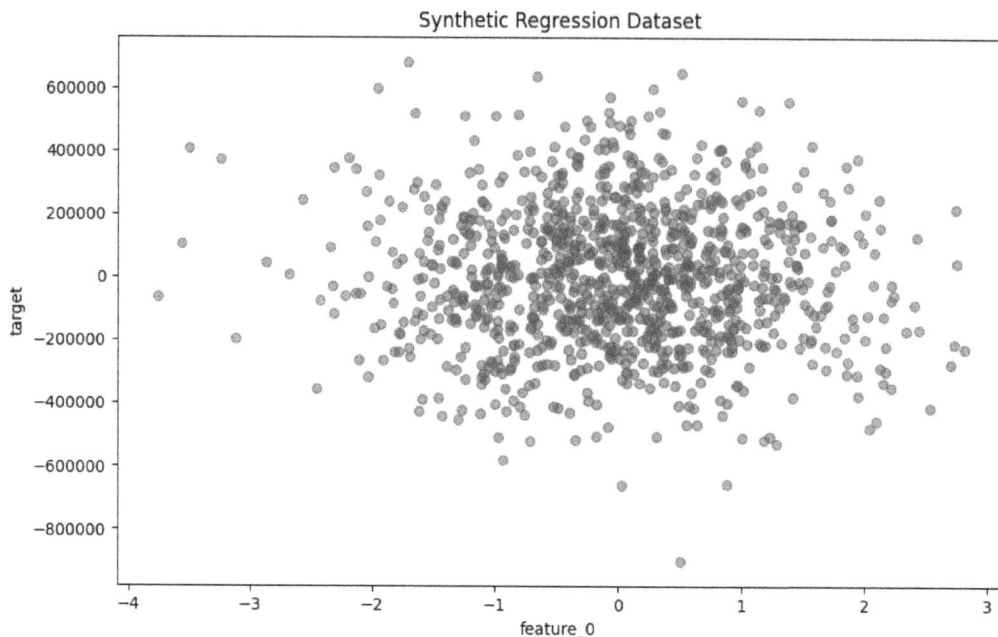

Figure 5.1 – A synthetic dataset for demonstrating linear regression

Now let's see whether we can find a linear equation that represents the general relationship between our features and target.

How to do it...

Implementation of a linear regression model is straightforward. We'll use the `train_test_split()` function to split the data into training and testing sets, and then fit a linear regression model to the training data. Finally, we'll evaluate the model's performance using the **mean squared error** (**MSE**) and **R-squared** (**R2**) metrics. We can also visualize the model's predictions on the test set to see how well it fits the data:

1. Load the following libraries:

```
from sklearn.model_selection import train_test_split
from sklearn.linear_model import LinearRegression
from sklearn.metrics import mean_squared_error, r2_score
```

2. Split the data into training and testing sets:

```
X_train, X_test, y_train, y_test = train_test_split(
    X, y, test_size=0.2,
    random_state=123
)
```

3. Create and fit a linear regression model:

```
linear_model = LinearRegression()
linear_model.fit(X_train, y_train)
```

4. Make predictions on the test set:

```
y_pred = linear_model.predict(X_test)
```

5. Evaluate the performance using the MSE and R^2:

```
mse = mean_squared_error(y_test, y_pred)
r2 = r2_score(y_test, y_pred)
print(f'Mean Squared Error: {mse:.2f}')
print(f'R-squared: {r2:.2f}')
```

6. Visualize the data and regression line (using `feature_0` for visualization):

```
plt.figure(figsize=(10, 6))
plt.scatter(
    X_test[:, 0], y_test, color='blue',
    alpha=0.5, label='Test Data'
)
plt.scatter(
    X_train[:, 0], y_train, color='green',
    alpha=0.5, label='Train Data'
)
```

7. Sort the data for a smooth line plot:

```
X_line = np.linspace(
    df['feature_0'].min(),
    df['feature_0'].max(), 100
).reshape(-1, 1)
X_line_full = np.zeros((100, len(feature_names)))
X_line_full[:, 0] = X_line.ravel()   # Set feature_0, leave
others as 0
y_line = linear_model.predict(pd.DataFrame(
    X_line_full, columns=feature_names))
plt.plot(X_line, y_line, color='red', label='Regression Line')
```

```
plt.xlabel('feature_0')
plt.ylabel('target')
plt.title('Linear Regression Fit')
plt.legend()
plt.show()
```

When we execute the code block, our plot shows our fitted regression line against both the training and testing datasets.

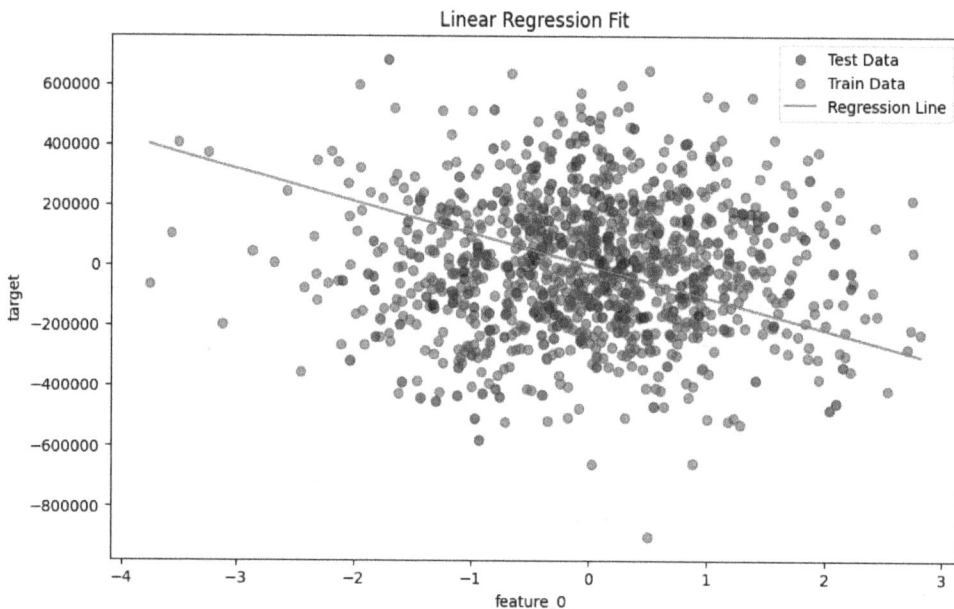

Figure 5.2 – A regression line fit to the training and testing data

Let's look more closely at the mathematics behind linear regression.

How it works...

Linear regression is a fundamental technique used to model relationships between a dependent variable (target) and one or more independent variables (features). The model assumes that there is a linear relationship between these variables, which can be expressed mathematically as follows:

$$y = \beta 0 + \beta 1x1 + \beta 2x2 + \cdots + \beta nxn + \epsilon y = \beta 0 + \beta 1x1 + \beta 2x2 + \cdots + \beta nxn + \epsilon$$

Here, we have the following:

- y is the predicted value
- $\beta 0$ is the intercept

- βi are the coefficients for each feature

- xi are the feature values

- ϵ is the error term

There's more...

Once you are comfortable with basic linear regression, you can explore more advanced techniques, such as the following:

- **Regularized regression**: Techniques such as ridge and Lasso regression help prevent overfitting by adding penalties to large coefficients

- **Logistic regression**: While primarily used for classification tasks, logistic regression is an extension of linear models that predicts probabilities of class membership

Hands-on exercises

To visualize these techniques, please refer to the GitHub repository (`https://github.com/PacktPublishing/scikit-learn-Cookbook-Third-Edition`). You will engage in hands-on exercises on linear regression. Although we've included the code examples in the repository, we encourage you to explore them on your own and try using these tools with different arguments to see the results. The following steps outline a general workflow:

1. Clone the GitHub repository and ensure all of the necessary libraries are installed.

2. Choose an appropriate dataset for regression tasks from scikit-learn or your own collection.

3. Clean your dataset by handling missing values and encoding categorical variables if necessary.

4. Load `LinearRegression()` from `sklearn.linear_model`.

5. Fit your model using training data with the `fit` method.

6. Use the `predict` method on your test data to generate predictions.

7. Calculate metrics such as the MSE and R^2 to assess how well your model performs.

8. Create plots to visualize predicted versus actual values or residuals.

Ridge and Lasso regression

Ridge and Lasso regression are two powerful techniques used to enhance the performance of linear regression models through what's called **regularization**. Regularization helps prevent overfitting by adding a *penalty term* to the loss function, which discourages overly complex models. We'll discuss this in more detail later on.

In this recipe, we will learn about the fundamentals of these two powerful regression techniques, how they differ from standard linear regression, and how to implement and compare these models using scikit-learn.

Getting ready

In order to implement ridge and Lasso regression, we'll use the ridge and Lasso classes from the `sklearn.linear_model` module. These classes are similar to `LinearRegression()`, but they include an additional parameter called `alpha`, which controls the strength of the regularization. We can use the same dataset created in the *Introduction to linear models* recipe to demonstrate the implementation of ridge and Lasso regression.

How to do it...

Let's fit both a ridge and Lasso regression model to the data and compare the results with the linear regression model we created in the *Introduction to linear models* recipe. You'll notice that the ridge and Lasso models perform better than the linear regression model, but the difference is not as significant as you might expect. This is because the data is highly multicollinear and the features are highly correlated with each other.

1. Load the following libraries:

```
from sklearn.linear_model import Ridge, Lasso
from sklearn.metrics import mean_squared_error, r2_score
```

2. Create and fit the ridge regression model:

```
ridge_model = Ridge(alpha=1.0)  # alpha controls regularization
strength
ridge_model.fit(X_train, y_train)
```

3. Create and fit the Lasso regression model with increased iterations and `alpha`:

```
lasso_model = Lasso(alpha=10.0, max_iter=10000, tol=0.001)
lasso_model.fit(X_train, y_train)

# Make predictions with both models
y_pred_ridge = ridge_model.predict(X_test)
y_pred_lasso = lasso_model.predict(X_test)
```

4. Evaluate the performance:

```
y_pred_linear = linear_model.predict(X_test)
```

5. Calculate metrics for all models:

```
metrics = {
    'Model': [
        'Ridge Regression',
        'Lasso Regression',
        'Linear Regression'
    ],
    'Mean Squared Error': [
        mean_squared_error(y_test, y_pred_ridge),
        mean_squared_error(y_test, y_pred_lasso),
        mean_squared_error(y_test, y_pred_linear)
    ],
    'R-squared': [
        r2_score(y_test, y_pred_ridge),
        r2_score(y_test, y_pred_lasso),
        r2_score(y_test, y_pred_linear)
    ]
}
```

6. Create a DataFrame and sort by the MSE:

```
metrics_df = pd.DataFrame(metrics)
metrics_df = metrics_df.sort_values(
    'Mean Squared Error', ascending=True)
```

7. Format the numeric columns:

```
metrics_df['Mean Squared Error'] = metrics_df[
    'Mean Squared Error'
].map('{:.2f}'.format)
metrics_df['R-squared'] = metrics_df[
    'R-squared'
].map('{:.2f}'.format)
display(metrics_df)
```

Here is a comparison of all three approaches using our regression evaluation metrics:

	Model	Mean Squared Error	R-squared
0	Ridge Regression	44396382506.70	0.11
1	Lasso Regression	45382227698.75	0.09
2	Linear Regression	45489296387.79	0.09

Figure 5.3 – Comparison of regularization techniques

8.   Visualize the results (using `feature_0` for visualization):

```
plt.figure(figsize=(10, 6))
plt.scatter(
    X_test[:, 0], y_test, color='blue',
    alpha=0.5, label='Test Data'
)
```

9.   Sort the data for smooth line plots:

```
X_line = np.linspace(
    df['feature_0'].min(),
    df['feature_0'].max(), 100
).reshape(-1, 1)
X_line_full = np.zeros((100, len(feature_names)))
X_line_full[:, 0] = X_line.ravel()
X_line_df = pd.DataFrame(X_line_full, columns=feature_names)
```

10. Generate predictions for the line:

```
y_line_ridge = ridge_model.predict(X_line_df)
y_line_lasso = lasso_model.predict(X_line_df)
y_line_linear = linear_model.predict(X_line_df)
plt.plot(X_line, y_line_ridge, color='red',
         label='Ridge Regression')
plt.plot(X_line, y_line_lasso, color='green',
         linestyle='--', label='Lasso Regression')
plt.plot(X_line, y_line_linear, color='purple',
         label='Linear Regression')
plt.xlabel('feature_0')
plt.ylabel('target')
plt.title('Ridge, Lasso, and Linear Regression Comparison')
plt.legend()
plt.show()
```

Executing the code block produces the following plot of all three techniques.

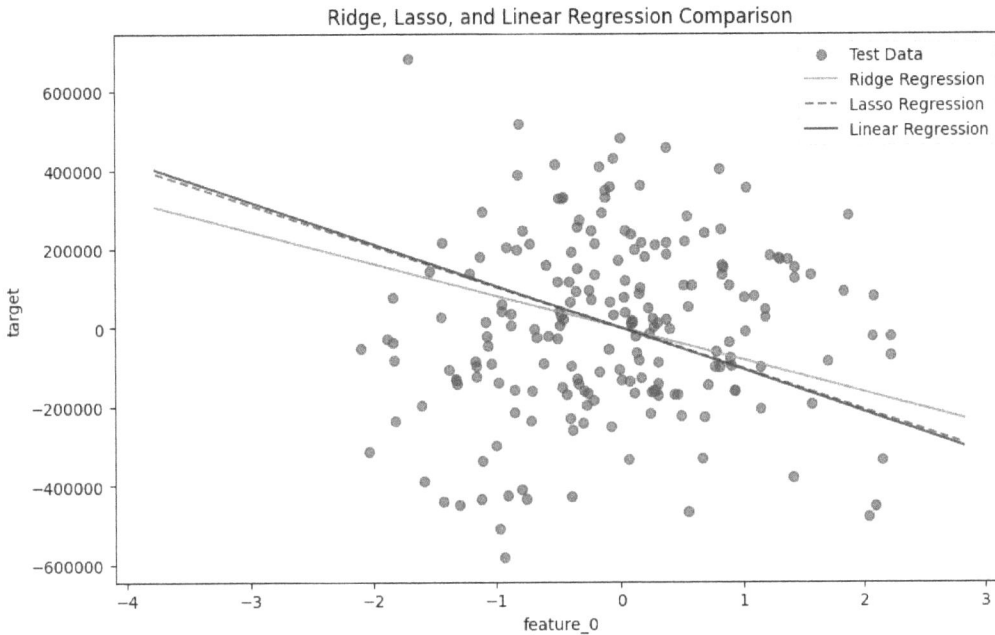

Figure 5.4 – Comparison of linear, ridge, and Lasso regression

As you can see, the difference in this case is negligible, but even small differences in predictive power can have significant impacts on real-world use cases!

How it works...

If we look more closely at both ridge and Lasso regularization, we can see that they do not differ all that much in their approach to shrinking coefficients in our linear regression equation:

- **Ridge regression**: Adds an L2 penalty term to the loss function of OLS regression:

$$Loss = \sum i = 1n(yi - y^\wedge i)2 + \alpha \sum j = 1p\beta j2 Loss = i = 1\sum n(yi - y^\wedge i)2 + \alpha j = 1\sum p\beta j2$$

Here, we have the following:

- α is a tuning parameter that controls the strength of regularization
- βj refers to the coefficients of the features

This penalty discourages large coefficients in order to reduce model complexity and prevent overfitting.

- **Lasso regression**: Incorporates an L1 penalty term:

$$Loss = \sum i = 1n(yi - y\hat{}i)2 + \alpha\sum j = 1p \mid \beta j \mid \; Loss = i = 1\sum n(yi - y\hat{}i)2 + \alpha j = 1\sum p \mid \beta j \mid$$

The L1 penalty not only helps prevent overfitting but also performs feature selection by shrinking some coefficients to 0, effectively removing them from the model.

So, how should we determine when to use one approach versus the other? **Ridge regression** is useful when you want to keep all features but reduce their impact through regularization.

Lasso regression, on the other hand, is beneficial when you suspect that many features are irrelevant or redundant since it can eliminate them entirely from consideration.

Hands-on exercises

To visualize these techniques, please refer to the GitHub repository (`https://github.com/PacktPublishing/scikit-learn-Cookbook-Third-Edition`). You will engage in hands-on exercises using ridge and Lasso regression. Although we've included the code examples in the repository, we encourage you to explore them on your own and try using these tools with different arguments to see the results. The following steps outline a general workflow:

1. **Download and set up your environment**: Clone the GitHub repository and ensure all of the necessary libraries are installed.

2. **Load your dataset**: Choose an appropriate dataset for regression tasks from scikit-learn or your own collection.

3. **Preprocess your data**: Clean your dataset by handling missing values and encoding categorical variables if necessary.

4. Load ridge from `sklearn.linear_model`.

5. Train your model on training data.

6. Calculate metrics such as the MSE and R^2.

7. Load Lasso from `sklearn.linear_model`.

8. Train your model on training data.

9. Calculate metrics such as the MSE and R^2.

10. Analyze how regularization affects each model's performance based on the evaluation metrics.

ElasticNet and regularization

ElasticNet is a hybrid of ridge and Lasso regression that combines their strengths to handle different types of data. With ElasticNet, we can control the strength of the regularization using the `alpha` parameter, which is similar to the `alpha` parameter in ridge and Lasso regression. We can also control the mix of ridge and Lasso regularization using the `l1_ratio` parameter, which controls the proportion of ridge and Lasso regularization in the model. This is useful when we have a dataset with a mix of features that are highly correlated with each other and some that are not. This recipe will introduce you to a technique that blends the benefits of both regularization techniques we covered previously.

Getting ready

In order to implement ElasticNet regression, we'll use the `ElasticNet()` class from the `sklearn.linear_model` module. This class is similar to ridge and Lasso regression, but it combines their strengths to handle different types of data. We can use the same dataset created in the *Ridge and Lasso regression* recipe to demonstrate the implementation of ElasticNet regression.

How to do it...

We will create a range of `alpha` and `l1_ratio` values to test and plot the coefficient paths for each combination. This is the main purpose of ElasticNet: to handle the multicollinearity and high-dimensional data that is common in real-world datasets. The resulting visualization is called a *coefficient path plot*, and it shows the relationship between the alpha and the coefficient for each feature.

1. Load the following libraries:

   ```
   from sklearn.linear_model import ElasticNet
   ```

2. Create a range of alphas to test:

   ```
   alphas = [0.0001, 0.001, 0.01, 0.1, 1, 10, 100]
   l1_ratios = [0.1, 0.3, 0.5, 0.7, 0.9]
   ```

3. Store coefficients for plotting:

   ```
   coef_paths = []
   labels = []
   ```

4. Create and fit ElasticNet models with different parameters:

   ```
   plt.figure(figsize=(10, 6))
   for l1_ratio in l1_ratios:
       coefs = []
       for alpha in alphas:
   ```

5. Create and fit the ElasticNet model with increased `max_iter` and `tol` values:

```
elastic_model = ElasticNet(
    alpha=alpha, l1_ratio=l1_ratio,
    random_state=123, max_iter=10000, tol=1e-4
)
elastic_model.fit(X_train, y_train)
coefs.append(elastic_model.coef_)
```

6. Convert the model coefficients to an array and store them in the empty list:

```
coef_paths.append(np.array(coefs))
```

7. Plot the coefficient paths:

```
for feature_idx in range(X_train.shape[1]):
    plt.plot(
        np.log10(alphas),
        np.array(coefs)[:, feature_idx],
        label=(
            f'l1_ratio={l1_ratio}, '
            f'feature_{feature_idx}'
            if feature_idx == 0 else ""
        ),
        alpha=0.5,
        linestyle=[
            'solid', 'dashed',
            'dotted', 'dashdot', '-'
        ][l1_ratios.index(l1_ratio)])
plt.xlabel('log(alpha)')
plt.ylabel('Coefficient value')
plt.title('ElasticNet Coefficient Paths')
plt.legend(bbox_to_anchor=(1.05, 1), loc='upper left')
plt.grid(True)
plt.tight_layout()
plt.show()
```

8. Create a model with a balanced `l1_ratio` and moderate `alpha`:

```
elastic_model = ElasticNet(
    alpha=1.0, l1_ratio=0.5, random_state=123,
    max_iter=10000, tol=1e-4
)  # Increased iterations and adjusted tolerance
elastic_model.fit(X_train, y_train)
```

9. Calculate the mean squared error and r-squared metrics:

```
elastic_pred = elastic_model.predict(X_test)
elastic_mse = mean_squared_error(y_test, elastic_pred)
elastic_r2 = r2_score(y_test, elastic_pred)
```

10. Add the ElasticNet results to the `metrics` DataFrame. You can see that its performance is better than our three previous models:

```
new_row = pd.DataFrame({
    'Model': ['ElasticNet Regression'],
    'Mean Squared Error': [elastic_mse],
    'R-squared': [elastic_r2]
})
```

The model performance is shown in the following figure.

	Model	Mean Squared Error	R-squared
3	ElasticNet Regression	42652278983.56	0.14
0	Ridge Regression	44396382506.70	0.11
1	Lasso Regression	45382227698.75	0.09
2	Linear Regression	45489296387.79	0.09

Figure 5.5 – Comparison of regularization techniques with ElasticNet

11. Remove any existing ElasticNet entries before concatenating:

```
metrics_df = metrics_df[
    ~metrics_df['Model'].str.contains('ElasticNet')]
metrics_df = pd.concat(
    [metrics_df, new_row], ignore_index=True)
```

12. Sort the `metrics` DataFrame by MSE:

```
metrics_df = metrics_df.sort_values(
    'Mean Squared Error', ascending=True)
```

13. Display the updated metrics:

```
display(metrics_df)
```

Executing this code block will print a visualization illustrating the application of ElasticNet for shrinking the values of our model's coefficients.

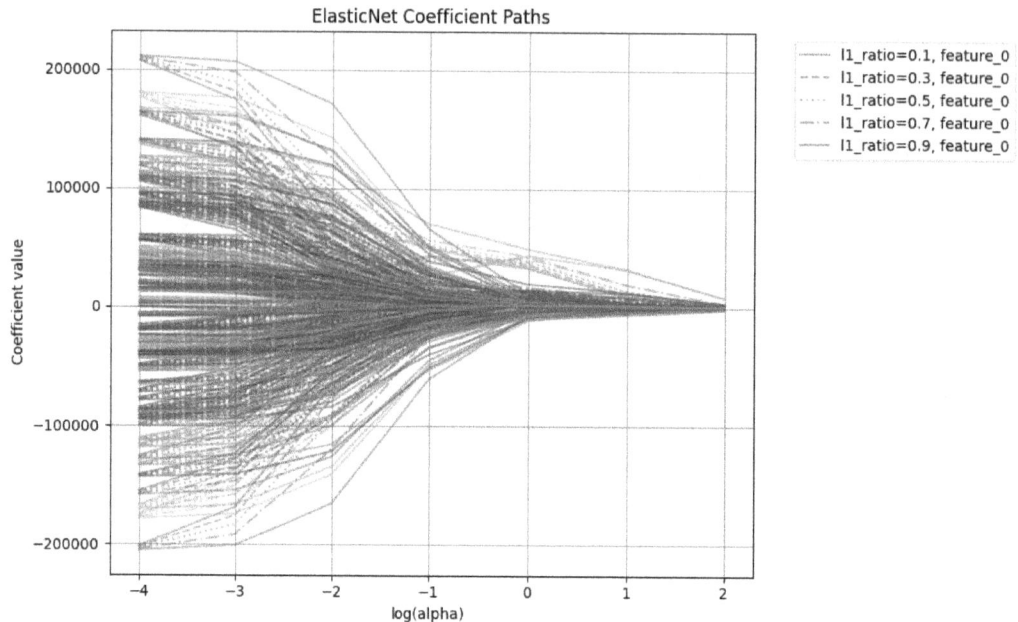

Figure 5.6 – Coefficient path plot showing the impact of regularization (log(alpha)) on coefficient values

The coefficient paths plot in the ElasticNet example visualizes how the model coefficients (feature weights) change as the regularization strength (alpha) varies. Here's a detailed explanation:

- **X axis (log(alpha))**:

  - Shows the regularization strength on a logarithmic scale

  - Ranges from very weak regularization (0.0001) to strong regularization (100)

- **Y axis (coefficient value)**:

  - Shows the magnitude of the feature coefficients

  - When coefficients are 0, it means those features have been eliminated from the model

- **Different lines**:

  - Each line represents how a feature's coefficient changes with different alpha values

  - Different line styles represent different `l1_ratio` values (0.1, 0.3, 0.5, 0.7, 0.9)

- `l1_ratio` controls the mix between ridge (L2) and Lasso (L1) regularization:

  - `l1_ratio` = `0.1`: More ridge-like behavior (tends to shrink coefficients)

  - `l1_ratio` = `0.9`: More Lasso-like behavior (tends to eliminate features)

- **Key insights from the plot**:

  - As the alpha increases (moving right), the coefficients generally get smaller

  - Some coefficients go to exactly 0, which means that ElasticNet, similar to both ridge and Lasso regression, is performing feature selection

  - Different `l1_ratio` values show different patterns of coefficient shrinkage

  - The paths help identify which features are most important (resistant to shrinkage) and which are least important (quickly go to 0)

Note that the plot in our example can be somewhat difficult to read since our dataset has 100 features, but the goal here is to give you a better idea of coefficient shrinkage. In a smaller, fewer-featured dataset, the results would be easier to read.

How it works...

ElasticNet combines both L1 (Lasso) and L2 (ridge) penalties in its loss function:

$$Loss = \sum_{i=1}^{n} (y_i - \hat{y}_i)^2 + \alpha(\lambda_1 \sum_{j=1}^{p} |\beta_j| + \lambda_2 \sum_{j=1}^{p} \beta_j^2) Loss = i$$
$$= 1 \sum_{n} (y_i - \hat{y}_i)^2 + \alpha(\lambda_1 j = 1 \sum_{p} |\beta_j| + \lambda_2 j = 1 \sum_{p} \beta_j^2)$$

Here, we have the following:

- α controls the overall strength of regularization

- λ_1 is associated with the L1 penalty

- λ_2 is associated with the L2 penalty

- β_j are the coefficients of the features

The `l1_ratio` parameter allows you to adjust the balance between Lasso and ridge penalties:

- If `l1_ratio` is 1, ElasticNet behaves like Lasso

- If `l1_ratio` is 0, it behaves like ridge

- Values between 0 and 1 allow for a combination of both penalties

There's more...

One of the significant advantages of using ElasticNet is its ability to perform feature selection automatically by shrinking some coefficients to 0 (similar to Lasso). This can be particularly useful in high-dimensional datasets where many features may not contribute meaningfully to predictions.

Hands-on exercises

To visualize these techniques, please refer to the GitHub repository (`https://github.com/PacktPublishing/scikit-learn-Cookbook-Third-Edition`). You will engage in hands-on exercises using ElasticNet regression. Although we've included the code examples in the repository, we encourage you to explore them on your own and try using these tools with different arguments to see the results. The following steps outline a general workflow:

1. **Download and set up your environment**: Clone the GitHub repository and ensure all of the necessary libraries are installed.

2. **Load your dataset**: Choose an appropriate dataset for regression tasks from scikit-learn or your own collection.

3. **Preprocess your data**: Clean your dataset by handling missing values and encoding categorical variables if necessary.

4. Load `ElasticNet()` from `sklearn.linear_model`.

5. Train your model on training data.

6. Calculate metrics such as the MSE and R^2.

7. Experiment with different values for `alpha` and `l1_ratio` to observe how they affect model performance.

8. Create plots to visualize predicted versus actual values or examine coefficient paths based on different hyperparameter settings.

Regularization theory and practice

Regularization is a technique that is almost always utilized in real-world applications of ML, so it's worth taking a closer look at it (after all, it's in the title of this chapter, so it must be worth exploring in depth!). Regularization is an important technique used to prevent overfitting and improve the generalization of models, or how well they can perform in nuanced datasets beyond those they were trained on.

It involves adding a penalty term to the loss function (the method we use to evaluate our model's performance) during the training process, which discourages the model from becoming too complex or relying too heavily on specific features. By doing so, regularization helps the model to capture the underlying patterns in the data rather than memorizing noise or peculiarities of the training set.

The main idea behind regularization is to strike a balance between model complexity and *goodness of fit*. Without regularization, a model might achieve near-perfect performance on the training data by creating an overly complex decision boundary or function. However, such a model would likely perform poorly on new, unseen data, which ultimately is the performance we care most about. Regularization addresses this by imposing constraints on the model parameters, effectively shrinking them toward 0 – or, in ML parlance, *encouraging sparsity*.

The choice between these techniques depends on the specific problem and the desired characteristics of the final model. Regardless of the method used, the goal of regularization remains the same: to create a model that generalizes well to new data by finding the right balance between fitting the training data and maintaining simplicity.

1. **Model complexity**: In ML, model complexity refers to the capacity of a model to fit a wide variety of functions. Complex models can capture intricate patterns in training data but may fail to generalize well to new data, leading to overfitting.

2. **Types of regularization**:

   - **L1 regularization (Lasso)**: Adds a penalty equal to the *absolute value* of the magnitude of the coefficients. This can lead to sparse models where some coefficients are exactly 0, effectively performing feature selection.

   - **L2 regularization (ridge)**: Adds a penalty equal to the *square* of the magnitude of the coefficients. This discourages large coefficients but does not set them to 0, allowing all features to contribute to the model.

   - **ElasticNet**: Combines both L1 and L2 penalties, providing a balance between feature selection and coefficient shrinkage.

How to do it...

Regularization techniques aim to reduce overfitting by adding a penalty term to the loss function used during training:

- In Lasso regression (L1), the penalty term encourages sparsity in the coefficient estimates

- In ridge regression (L2), the penalty term shrinks coefficients toward 0 but retains all features in the model

- ElasticNet combines both penalties, making it particularly useful when dealing with correlated features or when there are more predictors than observations

Bias-variance trade-off

Regularization plays a crucial role in managing the bias-variance trade-off:

- Adding regularization typically increases bias slightly (as it constrains the model), but it significantly reduces variance (the sensitivity of predictions to fluctuations in training data)

- The goal is to find an optimal level of regularization that minimizes overall prediction error on unseen data

There's more...

Beyond basic Lasso and ridge regression, consider exploring advanced techniques such as group Lasso for grouped feature selection or Bayesian regression methods that incorporate prior distributions on coefficients.

Regression and regularization

Let's move on and explore polynomial regression and spline interpolation. These methods extend the capabilities of traditional linear regression, allowing for more flexible modeling of complex relationships in data. By implementing these techniques, you can expand your toolbox of approaches to regression problems. This recipe allows us to model relationships that are exponential or curvilinear in nature.

Getting ready

We will look at two methods in this section: polynomial regression and spline interpolation. We will create a new dataset to demonstrate these methods. Ideally, these methods are used when we have a dataset with a non-linear relationship between the features and the target. In order to create this dataset, we will use the make_regression() function again, but this time we will add some non-linearity to the data by adding a sine wave and an exponential function to the target.

1. Load the following libraries:

    ```
    import pandas as pd
    import matplotlib.pyplot as plt
    import seaborn as sns
    ```

2. Create a synthetic dataset with non-linear relationships:

    ```
    np.random.seed(123)
    n_samples = 1000
    X = np.random.uniform(-50, 50, (n_samples, 1))
    ```

3. Create a target with non-linear components:

```
y = (2 * X[:, 0]   # linear component
    + 27 * np.sin(X[:, 0] / 8)
    + np.random.normal(0, 4, n_samples))   # noise
```

4. Create a DataFrame:

```
data = pd.DataFrame(X, columns=['feature1'])
data['target'] = y
```

5. Create a plot:

```
plt.figure(figsize=(10, 5))
sns.scatterplot(data=data, x='feature1', y='target')
plt.title('Feature 1 vs Target')
plt.tight_layout()
plt.show()
```

Executing this code block will give us a dataset that does not follow a traditionally linear path.

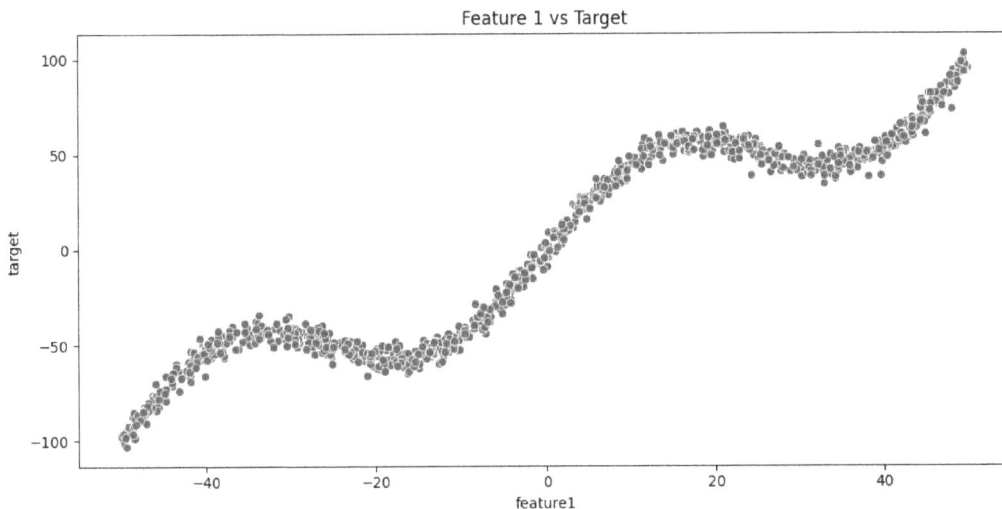

Figure 5.7 – A synthetic dataset with a non-linear component, a sine wave

While you might not often see a dataset with this particular structure in the real world, for our purposes, it provides a great opportunity to showcase polynomial regression.

How to do it...

In the following code, we will create a list of polynomial degrees to try and then fit a linear regression model on the polynomial features. We will then evaluate the model's performance using the MSE and R^2 metrics. Finally, we will visualize the different polynomial fits and the residuals for the best-performing model. Keep in mind that the best-performing model is not always the one with the highest R^2 value, but rather the one that best fits the data and has the lowest MSE. Also, the visualization is a bit messy, but it's a good starting point (you probably won't come across a dataset with such a clean relationship between the features and the target with a perfect sine wave non-linearity, anyway).

1. Load the following libraries:

    ```
    from sklearn.preprocessing import PolynomialFeatures
    from sklearn.model_selection import train_test_split
    from sklearn.linear_model import LinearRegression
    from sklearn.metrics import mean_squared_error, r2_score
    import pandas as pd
    import matplotlib.pyplot as plt
    ```

2. Use the synthetic dataset we just created:

    ```
    X = data[['feature1']]
    y = data['target']
    Create a list of polynomial degrees to try:
    degrees = [1, 2, 3, 4, 5]
    results = []
    ```

3. Try different polynomial degrees:

    ```
    for degree in degrees:
    ```

4. Transform the features to polynomial features:

    ```
    poly = PolynomialFeatures(degree=degree)
    X_poly = poly.fit_transform(X)
    ```

5. Split the data into training and testing sets:

    ```
    X_train, X_test, y_train, y_test = train_test_split(
        X_poly, y, test_size=0.2, random_state=123)
    ```

6. Create and fit the linear regression model on polynomial features:

    ```
    poly_model = LinearRegression()
    poly_model.fit(X_train, y_train)
    ```

7. Make predictions:

```
y_pred = poly_model.predict(X_test)
```

8. Calculate the mean squared error and r-squared metrics:

```
mse = mean_squared_error(y_test, y_pred)
r2 = r2_score(y_test, y_pred)
```

9. Store the results:

```
results.append({
    'Degree': degree,
    'MSE': mse,
    'R2': r2
})
```

10. Create a DataFrame of the results:

```
results_df = pd.DataFrame(results)
print("\nModel Performance Metrics:")
print(results_df.to_string(index=False))
```

11. Create a visualization of different polynomial fits:

```
fig, (ax1, ax2) = plt.subplots(1, 2, figsize=(20, 6))
```

12. Plot the data and polynomial fits:

```
ax1.scatter(X['feature1'], y, alpha=0.2, label='Data points')
```

13. Generate points for smooth curve plotting:

```
X_plot = np.linspace(
    X['feature1'].min(),
    X['feature1'].max(), 1000
).reshape(-1, 1)
colors = ['blue', 'green', 'red', 'purple', 'black']
for degree, color in zip(degrees, colors):
    poly = PolynomialFeatures(degree=degree)
    X_plot_poly = poly.fit_transform(X_plot)
    model = LinearRegression()
    model.fit(poly.fit_transform(X), y)
    y_plot = model.predict(X_plot_poly)
    ax1.plot(X_plot, y_plot, label=f'Degree {degree}',
             color=color, linewidth=2)
ax1.set_xlabel('Feature 1')
ax1.set_ylabel('Target')
```

```
ax1.set_title('Polynomial Regression Fits')
ax1.legend(loc='upper left')
```

14. Plot residuals for the best-performing model (based on R2):

```
best_degree = results_df.loc[
    results_df['R2'].idxmax(), 'Degree']
best_poly = PolynomialFeatures(degree=best_degree)
X_poly_best = best_poly.fit_transform(X)
X_train, X_test, y_train, y_test = train_test_split(
    X_poly_best, y, test_size=0.2, random_state=123)
best_model = LinearRegression()
best_model.fit(X_train, y_train)
y_pred = best_model.predict(X_test)
residuals = y_test - y_pred
ax2.scatter(y_pred, residuals, alpha=0.5)
ax2.axhline(y=0, color='r', linestyle='--')
ax2.set_xlabel('Predicted Values')
ax2.set_ylabel('Residuals')
ax2.set_title(
    f'Residual Plot (Best Model: Degree {best_degree})')
plt.tight_layout()
plt.show()
```

Let's visualize our five degrees of polynomial regression, keeping in mind that there will be some overlap, making some regression lines less visible.

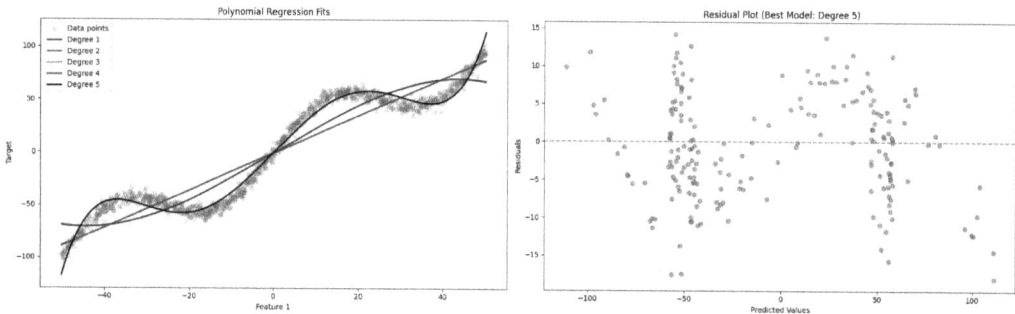

Figure 5.8 – Polynomial regression with different degrees applied
and residual plot of "best" fitting model (fifth degree)

Polynomial regression can seem like magic when working with non-linear datasets because of its ability to fit a regression line; however, you need to consider the recurring problem we've already spoken about: overfitting. We don't want our model to capture *noise* in our data because there is no guarantee that when we test it against real-world data, the same relationship will exist. So, looking solely at the MSE and R^2 can be problematic during model selection time.

Spline interpolation

Spline interpolation is a technique used to create a smooth curve that passes through a set of data points. It is a type of interpolation that uses piecewise polynomials to approximate the data. The basic idea is to divide the data into segments and then fit a polynomial to each segment. The resulting curve is smooth and continuous at the points where the segments meet.

scikit-learn provides a `SplineTransformer()` class that can be used to create spline interpolation. This class allows you to specify the number of *knots* (the points where the segments meet) and the degree of polynomial to use for each segment. The `SplineTransformer()` class is part of the `sklearn.preprocessing` module.

1. Load the following libraries:

```
from sklearn.preprocessing import SplineTransformer
from sklearn.pipeline import make_pipeline
from sklearn.metrics import mean_squared_error, r2_score
import pandas as pd
```

2. Create a spline transformer with different degrees of freedom:

```
n_knots = [3, 5, 7]   # Different numbers of knots to try
plt.figure(figsize=(12, 6))
```

3. Create lists to store metrics:

```
mse_scores = []
r2_scores = []
for n_knot, color in zip(n_knots, colors[:len(n_knots)]):
```

4. Create and fit the spline transformer:

```
spline = SplineTransformer(n_knots=n_knot, degree=3)
model = make_pipeline(spline, LinearRegression())
model.fit(X, y)
```

5. Generate the predictions:

```
y_pred = model.predict(X_plot)
y_pred_train = model.predict(X)
```

6. Calculate the metrics:

```
mse = mean_squared_error(y, y_pred_train)
r2 = r2_score(y, y_pred_train)
mse_scores.append(mse)
r2_scores.append(r2)
```

7. Plot the results:

```
plt.plot(X_plot, y_pred,
         label=f'Spline (knots={n_knot})',
         color=color,
         linewidth=2)
```

8. Plot the original data points:

```
plt.scatter(X, y, color='black', alpha=0.5,
            label='Data points')
plt.xlabel('Feature 1')
plt.ylabel('Target')
plt.title('Spline Interpolation with Different Numbers of
Knots')
plt.legend()
plt.grid(True, alpha=0.3)
plt.show()
```

Let's visualize the data:

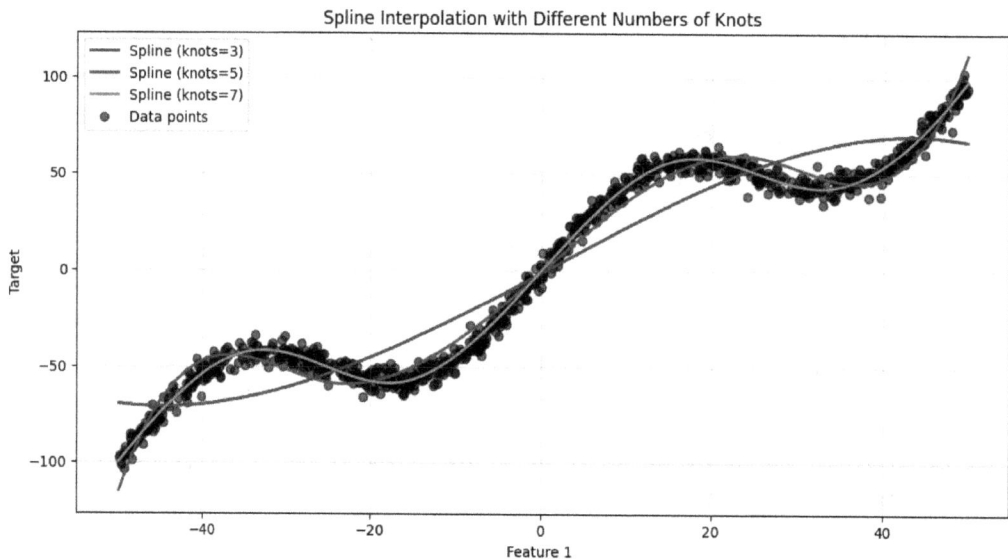

Figure 5.9 – Spline interpolation with several "knots" evaluated

9. Create and display the `metrics` DataFrame:

```
metrics_df = pd.DataFrame({
    'Number of Knots': n_knots,
    'MSE': mse_scores,
```

```
        'R-squared': r2_scores
    })
    display(metrics_df)
```

Let's print out our table.

	Number of Knots	MSE	R-squared
0	3	274.193682	0.904678
1	5	55.358587	0.980755
2	7	15.503780	0.994610

Figure 5.10 – Comparison of performance metrics at various knots

As the number of knots increases in our spline regression plot, our MSE decreases, indicating a better model fit.

How it works...

Polynomial regression extends linear regression by fitting a polynomial equation to the data. By transforming input features into polynomial terms (e.g., $x2x2$, $x3x3$), it allows capturing non-linear relationships between dependent and independent variables. The polynomial equation can be expressed as follows:

$$y = \beta0 + \beta1x + \beta2x2+\dots+\beta nxn + \epsilon y = \beta0 + \beta1x + \beta2x2+\dots+\beta nxn + \epsilon$$

Here, we have the following:

- y is the predicted value
- x represents input features
- βi refers to coefficients
- ϵ is the error term

Spline interpolation is a flexible method for fitting piecewise polynomials to data points. It allows for smooth transitions between segments while maintaining continuity at segment boundaries. This technique is particularly useful when dealing with complex datasets that exhibit non-linear trends.

There's more...

Beyond basic polynomial regression, consider exploring B-splines or natural splines for more sophisticated modeling of non-linear relationships.

Hands-on exercises

To visualize these techniques, please refer to the GitHub repository (`https://github.com/PacktPublishing/scikit-learn-Cookbook-Third-Edition`). You will engage in hands-on exercises focused on implementing polynomial regression and spline interpolation. Although we've included the code examples in the repository, we encourage you to explore them on your own and try using these tools with different arguments to see the results. The following steps outline a general workflow:

1. **Download and set up your environment**: Clone the GitHub repository and ensure all of the necessary libraries are installed.

2. **Load your dataset**: Choose an appropriate dataset for regression tasks from scikit-learn or your own collection.

3. **Preprocess your data**: Clean your dataset by handling missing values and encoding categorical variables if necessary.

4. Load `PolynomialFeatures()` from `sklearn.preprocessing`.

5. Train your model on transformed polynomial features.

6. Calculate metrics such as the MSE and R^2.

7. Load `SpineTransformer()` from `sklearn.preprocessing`.

8. Train your model on the training data.

9. Calculate metrics such as the MSE and R^2.

10. Analyze how both advanced techniques perform based on the evaluation metrics.

Practical exercises with regularization techniques

In this section, you will have the opportunity to apply your knowledge of regularization techniques through a series of practical exercises. These exercises will involve building, tuning, and evaluating regularized linear models – specifically ridge, Lasso, and ElasticNet – on different datasets. By engaging in these hands-on activities, you will reinforce your understanding of how regularization affects model performance and learn how to implement these techniques effectively in real-world scenarios.

Exercise 1: Implementing ridge regression

In the first exercise, we will create a new dataset and fit a ridge regression model to it. We will then evaluate the model's performance using the MSE and R^2 metrics. Finally, we will visualize the model's predictions on the test set to see how well it fits the data. When applicable, be sure to use `random_state=123` and/or `np.random.seed(123)` to ensure reproducibility.

The following are the implementation steps:

1. Load the libraries.

2. Generate a synthetic dataset with some noise.

3. Split the data into training and testing sets.

4. Create and fit a ridge regression model.

5. Make predictions.

6. Calculate the metrics.

7. Print the metrics.

8. Visualize the results.

9. Sort the X values for a smooth line plot.

Exercise 2: Implementing Lasso regression

This exercise is similar to the previous one, but we will implement Lasso regression instead. Compare the performance of the two when you're done.

The following are the implementation steps:

1. Load the libraries.

2. Generate synthetic data.

3. Split the data into training and testing sets.

4. Create and fit a Lasso regression model.

5. Make predictions.

6. Calculate the metrics.

7. Print the metrics.

8. Visualize the results.

9. Sort the X values for a smooth line plot.

Exercise 3: Implementing ElasticNet regression

Finally, ElasticNet regression combines the ridge and Lasso regularization techniques into a blended version. How well does this perform compared to the other two in isolation?

The following are the implementation steps:

1. Load the libraries.

2. Generate synthetic data.

3. Split the data into training and testing sets.

4. Create and fit the ElasticNet model.

5. Make predictions.

6. Calculate the metrics.

7. Print the metrics.

8. Visualize the results.

9. Sort the X values for a smooth line plot.

6

Advanced Logistic Regression and Extensions

Although most of us who have heard of or used regression modeling before tend to immediately think of its applications for predicting quantitative outcomes, regression modeling is actually quite robust and capable of also predicting qualitative, discrete outcomes like those found in classification problems. In fact, it is arguable that many traditional ML problems in business tend to be classification problems rather than regression ones. Therefore, we need to add some more regression techniques to our toolbox for just such occasions! In this chapter, we will deepen your understanding of logistic regression with advanced concepts such as multiclass and multilabel classification, regularization, and model evaluation metrics.

In this chapter, we're going to cover the following recipes:

- Overview of logistic regression
- Multiclass classification techniques
- Regularization in logistic regression
- Multilabel classification concepts
- Model evaluation metrics
- Implementation in scikit-learn

Technical requirements

It is advisable to create a Python environment for safely isolating your work from other Python installations/libraries. See the GitHub repository for more details (`https://github.com/PacktPublishing/scikit-learn-Cookbook-Third-Edition`).

- Git >=2.46.x

- Python >=3.9.x

- A cloned GitHub repository and Python environment built from the `requirements.txt` file

Overview of logistic regression

Logistic regression is a fundamental statistical method used for binary classification problems in machine learning (mostly, but as we'll see shortly, it can be extended to serve multiple classes and even instances where an observation may belong to multiple classes – multilabel classification).

Unlike linear regression, which predicts continuous outcomes, logistic regression predicts the probability that a given input point belongs to a particular category or class. This is achieved by applying the logistic function (also known as the **sigmoid function**) to the linear combination of the input features, which transforms the output into a value between 0 and 1. This makes logistic regression particularly useful for scenarios where the outcome variable is categorical, such as determining whether an email is spam or not, or predicting whether a patient has a certain disease based on medical measurements.

The mathematical foundation of logistic regression involves estimating the parameters of the model using **maximum likelihood estimation** (**MLE**). The logistic function can be expressed as:

$$P(Y = 1|X) = \frac{1}{1 + e^{-(\beta_0 + \beta_1 X_1 + \beta_2 X_2 \ldots \beta_n + X_n)}}$$

Here, $P(Y = 1 \mid X)$ represents the probability that the dependent variable Y equals 1 given the independent variables X, and $\beta0, \beta1, \ldots, \beta n$ are the coefficients to be estimated. The output of this function can be interpreted as the probability of belonging to the positive class

($Y = 1$), allowing us to classify observations based on a threshold (commonly set at 0.5 since this would indicate a probability greater than 50%, whereas anything at or less than 50% would indicate a chance probability of the predicted class).

Understanding logistic regression serves as a foundation for more advanced topics in classification and predictive modeling. As we explore its applications and underlying principles, we will also prepare for more complex models, such as regularized versions of logistic regression that help manage overfitting.

Getting ready

To get started, we'll need a classification dataset to illustrate the basics of logistic regression implementation in scikit-learn. We'll use the Breast Cancer dataset included in the scikit-learn library. This is also (yet another) commonly used toy dataset for illustrating ML applications.

1. Load the libraries:

```
from sklearn.datasets import load_breast_cancer
from sklearn.model_selection import train_test_split
from sklearn.linear_model import LogisticRegression
from sklearn.metrics import (
    accuracy_score, confusion_matrix,
    classification_report
)
import pandas as pd
```

2. Load the dataset:

```
data = load_breast_cancer()
X = data.data
y = data.target
```

3. Convert to a DataFrame for easier manipulation (optional):

```
df = pd.DataFrame(X, columns=data.feature_names)
df['target'] = y
```

4. Split the data:

```
X_train, X_test, y_train, y_test = train_test_split(
    df[data.feature_names], df['target'],
    test_size=0.2, random_state=2024
)
```

Now let's apply basic logistic regression.

How to do it...

As we've seen before (and will continue to see), loading a model in scikit-learn is as simple as instantiating the class in a variable and building from there.

1. Create a logistic regression model:

```
model = LogisticRegression(max_iter=10000) # Increase max_iter
if convergence issues occur
```

2. Train the model:

```
model.fit(X_train, y_train)
```

3. Make predictions:

```
y_pred = model.predict(X_test)
```

4. Evaluate the performance:

```
accuracy = accuracy_score(y_test, y_pred)
```

5. Generate and plot a confusion matrix:

```
class_names = ['Malignant', 'Benign']
cm = confusion_matrix(y_test, y_pred)
plt.figure(figsize=(8, 6))
sns.heatmap(cm, annot=True, fmt='d', cmap='Blues',
            xticklabels=class_names,
            yticklabels=class_names,
            cbar_kws={'label': 'Number of Samples'})
plt.xlabel('Predicted')
plt.ylabel('True')
plt.title('Confusion Matrix')
plt.show()
```

6. Get a classification report as a dictionary:

```
report_dict = classification_report(
    y_test, y_pred,
    target_names=class_names,
    output_dict=True
)
```

7. Create a DataFrame for better visualization:

```
report_df = pd.DataFrame(report_dict).transpose()
```

8. Style the DataFrame:

```
styled_df = (report_df
    .style
    .background_gradient(
        cmap='Blues',
        subset=['precision', 'recall', 'f1-score']
    )
    .format({
        'precision': '{:.3f}',
```

```
        'recall': '{:.3f}',
        'f1-score': '{:.3f}',
        'support': '{:.0f}'
    })
)
print(f'Accuracy: {accuracy:.2f}\n')
print("\nClassification Report:")
display(styled_df)

# Output:
Accuracy: 0.95
```

Even out of the box, logistic regression performs quite well in classifying our binary dataset:

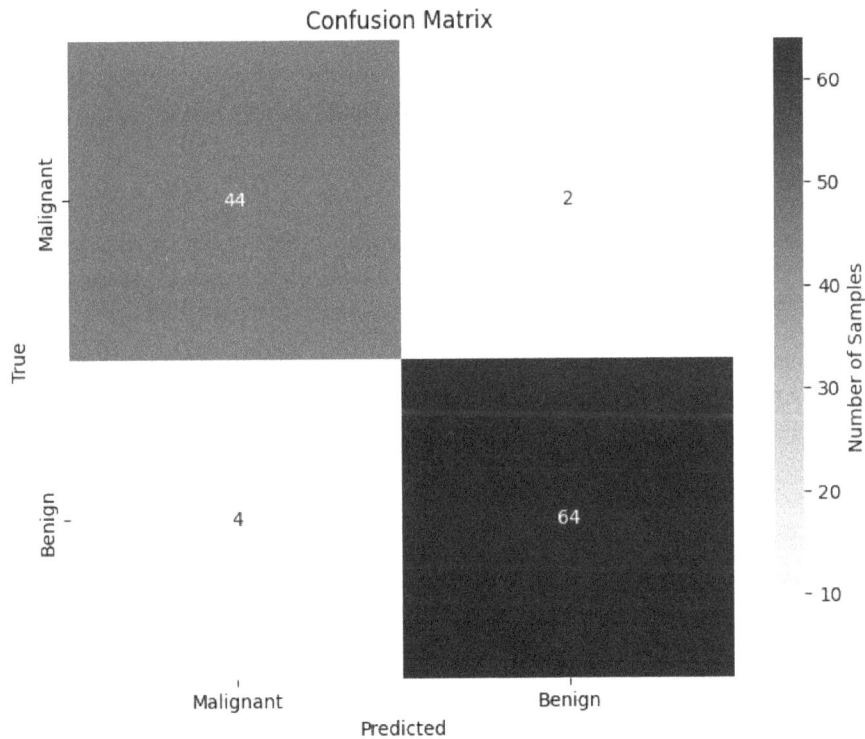

Figure 6.1 – Confusion matrix for logistic regression

The confusion matrix indicates that the model is able to easily infer **malignant** and **benign** records with very few misclassifications.

	precision	recall	f1-score	support
Malignant	0.917	0.957	0.936	46
Benign	0.970	0.941	0.955	68
accuracy	0.947	0.947	0.947	1
macro avg	0.943	0.949	0.946	114
weighted avg	0.948	0.947	0.948	114

Figure 6.2 – Classification report for logistic regression

In addition to the confusion matrix, the classification report also provides more granular detail on the performance of our model. Remember, a model's **accuracy** isn't always the best performance metric (especially in this case, where we are predicting the probability that a person has breast cancer). Based on your knowledge, what other metric represented in the chart might be better?

How it works...

Logistic regression operates by estimating probabilities through a linear combination of input features transformed by the logistic function. The coefficients obtained during training represent how much each feature contributes to predicting the probability of belonging to a particular class.

The decision boundary created by logistic regression is linear in terms of *log-odds* but can effectively separate classes in many binary classification scenarios. When visualizing results, plotting predicted probabilities against actual outcomes can provide insights into how well the model distinguishes between classes.

> Log-odds
>
> The "log-odds" of an event is the natural logarithm of its odds. We use the term "odds" often when talking about placing bets or predicting outcomes, but what exactly are "odds?" Odds are the ratio of the probability of an event happening to the probability of it not happening. We see this transformation used in statistical modeling, such as logistic regression, to convert a probability scale (bounded by 0 and 1) into a linear, unbounded scale ranging from negative to positive infinity.

Evaluating model performance

Evaluating logistic regression models involves assessing various metrics:

- **Accuracy score**: Represents the proportion of correctly classified instances

- **Confusion matrix**: Provides detailed insights into true positives, true negatives, false positives, and false negatives

- **Precision and recall**: Help understand how well the model performs in identifying positive cases versus all cases

- Visualizations such as **Receiver Operating Characteristic** (**ROC**) curves can also be beneficial in evaluating model performance across different thresholds

Hands-on exercises

To illustrate these techniques, please reference the GitHub repository (`https://github.com/PacktPublishing/scikit-learn-Cookbook-Third-Edition`). You will engage in hands-on exercises focused on implementing logistic regression models for binary classification tasks using the Breast Cancer dataset. Although we've included code examples, we encourage you to explore on your own and try using these tools with different arguments to see what results. The following steps outline a general workflow:

1. Clone the GitHub repository and ensure all necessary libraries are installed.
2. Load the Breast Cancer dataset using `load_breast_cancer()` from `sklearn.datasets`.
3. Clean your dataset by handling missing values, if applicable (not needed for this dataset).
4. Load `LogisticRegression()` from `sklearn.linear_model`.
5. Fit your model using training data with the `fit` method.
6. Use the `predict` method on your test data to generate predictions.
7. Calculate metrics such as accuracy score, confusion matrix, precision, recall, and F1-score to assess how well your model performs.
8. Create plots to visualize predicted probabilities versus actual outcomes, or examine ROC curves if applicable.

Multiclass classification techniques

Unfortunately, we live in a world where outcomes (in ML parlance, *classes*) are not always so polarized: 0 versus 1, night versus day, and so on. Therefore, we need techniques for predicting non-binary outcomes. Thankfully, logistic regression can still help us!

In this recipe, we introduce multiclass logistic regression techniques, focusing on **one-vs-rest (OvR)** (also known as **one-vs-all**) and multinomial logistic regression strategies. These methods extend binary logistic regression to handle classification problems with more than two classes. We will implement these techniques using scikit-learn, learning how to adapt and apply logistic regression to multiclass datasets.

Getting ready

To get started, we'll once again utilize a dataset we've used before: the Iris dataset. This dataset contains three classes, so it's perfect for this basic illustration of multiclass classification.

1. Load the libraries:

    ```
    from sklearn.datasets import load_iris
    from sklearn.model_selection import train_test_split
    from sklearn.linear_model import LogisticRegression
    from sklearn.metrics import (
        accuracy_score, classification_ report )
    from sklearn.inspection import DecisionBoundaryDisplay
    import pandas as pd
    import seaborn as sns
    import matplotlib.pyplot as plt
    ```

2. Load the Iris dataset:

    ```
    iris = load_iris()
    X = iris.data
    y = iris.target
    feature_names = iris.feature_names
    df = pd.DataFrame(X, columns=feature_names)
    df['target'] = y
    ```

3. Split the dataset:

    ```
    X_train, X_test, y_train, y_test = train_test_split(
        X, y, test_size=0.3, random_state=2024)
    ```

Now, let's apply multiclass classification by slightly modifying our logistic regression function's arguments.

How to do it...

We will implement both OvR and multinomial logistic regression:

1. Create and train an OvR logistic regression model. (Note: After version 1.7 of scikit-learn, the `multi_class` argument will be removed and the `multinomial` option will always be used when the predicted classes are greater than or equal to 3.)

    ```python
    ovr_model = LogisticRegression(solver='liblinear')
    ovr_model.fit(X_train, y_train)
    ```

2. Create and train a multinomial logistic regression model:

    ```python
    multinomial_model = LogisticRegression(
        multi_class='multinomial',
        solver='lbfgs', max_iter = 1000
    )
    multinomial_model.fit(X_train, y_train)
    ```

3. Make predictions with the OvR model:

    ```python
    y_pred_ovr = ovr_model.predict(X_test)
    ```

4. Make predictions with the multinomial model:

    ```python
    y_pred_multinomial = multinomial_model.predict(X_test)
    ```

5. Evaluate the OvR model:

    ```python
    accuracy_ovr = accuracy_score(y_test, y_pred_ovr)
    report_ovr = pd.DataFrame(classification_report(
        y_test, y_pred_ovr, output_dict=True)).transpose()
    print("One-vs-Rest (OvR) Logistic Regression:")
    styled_ovr = (report_ovr
        .style
        .background_gradient(
            cmap='Blues',
            subset=['precision', 'recall', 'f1-score']
        )
        .format({
            'precision': '{:.3f}',
            'recall': '{:.3f}',
            'f1-score': '{:.3f}',
            'support': '{:.0f}'
        })
    ```

```
)
display(styled_ovr)
```

Displayed in the following figure is our confusion matrix for OvR classification. What can you infer from these results? While you are already familiar with the term *accuracy*, you might not be familiar with *macro* and *weighted average*. Macro accuracy is a label-wise unweighted average, which does not take into account the number of samples (i.e., the *support* in the table), whereas *weighted average* does take these into account. Since our example includes such a small number of examples, these values aren't all that different.

	precision	recall	f1-score	support
0	1.000	1.000	1.000	18
1	0.917	0.917	0.917	12
2	0.933	0.933	0.933	15
accuracy	0.956	0.956	0.956	1
macro avg	0.950	0.950	0.950	45
weighted avg	0.956	0.956	0.956	45

Figure 6.3 – Classification report for OvR logistic regression

6. Evaluate the multinomial model:

```
accuracy_multinomial = accuracy_score(
    y_test, y_pred_multinomial)
report_multinomial = pd.DataFrame(classification_report(
    y_test, y_pred_multinomial,
    output_dict=True)).transpose()
print("Multinomial Logistic Regression:")
styled_multinomial = (report_multinomial
    .style
    .background_gradient(
        cmap='Blues',
        subset=['precision', 'recall', 'f1-score']
    )
    .format({
        'precision': '{:.3f}',
        'recall': '{:.3f}',
        'f1-score': '{:.3f}',
        'support': '{:.0f}'
    })
```

```
    )
display(styled_multinomial)
```

Here is the classification report for our next model. Even though we are using multinomial classification for a binary classification problem, the approach is slightly different in scikit-learn. OvR will fit a binary classification approach to each label, while multinomial will attempt to predict probabilities for each class even when there are only two classes.

	precision	recall	f1-score	support
0	1.000	1.000	1.000	18
1	0.846	0.917	0.880	12
2	0.929	0.867	0.897	15
accuracy	0.933	0.933	0.933	1
macro avg	0.925	0.928	0.926	45
weighted avg	0.935	0.933	0.934	45

Figure 6.4 – Classification report for multinomial logistic regression

The differences we see between these approaches in terms of their predictions are described next.

How it works...

We implemented two different approaches here, OvR and multinomial, so let's discuss them in more detail.

OvR logistic regression

OvR involves training a separate binary classifier for each class. For each classifier, the instances of that class are treated as the positive class, and the instances of all other classes are treated as the negative class. During prediction, the classifier with the highest confidence score is selected.

Multinomial logistic regression

Multinomial logistic regression, also known as **SoftMax regression**, directly models the probability of each class using a SoftMax function. It estimates multiple regression coefficients, one for each class, and optimizes them simultaneously. This approach is more suitable when the classes are mutually exclusive.

Key considerations

Keep these elements in mind when utilizing these techniques:

- **Solver selection**: Different solvers are suitable for different types of logistic regression. For OvR, **liblinear** is often a good choice, while for multinomial, **lbfgs** or **newton-cg** are common. Browse the scikit-learn documentation for more details.

- **Regularization**: Like binary logistic regression, multiclass logistic regression benefits from regularization to prevent overfitting.

- **Data preprocessing**: Scaling numerical features to a standard range can often improve the performance of logistic regression models.

There's more...

There are a variety of visualization methods available to visually inspect the results of our model, or sometimes just the dataset itself. The pairplot in the Python package seaborn can provide insights into how well the model separates the different classes.

1. Create a pairplot to visualize the data:

```
target_names = {0: 'Setosa',
                1: 'Versicolor',
                2: 'Virginica'}
df['target_name'] = df['target'].map(target_names)
sns.pairplot(df, hue='target_name', diag_kind='kde')
plt.show()
```

Let's visualize our pairplot.

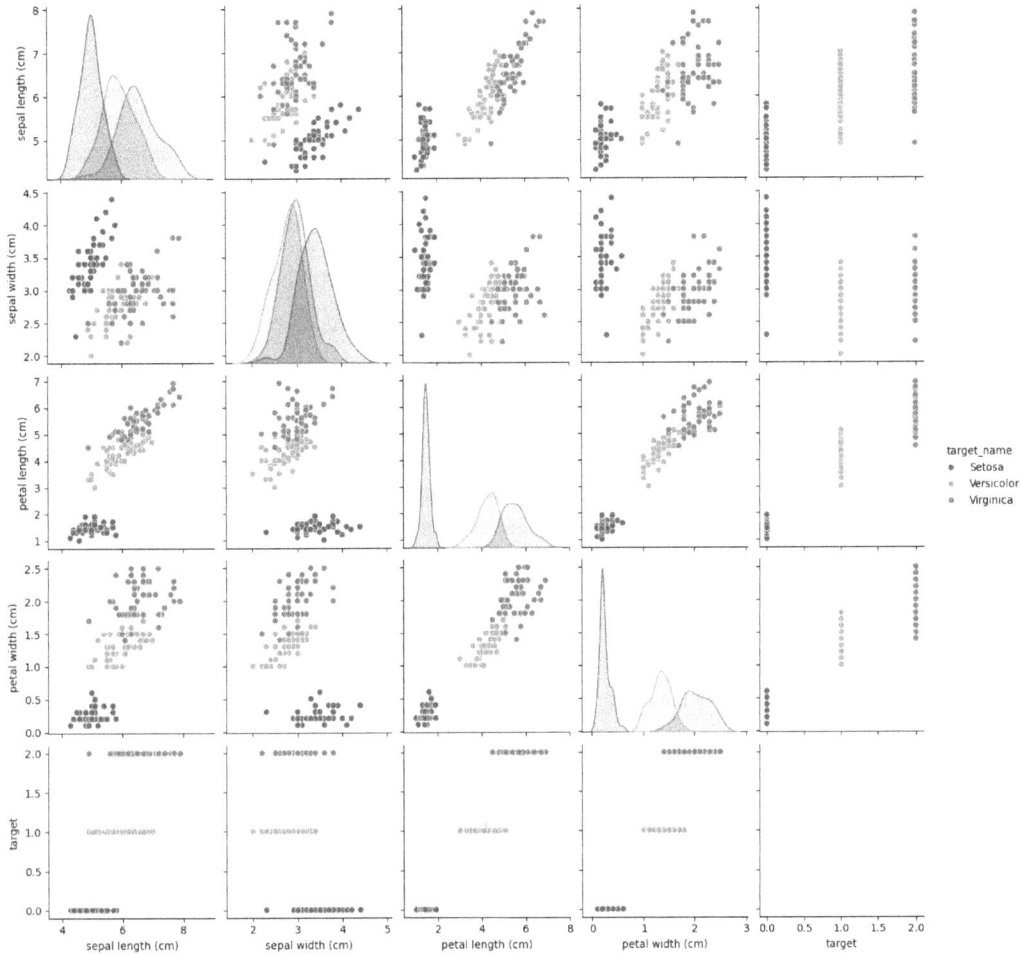

Figure 6.5 – Pairplot of Iris dataset

The pairplot provides a lot of valuable information visually. For example, we can see that "petal length" and "petal width" are distributed with a high kurtosis (e.g., concentrated at a small set of values, creating a highly narrow, peaked distribution). This confirms these features as highly valuable for our classification problem.

Hands-on exercises

To illustrate these techniques, please reference the GitHub repository (`https://github.com/PacktPublishing/scikit-learn-Cookbook-Third-Edition`). We will engage in hands-on exercises focused on implementing multiclass logistic regression models using the Iris dataset. Although we've included code examples, we encourage you to explore on your own and try using these tools with different arguments to see what results. The following steps outline a general workflow:

1. Clone the GitHub repository and ensure all necessary libraries are installed.

2. Load the `Iris` dataset using `load_iris()` from `sklearn.datasets`.

3. Clean the dataset by handling missing values and encoding categorical variables, if necessary (not needed for this dataset).

4. Load `LogisticRegression()` from `sklearn.linear_model`.

5. Implement OvR logistic regression and evaluate the performance using metrics such as accuracy score and classification report.

6. Implement multinomial logistic regression and evaluate the performance using the same metrics.

7. Compare the results of the two approaches and discuss their strengths and weaknesses in the context of the Iris dataset.

8. Generate a pairplot to visualize the relationships between the features in the Iris dataset.

9. Generate decision boundary plots for OvR and multinomial logistic regression.

Regularization in logistic regression

Let's take a closer look at the role of regularization in logistic regression. Remember, regularization is a crucial technique for preventing overfitting, especially when dealing with high-dimensional datasets or complex models. We'll focus on how Ridge (L2) and Lasso (L1) regularization, last seen in *Chapter 5*, can be applied to logistic regression to improve its generalization performance. By implementing regularized logistic regression models using scikit-learn, we will learn how to tune the regularization strength to achieve an optimal balance between bias and variance.

Getting ready

Before implementing regularized logistic regression, let's ensure we have the necessary Python libraries installed and the dataset loaded. We'll jump back to using the Breast Cancer dataset again.

1. Load the libraries:

```
from sklearn.model_selection import train_test_split
from sklearn.linear_model import LogisticRegression
```

```
from sklearn.metrics import (
    accuracy_score, classification_ report)
from sklearn.datasets import load_breast_cancer
import pandas as pd
import matplotlib.pyplot as plt
import numpy as np
from sklearn.preprocessing import StandardScaler
```

2. Load the dataset:

```
data = load_breast_cancer()
X = data.data
y = data.target
feature_names = data.feature_names
df = pd.DataFrame(X, columns=feature_names)
df['target'] = y
```

3. Split the dataset and scale it:

```
X_train, X_test, y_train, y_test = train_test_split(
    X, y, test_size=0.3, random_state=2024)
scaler = StandardScaler()
X_train = scaler.fit_transform(X_train)
X_test = scaler.transform(X_test)
```

How to do it...

Now, let's implement Ridge (L2) and Lasso (L1) regularized logistic regression models.

1. Create and train a Ridge (L2) regularized logistic regression model:

```
ridge_model = LogisticRegression(
    penalty='l2', solver='liblinear', C=0.1)
ridge_model.fit(X_train, y_train)
```

2. Create and train a Lasso (L1) regularized logistic regression model:

```
lasso_model = LogisticRegression(
    penalty='l1', solver='liblinear', C=0.1)
lasso_model.fit(X_train, y_train)
```

3. Make predictions with the Ridge model:

```
y_pred_ridge = ridge_model.predict(X_test)
```

4. Make predictions with the Lasso model:

```
y_pred_lasso = lasso_model.predict(X_test)
```

5. Evaluate the Ridge model:

```
accuracy_ridge = accuracy_score(y_test, y_pred_ridge)
report_ridge = pd.DataFrame(classification_report(
    y_test, y_pred_ridge, output_dict=True)).transpose()
print("Ridge (L2) Regularized Logistic Regression:")
styled_ridge = (report_ridge
    .style
    .background_gradient(
        cmap='Blues',
        subset=['precision', 'recall', 'f1-score']
    )
    .format({
        'precision': '{:.3f}',
        'recall': '{:.3f}',
        'f1-score': '{:.3f}',
        'support': '{:.0f}'
    })
)
display(styled_ridge)
```

Let's print our ridge regression classification report.

	precision	recall	f1-score	support
0	0.985	0.970	0.977	67
1	0.981	0.990	0.986	104
accuracy	0.982	0.982	0.982	1
macro avg	0.983	0.980	0.982	171
weighted avg	0.982	0.982	0.982	171

Figure 6.6 – Classification report for ridge regularization

6. Evaluate the Lasso model:

```
accuracy_lasso = accuracy_score(y_test, y_pred_lasso)
report_lasso = pd.DataFrame(classification_report(
    y_test, y_pred_lasso, output_dict=True)).transpose()
print("Lasso (L1) Regularized Logistic Regression:")
styled_lasso = (report_lasso
```

```
      .style
      .background_gradient(
          cmap='Blues',
          subset=['precision', 'recall', 'f1-score']
      )
      .format({
          'precision': '{:.3f}',
          'recall': '{:.3f}',
          'f1-score': '{:.3f}',
          'support': '{:.0f}'
      })
  )
display(styled_lasso)
```

Let's print our Lasso regression classification report. Both ridge and Lasso regression provide quality performance, but your final evaluation will be dependent on the metrics you choose.

	precision	recall	f1-score	support
0	0.930	0.985	0.957	67
1	0.990	0.952	0.971	104
accuracy	0.965	0.965	0.965	1
macro avg	0.960	0.968	0.964	171
weighted avg	0.966	0.965	0.965	171

Figure 6.7 – Classification report for Lasso regularization

Lasso regression has a slightly lower **accuracy** score, so it doesn't work as well for overall classification of *both* **malignant** and **benign** records; however, if we are using **precision** or **recall**, then we can see that ridge outperforms in **precision** while Lasso outperforms in **recall**.

How it works...

Regularization adds a penalty term to the loss function, which discourages the model from assigning overly large coefficients to the features. This helps prevent overfitting, where the model performs well on the training data but poorly on unseen data.

- **Ridge (L2) Regularization**: Adds a penalty proportional to the square of the magnitude of the coefficients. This shrinks the coefficients towards zero but rarely sets them exactly to zero.

- **Lasso (L1) Regularization**: Adds a penalty proportional to the absolute value of the coefficients. This can lead to sparse models by driving some coefficients to exactly zero, effectively performing feature selection.

The C parameter in `LogisticRegression()` controls the inverse of the regularization strength; smaller values specify stronger regularization.

Key considerations

Keep these elements in mind when utilizing these techniques:

- **Solver selection**: Different solvers have different support for regularization penalties. The **liblinear** solver is suitable for both L1 and L2 regularization with small datasets. For larger datasets, **saga** is often a good choice.

- **Data scaling**: Regularization is sensitive to the scale of the features, so it's important to scale the data before applying regularization.

- **Hyperparameter tuning**: The regularization strength, C, needs to be tuned to find the optimal balance between bias and variance. You can implement grid or random search techniques as you would any other hyperparameter selection process we've discussed so far.

There's more...

We can visualize the effect of regularization by plotting the coefficients of the logistic regression model as a function of the regularization strength.

1. Plot coefficients for different C values (Ridge).

```
C_values = np.array(
    [0.0001, 0.001, 0.01, 0.1, 1, 10, 100, 1000])
coefs_ridge = []
for C in C_values:
    ridge_model = LogisticRegression(
        penalty='l2', solver='liblinear', C=C)
    ridge_model.fit(X_train, y_train)
    coefs_ridge.append(ridge_model.coef_[0])
plt.figure(figsize=(12, 6))
for i in range(X.shape[1]):
    plt.plot(
        C_values, [coef[i] for coef in coefs_ridge],
        label=feature_names[i]
    )
plt.xscale('log')
plt.xlabel('C (Inverse Regularization Strength)')
plt.ylabel('Coefficient Value')
plt.title('Ridge Regression: Coefficient Values vs. C')
plt.legend(
    bbox_to_anchor=(0.5, -0.35),
```

```
        ncol=6, loc='lower center', fontsize=8
)
plt.tight_layout()
plt.show()
```

The output plot visualizes the impact of coefficient shrinkage using L2 (i.e., Ridge) regularization.

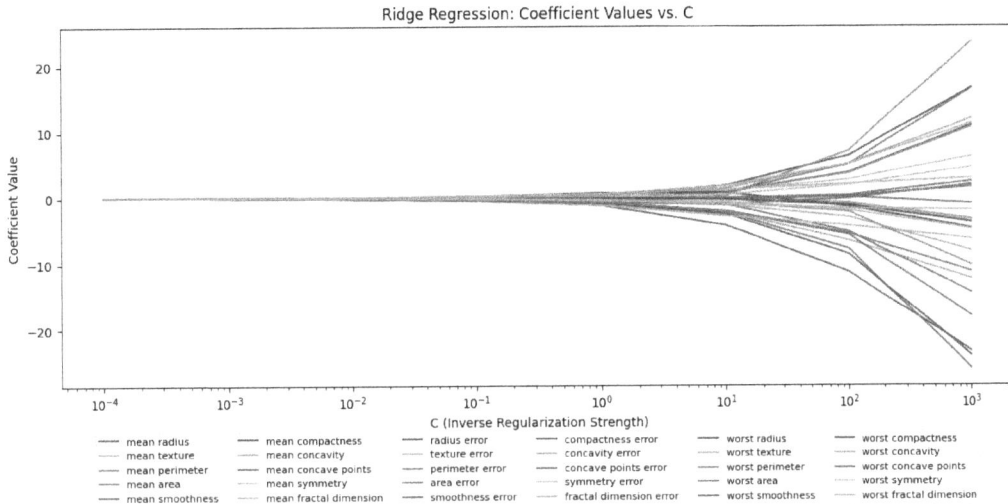

Figure 6.8 – Regularization plot for Ridge regularization

2. Plotting coefficients for different C values (Lasso):

```
C_values = np.array(
    [0.0001, 0.001, 0.01, 0.1, 1, 10, 100, 1000])
coefs_lasso = []
for C in C_values:
    lasso_model = LogisticRegression(
        penalty='l1', solver='liblinear', C=C)
    lasso_model.fit(X_train, y_train)
    coefs_lasso.append(lasso_model.coef_[0])
plt.figure(figsize=(12, 6))
for i in range(X.shape[1]):
    plt.plot(
        C_values, [coef[i] for coef in coefs_lasso],
        label=feature_names[i]
    )
plt.xscale('log')
plt.xlabel('C (Inverse Regularization Strength)')
plt.ylabel('Coefficient Value')
```

```
plt.title('Lasso Regression: Coefficient Values vs. C')
plt.legend(
    bbox_to_anchor=(0.5, -0.35), ncol=6,
    loc='lower center', fontsize=8
)
plt.tight_layout()
plt.show()
```

This visualization shows the results of applied L1 (i.e., LASSO) regularization.

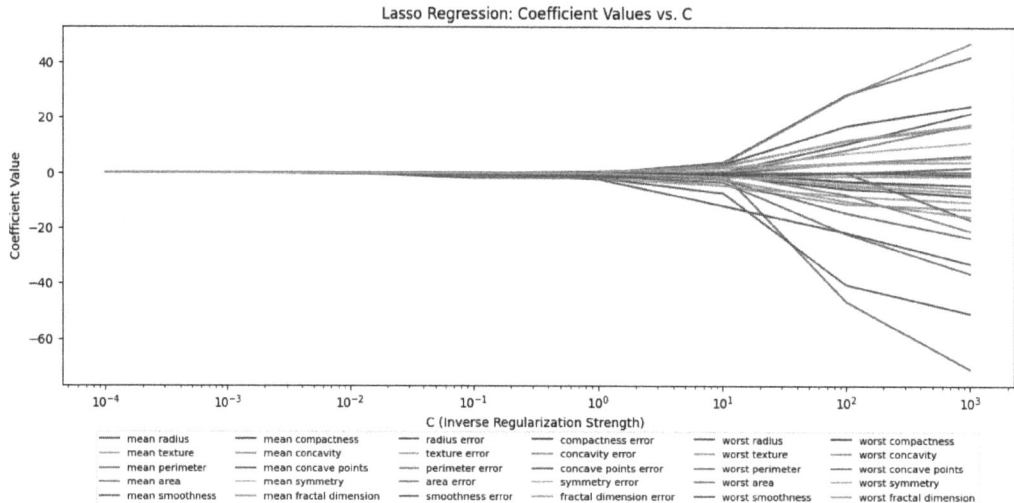

Figure 6.9 – Regularization plot for Lasso regularization

These visualizations will help us understand how the coefficients change as we vary the regularization strength, providing insights into the impact of regularization on feature importance.

Hands-on exercises

To illustrate these techniques, please reference the GitHub repository (https://github.com/PacktPublishing/scikit-learn-Cookbook-Third-Edition). We will engage in hands-on exercises focused on implementing regularized logistic regression models using the Breast Cancer dataset. Although we've included code examples, we encourage you to explore on your own and try using these tools with different arguments to see what results. The following steps outline a general workflow:

1. Clone the GitHub repository and ensure all necessary libraries are installed.

2. Load the Breast Cancer dataset using load_breast_cancer() from sklearn.datasets.

3. Scale your data using StandardScaler() from sklearn.preprocessing.

4. Load `LogisticRegression()` from `sklearn.linear_model`.

5. Implement Ridge (L2) regularized logistic regression and evaluate performance using metrics such as accuracy score and classification report.

6. Implement Lasso (L1) regularized logistic regression and evaluate performance using the same metrics.

7. Compare the results of the two approaches and discuss their strengths and weaknesses in the context of the Breast Cancer dataset.

8. Generate plots to visualize the relationships between the **C (Inverse Regularization Strength)** and the model coefficients, as seen in *Figure 6.9*.

Multilabel classification concepts

Multilabel classification is an advanced machine learning technique where each instance can belong to multiple classes simultaneously. Unlike traditional classification tasks that assign a single label to each instance, multilabel classification allows for a more nuanced approach, making it suitable for various applications such as text categorization, image tagging, and bioinformatics. In this recipe, we will explore how to set up and implement multilabel logistic regression models in scikit-learn, gaining valuable experience with this complex classification problem.

Getting ready

Before we start implementing multilabel classification techniques, let's ensure we have the necessary Python libraries installed and the dataset loaded. We're going to generate our own dataset for this example recipe.

1. Load the libraries:

```
from sklearn.datasets import make_multilabel_classification
from sklearn.model_selection import train_test_split
from sklearn.linear_model import LogisticRegression
from sklearn.metrics import (
    accuracy_score, classification_report, confusion_matrix)
import pandas as pd
import numpy as np
import seaborn as sns
import matplotlib.pyplot as plt
```

2. Load the dataset:

    ```
    X,  y = make_multilabel_classification(
        n_samples=1000, n_features=20,
        n_classes=5, n_labels=2, random_state=2024
    )
    df = pd.DataFrame(
        X,
        columns=[f'feature_{i}' for i in range(X.shape[1])]
    )
    df['target'] = list(y)
    ```

3. Split the data:

    ```
    X_train, X_test, y_train, y_test = train_test_split(
        X, y, test_size=0.3, random_state=2024)
    ```

Now we have a synthetic dataset with several classes (n_classes=5) and multiple classes for each record (n_labels=2). (Note: the n_labels argument does *not* guarantee that number of labels per record; it merely *allows* each record to have that number of labels).

How to do it...

Now let's implement multilabel logistic regression using the OvR strategy.

1. Since we have multiple labels, we need to train a separate model for each label:

    ```
    models = []
    y_pred_all = []
    ```

2. Train the model for each label (column) in *y*:

    ```
    for i in range(y_train.shape[1]):
        # Create and train model for this label
        model = LogisticRegression(solver='liblinear')
        model.fit(X_train, y_train[:, i])
        models.append(model)
        # Make predictions for this label
        y_pred_label = model.predict(X_test)
        y_pred_all.append(y_pred_label)
    ```

3. Convert the predictions list to an array and transpose it to match the original format:

    ```
    y_pred = np.array(y_pred_all).T
    ```

4. Evaluate the model:

```
accuracy = accuracy_score(y_test, y_pred)
report = pd.DataFrame(classification_report(
    y_test, y_pred, zero_division=1,
    output_dict=True
)).transpose()
print("Classification Report:")
styled_report = (report
    .style
    .background_gradient(
        cmap='Blues',
        subset=['precision', 'recall', 'f1-score']
    )
    .format({
        'precision': '{:.3f}',
        'recall': '{:.3f}',
        'f1-score': '{:.3f}',
        'support': '{:.0f}'
    })
)
display(styled_report)
```

Let's display our classification report.

	precision	recall	f1-score	support
0	0.808	0.813	0.811	166
1	0.801	0.845	0.823	181
2	0.674	0.333	0.446	93
3	0.750	0.176	0.286	34
4	0.575	0.477	0.522	88
micro avg	0.757	0.653	0.701	562
macro avg	0.722	0.529	0.577	562
weighted avg	0.744	0.653	0.677	562
samples avg	0.787	0.782	0.680	562

Figure 6.10 – Classification report for multilabel classification

Our multilabel classification problem is a bit more challenging than the binary classification problems we saw earlier in the chapter.

How it works...

Multilabel classification involves predicting multiple binary labels for each instance. In our implementation using logistic regression with the OvR strategy, we train a separate binary classifier for each class label. Each classifier learns to distinguish between instances that belong to its respective class and those that do not.

The `make_multilabel_classification()` function generates synthetic datasets suitable for multilabel problems. The generated dataset consists of features and corresponding labels indicating the presence or absence of each class.

When evaluating our model's performance, metrics such as accuracy score and classification report provide insights into how well our model predicts multiple labels. The classification report includes precision, recall, and F1-score for each class label, allowing us to assess performance comprehensively.

MultiOutputClassifier()

scikit-learn provides a class called `MultiOutputClassifier()` as a shortcut that can be applied to problems requiring multilabel classification. The class takes a classifier as the first argument (for example, `LogisticRegression()`) and applies it to each target. This can reduce the code needed and remove the need to select a *solver* specific to multilabel classification, like we applied in the example previously.)

Visualizing results

Visualizations can enhance our understanding of how well our model performs across different classes. For instance, we can create a co-occurrence matrix (similar to a confusion matrix) that shows which labels frequently appear together.

1. Create a detailed label co-occurrence visualization:

   ```
   def plot_label_cooccurrence(
       y, title="Label Co-occurrence Analysis"):
   ```

   I.   Compute raw co-occurrence counts:

   ```
   cooccurrence = y.T @ y
   ```

   II.   Compute relative co-occurrence (normalized by diagonal). This shows what percentage of time label i occurs with label j:

   ```
   diag = np.diag(cooccurrence)
   relative_cooccurrence = cooccurrence / diag[:, None]
   ```

III. Create a figure with two subplots:

```
fig, (ax1, ax2) = plt.subplots(1, 2, figsize=(15, 6))
```

IV. Plot raw co-occurrence:

```
sns.heatmap(
    cooccurrence, annot=True, fmt='d',
    cmap='Blues', ax=ax1, annot_kws={"fontsize": 15}
)
ax1.set_title('Raw Co-occurrence Counts')
ax1.set_xlabel('Label')
ax1.set_ylabel('Label')
```

V. Plot relative co-occurrence:

```
sns.heatmap(
    relative_cooccurrence, annot=True,
    fmt='.2f',cmap='RdYlBu_r', ax=ax2,
    annot_kws={"fontsize": 15}
    vmin=0, vmax=1
)
ax2.set_title('Relative Co-occurrence (Normalized)')
ax2.set_xlabel('Label')
ax2.set_ylabel('Label')
plt.suptitle(title, y=1.05)
plt.tight_layout()
```

VI. Print additional statistics:

```
print("\nLabel Statistics:")
print(f"Total samples: {len(y)}")
print("\nLabel frequencies:")
for i in range(y.shape[1]):
    count = y[:, i].sum()
    percentage = count / len(y) * 100
    print(f"Label {i}: {count} samples ({percentage:.1f}%)")
print("\nMost common label combinations:")
```

VII. Get unique combinations and their counts:

```
unique_combinations = np.unique(
    y, axis=0, return_counts=True)
sorted_idx = np.argsort(
    -unique_combinations[1]
)  # Sort by count (descending)
```

```
        for combo, count in zip(
            unique_combinations[0][sorted_idx][:5],
            unique_combinations[1][sorted_idx][:5]
        ):
            percentage = count / len(y) * 100
            print(f"Combination {combo}: "
                    f"{count} samples ({percentage:.1f}%)")
```

2. Use the function on your test data:

```
plot_label_cooccurrence(
    y_test, "Test Set Label Co-occurrence Analysis")
Label Statistics: Total samples: 300
Label frequencies:
Label 0: 166 samples (55.3%)
Label 1: 181 samples (60.3%)
Label 2: 93 samples (31.0%)
Label 3: 34 samples (11.3%)
Label 4: 88 samples (29.3%)

# Output:
Most common label combinations:
Combination [0 0 0 0 0]: 52 samples (17.3%)
Combination [0 1 0 0 0]: 34 samples (11.3%)
Combination [1 1 0 0 0]: 28 samples (9.3%)
Combination [1 1 1 0 0]: 25 samples (8.3%)
Combination [1 1 0 0 1]: 24 samples (8.0%)
```

Our output gives us both numeric performance data and our heatmaps.

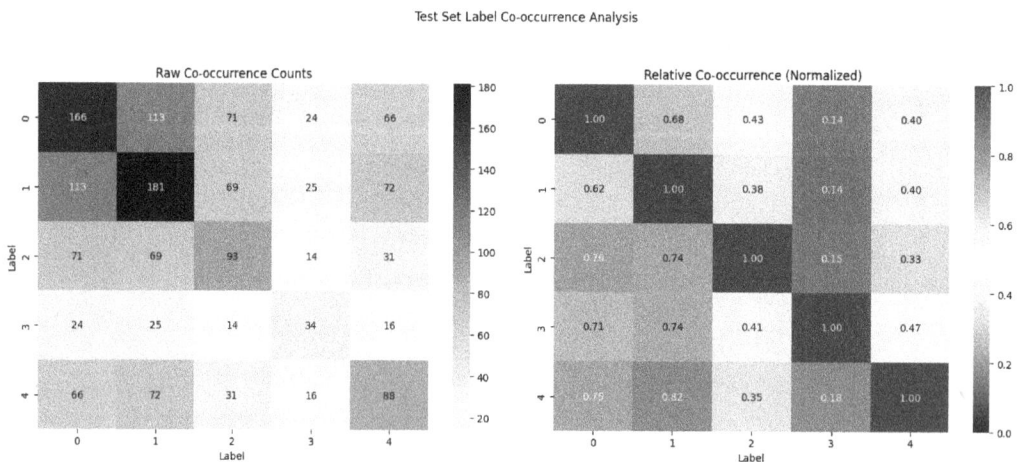

Figure 6.11 – Test set label co-occurrence analysis

This visualization provides the following:

I.   Raw co-occurrence matrix (left plot):

II.   Each cell shows how many times label i and j appear together.

  • The diagonal shows how many times each label appears in total.

III.   Higher numbers indicate labels that frequently occur together, so in this example, labels 0 and 1 occur together most often.

IV.   Relative co-occurrence matrix (right plot):

V.   Each cell shows what *percentage* of time label i occurs when label j is present.

  • Values are normalized and range from 0.00 to 1.00 (0% to 100%).

VI.   This helps us identify conditional relationships between labels, where we can see, in this example, labels 0 and 1 co-occur most often with all other labels.

VII.   Additional statistics:

  • Total number of samples, 300

  • Individual label frequencies

  • Most common label combinations, where a **0** indicates a label was not present and a **1** indicates presence. The array in the output can be read from left to right by label. So, for example, combination [1 1 0 0 0] indicates records with labels **0** and **1** without **2**, **3**, or **4**.

VIII. Reading the matrices:

  • If cell (**i**, **j**) in the relative matrix is close to **1**, it means when label **i** appears, label **j** almost always appears too.

  • If cell (**i**, **j**) is close to 0, it means labels **i** and **j** rarely occur together.

  • Asymmetric patterns in the relative matrix can reveal interesting dependencies (e.g., label A might always come with label B, but label B might occur without label A).

There's more...

Beyond OvR, other strategies such as binary relevance or classifier chains can also be employed for multilabel classification tasks. Each approach has its strengths and weaknesses depending on the specific characteristics of the dataset and the relationships between classes.

Hands-on exercises

To illustrate these techniques, please reference the GitHub repository (`https://github.com/PacktPublishing/scikit-learn-Cookbook-Third-Edition`). We will engage in hands-on exercises focused on implementing multilabel logistic regression models using synthetic datasets created with `make_multilabel_classification()`. Although we've included code examples, we encourage you to explore on your own and try using these tools with different arguments to see what results. The following steps outline a general workflow:

1. Clone the GitHub repository and ensure all necessary libraries are installed.
2. Use `make_multilabel_classification()` from `sklearn.datasets` to generate a synthetic dataset.
3. Clean your dataset by ensuring there are no missing values.
4. Load `LogisticRegression()` from `sklearn.linear_model`.
5. Fit your model using training data with the `fit` method.
6. Use the predict method on your test data to generate predictions.
7. Calculate metrics such as accuracy score and generate a classification report to assess how well your model performs.
8. Create visualizations such as confusion matrices or heatmaps to better understand model performance across different classes.

Model evaluation metrics

Let's look at different metrics for evaluating logistic regression models. Evaluating model performance is central for understanding how well our models are generalizing to new data and identifying areas for improvement. In this recipe, we will explore various metrics for evaluating logistic regression models, including precision, recall, F1-score, and ROC curves – metrics and techniques you should already be familiar with from *Chapter 4*, where we applied them to KNN. We will apply these metrics to assess the performance of our models and learn to interpret the results effectively.

Getting ready

By now, you probably have a fairly good idea what we need to do in order to evaluate our models using scikit-learn's methods.

1. Load the libraries:

    ```
    from sklearn.model_selection import train_test_split
    from sklearn.linear_model import LogisticRegression
    from sklearn.metrics import (
        accuracy_score, classification_report,
    ```

```
        precision_score, recall_score,
        f1_score, roc_curve, auc
    )
    from sklearn.datasets import load_breast_cancer
    import pandas as pd
    import matplotlib.pyplot as plt
```

2. Load the dataset:

```
    data = load_breast_cancer()
    X = data.data
    y = data.target
    feature_names = data.feature_names
    df = pd.DataFrame(X, columns=feature_names)
    df['target'] = y
```

3. Split the data:

```
    X_train, X_test, y_train, y_test = train_test_split(
        X, y, test_size=0.3, random_state=2024)
```

Let's model logistic regression with the *liblinear* solver approach.

How to do it...

Now let's implement logistic regression and evaluate its performance using various metrics.

1. Load the model:

```
    model = LogisticRegression(solver='liblinear')
```

2. Train the model:

```
    model.fit(X_train, y_train)
```

3. Make predictions:

```
    y_pred = model.predict(X_test)
    y_prob = model.predict_proba(X_test)[:, 1]
```

4. Calculate evaluation metrics:

```
    accuracy = accuracy_score(y_test, y_pred)
    precision = precision_score(y_test, y_pred)
    recall = recall_score(y_test, y_pred)
    f1 = f1_score(y_test, y_pred)
    fpr, tpr, thresholds = roc_curve(y_test, y_prob)
```

```
roc_auc = auc(fpr, tpr)
report = classification_report(y_test, y_pred)
```

5. Print the metrics:

```
print(f"Accuracy {accuracy:.2f}")
print(f"Precision {precision:.2f}")
print(f"Recall {recall:.2f}")
print(f"F1 Score {f1:.2f}")
print(f"ROC AUC {roc_auc:.2f}")
print("Classification Report")
print(report)

# Output:
Accuracy 0.94
Precision 0.94
Recall 0.95
F1 Score 0.95
ROC AUC 0.99
```

Here is our classification report. Most of our performance metrics are comparable.

	precision	recall	f1-score	support
0	0.924	0.910	0.917	67
1	0.943	0.952	0.947	104
accuracy	0.936	0.936	0.936	1
macro avg	0.934	0.931	0.932	171
weighted avg	0.936	0.936	0.936	171

Figure 6.12 – Classification report for logistic regression model evaluation metrics

6. Plot the ROC curve:

```
plt.figure(figsize=(8, 6))
plt.plot(fpr, tpr, color='darkorange', lw=2,
         label=f'ROC curve (area = {roc_auc:.2f})')
plt.plot([0, 1], [0, 1], color='navy',
         lw=2, linestyle='--')
plt.xlabel('False Positive Rate')
plt.ylabel('True Positive Rate')
plt.title('Receiver Operating Characteristic (ROC)')
plt.legend(loc="lower right")
plt.show()
```

Let's plot our ROC curve for analysis.

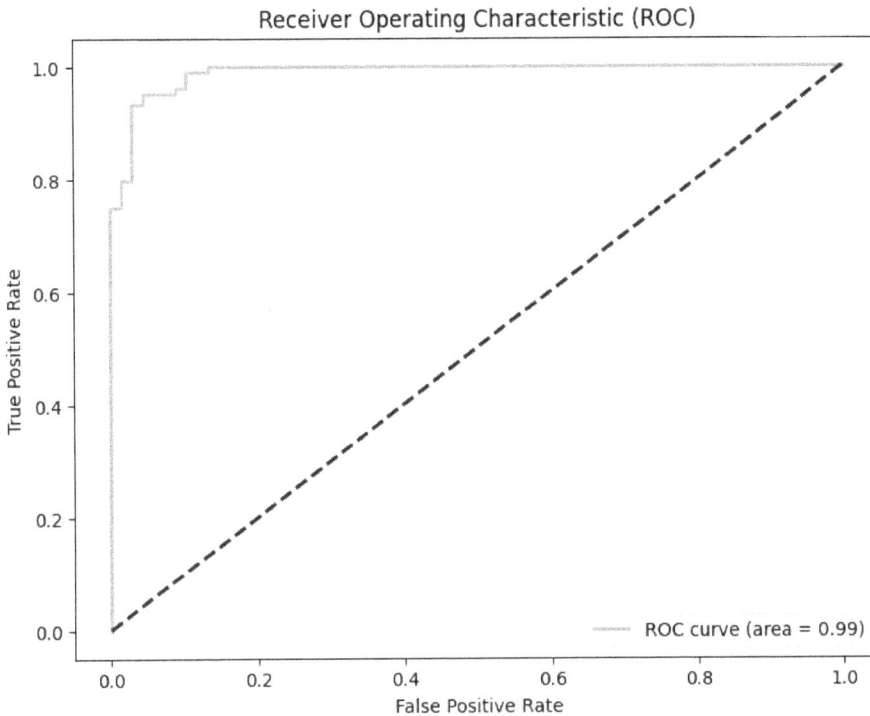

Figure 6.13 – ROC curve for logistic regression model evaluation metrics

The ROC curve indicates a fairly solid performance from our classification model.

How it works...

You should already be familiar with these metrics, but just to reiterate, let's cover them again.

- **Accuracy**: Measures the overall correctness of the model's predictions
- **Precision**: Measures the proportion of positive identifications that were actually correct
- **Recall**: Measures the proportion of actual positives that were correctly identified
- **F1-score**: The harmonic mean of precision and recall, providing a balanced measure of the model's performance
- **ROC Curve**: Plots the true positive rate against the false positive rate at various threshold settings
- **Area Under the Curve (AUC)**: Quantifies the overall ability of the model to discriminate between positive and negative instances

Visualizing model performance

The ROC curve visualizes the trade-off between the true positive rate and the false positive rate. The AUC provides a single scalar value that summarizes the performance of the classifier across all possible threshold settings. A higher AUC indicates better performance.

There's more...

The choice of evaluation metric depends on the specific goals of the classification task and the characteristics of the dataset. For example, in situations where false positives are costly, precision may be more important than recall. In situations where it is important to capture as many positive instances as possible, recall may be more important than precision.

Hands-on exercises

To illustrate these techniques, please reference the GitHub repository (`https://github.com/PacktPublishing/scikit-learn-Cookbook-Third-Edition`). We will engage in hands-on exercises focused on evaluating logistic regression models using various metrics. Although we've included code examples, we encourage you to explore on your own and try using these tools with different arguments to see what results. The following steps outline a general workflow.

1. Clone the GitHub repository and ensure all necessary libraries are installed.
2. Load the Breast Cancer dataset using `load_breast_cancer()` from `sklearn.datasets`.
3. Load `LogisticRegression()` from `sklearn.linear_model`.
4. Fit your model using training data with the `fit` method.
5. Use the `predict` method and the `predict_proba()` method on your test data to generate predictions.
6. Calculate metrics such as accuracy score, precision, recall, F1-score, and ROC AUC to assess how well your model performs.
7. Generate plots to visualize ROC curves to visually assess model performance.

Practical exercises with advanced logistic regression

In this final section, we will engage in practical exercises that involve building, tuning, and evaluating logistic regression models for various datasets. These exercises are designed to reinforce the concepts learned throughout the chapter and demonstrate how to effectively apply logistic regression and its extensions in real-world scenarios. By the end of this section, we will have hands-on experience that can be leveraged in our own machine learning projects.

Exercise 1: Building a regularized logistic regression model

In this exercise, we will build a logistic regression model using the Breast Cancer dataset, applying both Lasso and Ridge regularization techniques.

Here are the implementation steps:

1. Load the libraries.
2. Load the dataset.
3. Split the data.
4. Create and train a Lasso regularized logistic regression model.
5. Make predictions with the Lasso model.
6. Evaluate the Lasso model performance.

Exercise 2: Evaluating multiclass logistic regression

In this exercise, we will implement a multinomial logistic regression model using the Iris dataset.

Here are the implementation steps:

1. Load the libraries.
2. Load the dataset.
3. Split the data.
4. Create and train a multinomial logistic regression model.
5. Make predictions with the multinomial model.
6. Evaluate the multinomial model performance.

Exercise 3: Visualizing logistic regression results

In this exercise, we will visualize the decision boundaries of a logistic regression model trained on a synthetic dataset.

Here are the implementation steps:

1. Load libraries for visualization and dataset creation.
2. Create a synthetic dataset for binary classification.
3. Split the data.
4. Create and train a logistic regression model.
5. Create a mesh grid for plotting decision boundaries.

6. Predict class probabilities across the grid.

7. Plot decision boundaries.

Get This Book's PDF Version and Exclusive Extras

UNLOCK NOW

Scan the QR code (or go to packtpub.com/unlock). Search for this book by name, confirm the edition, and then follow the steps on the page.

Note: Keep your invoice handy. Purchases made directly from Packt don't require an invoice.

7

Support Vector Machines and Kernel Methods

Up to this point, our recipes for training models have used datasets designed for easy class separability. These are great for illustration, but when we enter the real world, we'll find that problems requiring **machine learning** (**ML**) solutions are rarely as cut-and-dry – we need additional tools in our toolchest for handling datasets where the boundaries between classes aren't so well defined. In this chapter, we'll explore methods that allow us to transform our dataset prior to training in a way that maps our original dataset onto a higher-dimensional representation, allowing for easier class separability when using a straight line just won't cut it (pun slightly intended). In this chapter, we will explore **support vector machines** (**SVMs**) and kernel methods, focusing on theory, practical applications, and tuning techniques for high-dimensional data. Exercises include building SVM models and experimenting with various kernel functions.

In this chapter, we're going to cover the following recipes:

- Introduction to SVMs
- Kernel functions and their applications
- Tuning SVM parameters
- SVMs in high-dimensional spaces
- Evaluating SVM models

Technical requirements

It is advisable to create a Python environment for safely isolating your work from other Python installations/libraries. See the GitHub repository for more details (`https://github.com/PacktPublishing/scikit-learn-Cookbook-Third-Edition`). You will need the following for this chapter:

- Git >=2.46.x

- Python >=3.9.x

- Cloned GitHub repository and Python environment built from the `requirements.txt` file

Introduction to SVMs

SVMs are ML models used for both classification and regression tasks. SVMs are particularly effective in situations where the number of features is large compared to the number of samples, or when the data is high-dimensional. Additionally, SVMs excel in classification problems where classes are not easily separable using their existing feature set. The core idea behind SVMs is to find the **hyperplane** that maximizes the margin between classes, which helps in achieving better generalization performance. In this recipe, we will explore the basics of SVMs, their role in classification and regression, and how they work.

> **What is a hyperplane?**
>
> In the context of SVMs, a hyperplane serves as a decision boundary – a *non-linear line* (i.e., a curved line in two or more dimensions) that separates data points into different classes. SVMs are primarily used for binary classification tasks, although they can also be applied to regression problems.
>
> The hyperplane acts as a plane that divides feature space into regions corresponding to different classes. The primary objective of SVMs is to find the optimal hyperplane that maximizes the margin, or distance, between the closest data points (which are referred to as **support vectors**) from each class. This margin represents the distance between the hyperplane and the nearest data points of each class.
>
> By maximizing this margin, SVMs aim to reduce the generalization error of the classifier, so we make fewer misclassification mistakes when predicting on new data – the main goal behind ML. The larger the margin, the better the classifier is expected to perform on new, unseen data.

Getting ready

Before implementing SVMs, let's ensure we have the necessary Python libraries installed and the dataset loaded:

1. Load the libraries:

    ```
    from sklearn.model_selection import train_test_split
    from sklearn.svm import SVC, SVR
    from sklearn.datasets import load_iris
    from sklearn.metrics import (
        accuracy_score, classification_ report)
    import pandas as pd
    ```

2. Load the dataset:

    ```
    iris = load_iris()
    X = iris.data
    y = iris.target
    feature_names = iris.feature_names
    df = pd.DataFrame(X, columns=feature_names)
    df['target'] = y
    ```

3. Split the data:

    ```
    X_train, X_test, y_train, y_test = train_test_split(
        X, y, test_size=0.3, random_state=2024)
    ```

By now, it should be well-instilled in your brain how scikit-learn manages the train/test split!

How to do it...

Now, let's implement an SVM for classification and regression tasks:

1. Load the model:

    ```
    svm_classifier = SVC(kernel='linear')
    ```

2. Train the model:

    ```
    svm_classifier.fit(X_train, y_train)
    ```

3. Make predictions:

    ```
    y_pred = svm_classifier.predict(X_test)
    ```

4. Evaluate the model:

```
accuracy = accuracy_score(y_test, y_pred)
report = classification_report(y_test, y_pred, output_dict=True)
report_df = pd.DataFrame(report).transpose()
```

5. Stylize the DataFrame:

```
styled_df = (report_df
    .style
    .background_gradient(
        cmap='Blues',
        subset=['precision', 'recall', 'f1-score']
    )
    .format({
        'precision': '{:.3f}',
        'recall': '{:.3f}',
        'f1-score': '{:.3f}',
        'support': '{:.0f}'
    })
)
print(f"Accuracy: {accuracy:.2f}")
styled_df
```

Our SVM is able to achieve some fairly impressive classification performance, even with its default parameters. One of the positive aspects of the implementation of several scikit-learn ML algorithms is that, often, their default arguments work well without fine-tuning!

	precision	recall	f1-score	support
0	1.000	1.000	1.000	18
1	0.909	0.833	0.870	12
2	0.875	0.933	0.903	15
accuracy	0.933	0.933	0.933	1
macro avg	0.928	0.922	0.924	45
weighted avg	0.934	0.933	0.933	45

Figure 7.1 – SVM classification report (linear kernel)

With default arguments, the SVM classifier works rather well, with 93% predictive accuracy.

Now, let's use an SVM for a simple regression problem:

1. Load the model:

    ```
    svm_regressor = SVR(kernel='rbf')
    ```

2. Train the model:

    ```
    svm_regressor.fit(X_train[:, :2], y_train)
    ```

3. Make predictions:

    ```
    y_pred_reg = svm_regressor.predict(X_test[:, :2])
    ```

4. Evaluate the model:

    ```
    # Note: For regression,
    # we typically use metrics like MSE or R-squared
    from sklearn.metrics import mean_squared_error
    mse = mean_squared_error(y_test, y_pred_reg)
    print(f"MSE: {mse:.2f}")

    # Output:
    MSE: 0.20
    ```

Remember, for regression metrics such as MSE, MAE, MAPE, and others, the *lower* the value of these metrics, the better the performance. How low is acceptable is often a business-oriented question in real-world applications.

How it works...

SVMs work by finding the hyperplane that maximizes the margin or distance (or, for another synonym, space) between classes in our dataset. As mentioned earlier, the margin is the distance between the hyperplane and the nearest data points of each class, known as support vectors. SVMs can handle non-linearly separable data by using kernel functions, which map the data into higher-dimensional spaces where it becomes linearly separable. Up to this point, we've been spending most of our time reducing the number of dimensions in our datasets, but sometimes increasing them is more useful!

*   **Kernel functions**: Common kernels include linear, polynomial, and **radial basis function (RBF)**. The choice of kernel depends on the complexity of the data and the problem at hand.

*   **Soft margin**: SVMs can tolerate some misclassifications by introducing *slack variables*, allowing for a *soft margin* that improves robustness against outliers. Think of *slack* like you would with a rope: we loosen how taut a rope is to allow for more flexibility, but in this case, the rope is our hyperplane and support vectors.

Visualizing SVM decision boundaries

Visualizing the decision boundaries of SVMs can provide insights into how they classify data. For linear SVMs, the decision boundary is a line that maximizes the margin between classes.

To visualize SVM decision boundaries, follow these steps:

1. Load the libraries:

    ```
    import matplotlib.pyplot as plt
    import numpy as np
    from sklearn.inspection import DecisionBoundaryDisplay
    ```

2. Create a mesh grid:

    ```
    x_min, x_max = X[:, 0].min() - 1, X[:, 0].max() + 1
    y_min, y_max = X[:, 1].min() - 1, X[:, 1].max() + 1
    xx, yy = np.meshgrid(np.arange(x_min, x_max, 0.01),
                         np.arange(y_min, y_max, 0.01))
    ```

3. Adjust the input to match the expected number of features (use all four features for prediction, but only visualize the first two):

    ```
    grid_points = np.c_[
        xx.ravel(), yy.ravel(),
        np.zeros((xx.ravel().shape[0], 2))
    ]
    ```

4. Plot decision boundaries using `DecisionBoundaryDisplay`:

    ```
    fig, ax = plt.subplots()
    disp = DecisionBoundaryDisplay.from_estimator(
        svm_regressor,
        grid_points[:, :2],
        response_method="predict",
        plot_method="contourf",
        cmap=plt.cm.coolwarm,
        alpha=0.8,
        ax=ax
    )
    ```

5. Plot the data points:

    ```
    ax.scatter(
        X[:, 0], X[:, 1], c=y, edgecolors='k',
        marker='o', cmap=plt.cm.coolwarm
    )
    ```

```
ax.set_title("SVM Decision Boundary")
ax.set_xlabel("Feature 1")
ax.set_ylabel("Feature 2")
ax.set_xlim(xx.min(), xx.max())
ax.set_ylim(yy.min(), yy.max())
ax.set_xticks(())
ax.set_yticks(())
plt.show()
```

The resulting contour graph produced by this code illustrates an SVM's ability to find non-linear boundaries between classes. In this graph, the darker regions indicate areas in our feature space where the trained SVM is more certain to belong to a given class, with the region in between indicating more uncertainty and, hence, lighter shading.

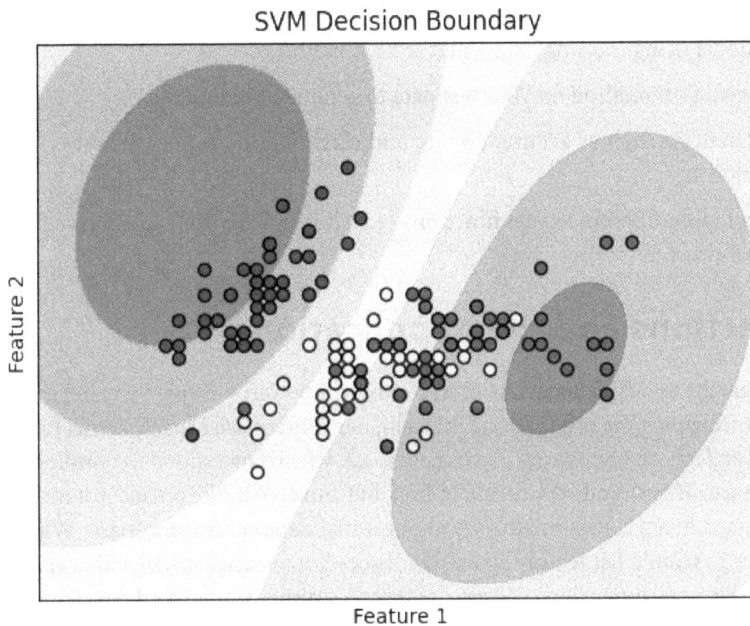

Figure 7.2 – SVM decision boundaries

This visualization (sometimes called a **contour plot**) showcases the non-linear classification boundaries that the SVM is capable of estimating using the *kernel trick*. Keep in mind that these boundaries are estimated in a higher-dimensional space than the two dimensions portrayed in the graph, so what you see is a *squashed* version.

Hands-on exercises

To illustrate these techniques, please refer to the GitHub repository (`https://github.com/PacktPublishing/scikit-learn-Cookbook-Third-Edition`). We will engage in hands-on exercises focused on implementing SVM models for classification and regression tasks using the *Iris* dataset. Although we've included code examples, we encourage you to explore on your own and try using these tools with different arguments to see the results. The following steps outline a general workflow:

1. Clone the GitHub repository and ensure that all the necessary libraries are installed.

2. Load the *Iris* dataset using `load_iris()` from `sklearn.datasets`.

3. Clean your dataset by handling missing values and encoding categorical variables if necessary.

4. Load SVC from `sklearn.svm` for classification tasks.

5. Fit your model using training data with the `fit` method.

6. Use the `predict` method on your test data to generate predictions.

7. Calculate metrics such as accuracy score and classification report to assess how well your model performs.

8. Experiment with different kernel functions (e.g., linear, RBF, etc.) to observe their effects on model performance.

Kernel functions and their applications

Kernel functions are the critical element that gives SVMs their power, allowing them to handle non-linear data effectively. By mapping the original data into a higher-dimensional space, kernel functions enable SVMs to find linear decision boundaries in this new space, which correspond to non-linear boundaries in the original space. This sounds confusing at first, but think of it like an accordion: the accordion starts off compressed in a flat state analogous to our initial dataset's feature space. When we expand the accordion, we go from a flat feature space to a three-dimensional space, which spreads our data points out along this new dimension. We can use this new dimension to find our decision boundary and then squeeze our accordion back to its original flat state. The linear boundary we found when the accordion was stretched out will also collapse into a potentially non-linear (i.e., curved) state.

In this recipe, we will explore different types of kernels, including linear, polynomial, and RBF, and learn how to apply them using scikit-learn.

Getting ready

Before implementing kernel functions with SVMs, let's ensure we have the necessary Python libraries installed and the dataset loaded:

1. Load the libraries:

    ```
    from sklearn.model_selection import train_test_split
    from sklearn.svm import SVC
    from sklearn.datasets import load_iris
    from sklearn.metrics import (
        accuracy_score, classification_ report)
    import pandas as pd
    import numpy as np
    import matplotlib.pyplot as plt
    ```

2. Load the dataset:

    ```
    iris = load_iris()
    X = iris.data
    y = iris.target
    feature_names = iris.feature_names
    df = pd.DataFrame(X, columns=feature_names)
    df['target'] = y
    ```

3. Split the data:

    ```
    X_train, X_test, y_train, y_test = train_test_split(
        X, y, test_size=0.3, random_state=2024)
    ```

Let's apply our first kernel example.

How to do it...

Now, let's implement SVMs using different kernel functions. We already used the linear kernel in the first example, so now let's use the polynomial kernel:

1. Load the model:

    ```
    svm_poly = SVC(kernel='poly', degree=3)
    ```

2. Train the model:

    ```
    svm_poly.fit(X_train, y_train)
    ```

3.   Make predictions:

```
y_pred_poly = svm_poly.predict(X_test)
```

4.   Evaluate the model:

```
accuracy_poly = accuracy_score(y_test, y_pred_poly)
report_poly = classification_report(
    y_test, y_pred_poly, output_dict=True)
report_df_poly = pd.DataFrame(report_poly).transpose()
```

5.   Stylize the DataFrame:

```
styled_df_poly = (report_df_poly
    .style
    .background_gradient(
        cmap='Blues',
        subset=['precision', 'recall', 'f1-score']
    )
    .format({
        'precision': '{:.3f}',
        'recall': '{:.3f}',
        'f1-score': '{:.3f}',
        'support': '{:.0f}'
    })
)
print(f"Polynomial Kernel Accuracy: {accuracy_poly:.2f}")
styled_df_poly
```

The results are slightly better this time than with our linear kernel.

	precision	recall	f1-score	support
0	1.000	1.000	1.000	18
1	1.000	0.833	0.909	12
2	0.882	1.000	0.938	15
accuracy	0.956	0.956	0.956	1
macro avg	0.961	0.944	0.949	45
weighted avg	0.961	0.956	0.955	45

Figure 7.3 – SVM classification report (polynomial kernel)

Utilizing the polynomial kernel elicits slightly better performance than the default linear approach. This tells us that the underlying data probably has a structure that is better represented in a way that allows for more complex decision boundaries using feature combinations that employ polynomials.

Finally, let's try the RBF:

1. Load the model:

    ```
    svm_rbf = SVC(kernel='rbf')
    ```

2. Train the model:

    ```
    svm_rbf.fit(X_train, y_train)
    ```

3. Make predictions:

    ```
    y_pred_rbf = svm_rbf.predict(X_test)
    ```

4. Evaluate the model:

    ```
    accuracy_rbf = accuracy_score(y_test, y_pred_rbf)
    report_rbf = classification_report(
        y_test, y_pred_rbf, output_dict=True)
    report_df_rbf = pd.DataFrame(report_rbf).transpose()
    ```

5. Stylize the DataFrame:

    ```
    styled_df_rbf = (report_df_rbf
        .style
        .background_gradient(
            cmap='Blues',
            subset=['precision', 'recall', 'f1-score']
        )
        .format({
            'precision': '{:.3f}',
            'recall': '{:.3f}',
            'f1-score': '{:.3f}',
            'support': '{:.0f}'
        })
    )
    print(f"RBF Kernel Accuracy: {accuracy_rbf:.2f}")
    styled_df_rbf
    ```

RBF results are a little worse than our polynomial kernel-based SVM model.

	precision	recall	f1-score	support
0	1.000	1.000	1.000	18
1	0.786	0.917	0.846	12
2	0.923	0.800	0.857	15
accuracy	0.911	0.911	0.911	1
macro avg	0.903	0.906	0.901	45
weighted avg	0.917	0.911	0.911	45

Figure 7.4 – SVM classification report (RBF kernel)

The RBF kernel performs the worst out of the three approaches; however, we are using all default arguments in our SVM estimator. Once we look at hyperparameter optimization, we may be able to achieve better results.

How it works...

Kernel functions allow SVMs to operate in higher-dimensional spaces without explicitly computing the coordinates of the data in that space. This is achieved by using the kernel trick, which involves computing the dot product of the data points in the higher-dimensional space using only the original data. Feel free to brush up on your linear algebra concepts and definitions if some of these terms are foreign to you!

- **Linear kernel**: Maps the data linearly into a higher-dimensional space. It is the simplest form of kernel and is used when the data is linearly separable.

- **Polynomial kernel**: Maps the data into a higher-dimensional space using a polynomial function. It is useful for data that has a polynomial relationship between features.

- **RBF kernel**: Maps the data into a higher-dimensional space using a Gaussian function (such as a normal distribution). It is one of the most commonly used kernels due to its ability to handle complex relationships between features.

Visualizing kernel effects

Visualizing the decision boundaries of SVMs with different kernels can provide insights into how they classify data.

To visualize the decision boundaries, follow these steps:

1. Create a mesh grid:

```
x_min, x_max = X_train[:, 0].min() - 1, X_train[:, 0].max() + 1
y_min, y_max = X_train[:, 1].min() - 1, X_train[:, 1].max() + 1
xx, yy = np.meshgrid(np.arange(x_min, x_max, 0.01),
                     np.arange(y_min, y_max, 0.01))
```

2. Use only the first two features for prediction:

```
X_train_2d = X_train[:, :2]
```

3. Train new SVM models using only the first two features:

```
svm_linear_2d = SVC(kernel='linear').fit(X_train_2d, y_train)
svm_poly_2d = SVC(kernel='poly').fit(X_train_2d, y_train)
svm_rbf_2d = SVC(kernel='rbf').fit(X_train_2d, y_train)
```

4. Predict class probabilities across the grid for each kernel using only the first two features:

```
Z_linear = svm_linear_2d.predict(
    np.c_[xx.ravel(), yy.ravel()])
Z_poly = svm_poly_2d.predict(
    np.c_[xx.ravel(), yy.ravel()])
Z_rbf = svm_rbf_2d.predict(
    np.c_[xx.ravel(), yy.ravel()])
Z_linear = Z_linear.reshape(xx.shape)
Z_poly = Z_poly.reshape(xx.shape)
Z_rbf = Z_rbf.reshape(xx.shape)
```

5. Plot the decision boundaries:

```
 fig, axes = plt.subplots(1, 3, figsize=(18, 6))
axes[0].contourf(xx, yy, Z_linear, alpha=0.8)
axes[0].scatter(
    X_train_2d[:, 0], X_train_2d[:, 1],
    c=y_train, edgecolors='k', marker='o'
)
axes[0].set_title("Linear Kernel")
axes[1].contourf(xx, yy, Z_poly, alpha=0.8)
axes[1].scatter(
    X_train_2d[:, 0], X_train_2d[:, 1],
    c=y_train, edgecolors='k', marker='o'
)
axes[1].set_title("Polynomial Kernel")
axes[2].contourf(xx, yy, Z_rbf, alpha=0.8)
```

```
axes[2].scatter(
    X_train_2d[:, 0], X_train_2d[:, 1],
    c=y_train, edgecolors='k', marker='o'
)
axes[2].set_title("RBF Kernel")
plt.tight_layout()
plt.show()
```

While not very different at first glance, each of our different kernel methods provides a slightly different estimate of class boundaries. While this may seem trivial, always keep in mind that, in the real world, the difference between a correct classification and a false classification can have substantial implications for a business!

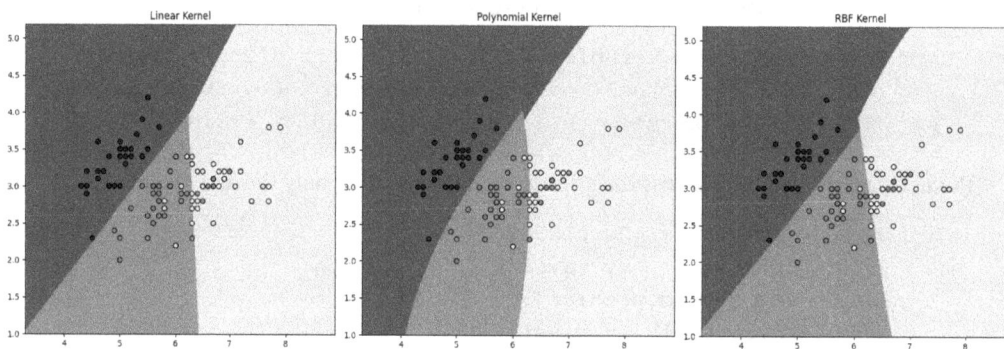

Figure 7.5 – SVM kernel comparison

This visualization shows how different kernels affect the decision boundaries of the SVM model. The linear kernel will produce a linear boundary, while the polynomial and RBF kernels will produce more complex, non-linear boundaries.

There's more...

Beyond linear, polynomial, and RBF kernels, consider experimenting with sigmoid kernels for specific types of data or custom kernel functions for unique problem domains.

Hands-on exercises

To illustrate these techniques, please refer to the GitHub repository (https://github.com/ PacktPublishing/scikit-learn-Cookbook-Third-Edition). We will engage in hands-on exercises focused on implementing SVM models with different kernel functions using the *Iris* dataset. Although we've included code examples, we encourage you to explore on your own and try using these tools with different arguments to see what results.

The following steps outline a general workflow:

1. Clone the GitHub repository and ensure that all the necessary libraries are installed.

2. Load the *Iris* dataset using `load_iris()` from `sklearn.datasets`.

3. Clean your dataset by handling missing values and encoding categorical variables if necessary.

4. Load SVC from `sklearn.svm`.

5. Implement SVM models using linear, polynomial, and RBF kernels.

6. Evaluate model performance using metrics such as accuracy score and classification report.

7. Visualize the decision boundaries for each kernel type to compare their effects on model classification.

8. Experiment with different kernel parameters (e.g., degree for polynomial, and gamma for RBF) to observe their impact on model performance.

Tuning SVM parameters

As we've seen with all other ML models up to this point, hyperparameter tuning and optimization are key steps in improving the performance of SVMs. By adjusting hyperparameters, we can significantly improve the accuracy and robustness of SVM models. In this recipe, we will discover how to use classic grid search and cross-validation techniques to optimize SVM models using scikit-learn.

Getting ready

Before tuning SVM parameters, let's ensure that we have the necessary Python libraries installed and the dataset loaded:

1. Load the libraries:

```
from sklearn.model_selection import (
    train_test_split, GridSearchCV)
from sklearn.svm import SVC
from sklearn.datasets import load_iris
from sklearn.metrics import (
    accuracy_score, classification_ report)
import pandas as pd
```

2. Load the dataset:

```
iris = load_iris()
X = iris.data
y = iris.target
feature_names = iris.feature_names
df = pd.DataFrame(X, columns=feature_names)
df['target'] = y
```

3. Split the data:

```
X_train, X_test, y_train, y_test = train_test_split(
    X, y, test_size=0.3, random_state=2024)
```

We are now ready to start fine-tuning.

How to do It...

Now, let's implement SVM parameter tuning using grid search and cross-validation:

1. Define the parameter grid:

```
param_grid = {
    'C': [0.1, 1, 10],
    'kernel': ['linear', 'rbf', 'poly'],
    'degree': [2, 3, 4]
}
```

2. Perform grid search with cross-validation:

```
grid_search = GridSearchCV(SVC(), param_grid, cv=5)
grid_search.fit(X_train, y_train)
```

3. Get the best hyperparameters and score:

```
best_params = grid_search.best_params_
best_score = grid_search.best_score_
print(f"Best Parameters: {best_params}")
print(f"Best Cross-Validation Score: {best_score:.2f}")
```

4. Train a new model with the best hyperparameters:

```
best_model = SVC(**best_params)
best_model.fit(X_train, y_train)
```

5. Make predictions with the best model:

```
y_pred = best_model.predict(X_test)
```

6. Evaluate the best model:

```
accuracy = accuracy_score(y_test, y_pred)
report_df = pd.DataFrame(classification_report(
    y_test, y_pred, output_dict=True)
).transpose()
```

7. Stylize the DataFrame:

```
styled_report_df = (report_df
    .style
    .background_gradient(
        cmap='Blues',
        subset=['precision', 'recall', 'f1-score']
    )
    .format({
        'precision': '{:.3f}',
        'recall': '{:.3f}',
        'f1-score': '{:.3f}',
        'support': '{:.0f}'
    })
)
print(f"Accuracy: {accuracy:.2f}")
styled_report_df
```

The output from hyperparameter tuning provides both the optimal parameters that were found as well as our classification report. You'll notice that the results are almost the same as what we were able to achieve earlier with just our default parameters. This is not a failure of hyperparameter optimization, but rather a reflection of the simplicity of our dataset when it comes to classification:

```
Best Parameters: {'C': 0.1, 'degree': 4, 'kernel': 'poly'}
Best Cross-Validation Score: 0.99
Accuracy: 0.93
```

	precision	recall	f1-score	support
0	1.000	1.000	1.000	18
1	0.909	0.833	0.870	12
2	0.875	0.933	0.903	15
accuracy	0.933	0.933	0.933	1
macro avg	0.928	0.922	0.924	45
weighted avg	0.934	0.933	0.933	45

Figure 7.6 – SVM classification report (optimized hyperparameters)

In this example, we only used grid search, but you could also apply random search.

How it works...

Grid search is a systematic approach to hyperparameter tuning that involves evaluating all possible combinations of parameters specified in a grid. Cross-validation is used to assess the performance of each (and every) combination, ensuring that the model generalizes well to unseen data. This is an exhaustive process, so the more hyperparameters you select to use in your code, the longer the operation will take.

- **Regularization parameter** (C): Controls the trade-off between margin and misclassification error. A high C value means the model is less tolerant of misclassifications.

- **Kernel parameters**: Different kernels and their parameters (e.g., degree for polynomial, gamma for RBF) affect how the data is mapped into higher-dimensional spaces.

Visualizing hyperparameter effects

Visualizing how different hyperparameters affect model performance can provide insights into the tuning process.

To visualize the effect of hyperparameters, follow these steps:

1. Perform a grid search with a range of C values for a specific kernel:

```
param_grid_c = {
    'C': np.logspace(-4, 4, 10),
    'kernel': ['rbf']
}
grid_search_c = GridSearchCV(SVC(), param_grid_c, cv=5)
grid_search_c.fit(X_train, y_train)
```

2. Plot the cross-validation scores against the C values:

```
plt.figure(figsize=(8, 6))
plt.plot(
    grid_search_c.param_grid['C'],
    grid_search_c.cv_results_['mean_test_score']
)
plt.xscale('log')
plt.xlabel('C (Regularization Parameter)')
plt.ylabel('Cross-Validation Score')
plt.title('Effect of C on Model Performance')
plt.show()
```

We can see diminishing returns when utilizing the regularization parameter and model performance plateaus around $C = 10^1$:

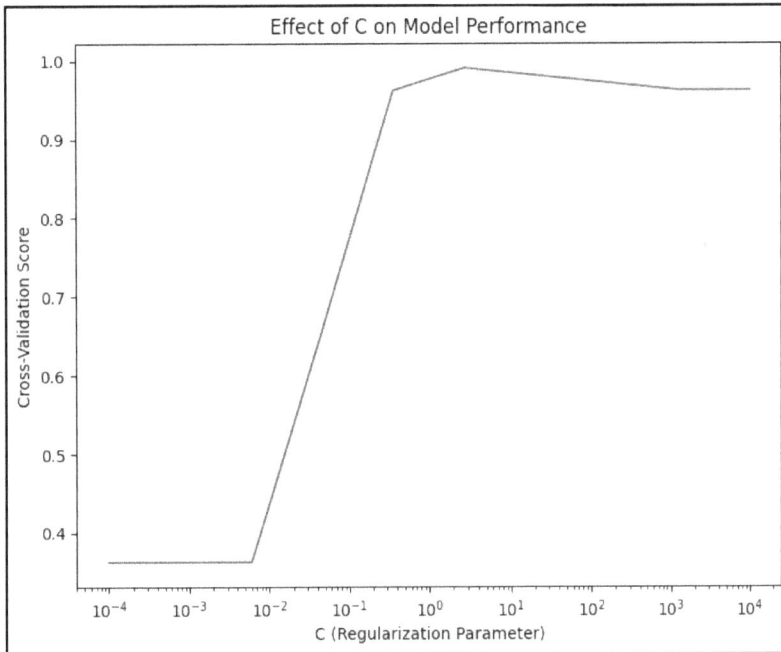

Figure 7.7 – Impact of different values of C

The preceding visualization shows the model's performance, helping us understand the impact of C on the trade-off between margin and misclassification error. Changes in performance may appear subtle, but remember that even minor performance improvements (or declines for that matter) can have a significant impact in real-world applications.

There's more...

Beyond grid search, randomized search can be used to sample a subset of hyperparameters randomly, which can be more efficient for large parameter spaces.

Hands-on exercises

To illustrate these techniques, please refer to the GitHub repository (`https://github.com/PacktPublishing/scikit-learn-Cookbook-Third-Edition`). We will engage in hands-on exercises focused on tuning SVM parameters using grid search and cross-validation. Although we've included code examples, we encourage you to explore on your own and try using these tools with different arguments to see what results.

The following steps outline a general workflow:

1. Clone the GitHub repository and ensure that all the necessary libraries are installed.

2. Load the *Iris* dataset using `load_iris()` from `sklearn.datasets`.

3. Clean your dataset by handling missing values and encoding categorical variables if necessary.

4. Load SVC from `sklearn.svm`.

5. Define a parameter grid for hyperparameter tuning.

6. Perform grid search with cross-validation using `GridSearchCV`.

7. Train a new model with the best parameters obtained from grid search.

8. Evaluate the model's performance using metrics such as accuracy score and classification report.

9. Create plots to visualize how different hyperparameters affect model performance.

SVMs in high-dimensional spaces

SVMs are particularly effective in handling high-dimensional data, where the number of features is large compared to the number of samples. For example, maybe you are measuring a rare event but have several powerful instruments to gather hundreds of data points about it once they do occur. We call this a *wide* dataset. In this recipe, we will look more closely at how SVMs can be applied to high-dimensional data, both synthetically generated and from real-world datasets.

Getting ready

Before applying SVMs to high-dimensional data, let's ensure that we have the necessary Python libraries installed and the dataset loaded:

1. Load the libraries:

    ```
    from sklearn.model_selection import train_test_split
    from sklearn.svm import SVC
    from sklearn.datasets import make_classification
    from sklearn.metrics import (
        accuracy_score, classification_ report)
    import pandas as pd
    import numpy as np
    ```

2. Create a synthetic high-dimensional dataset:

    ```
    X, y = make_classification(
        n_samples=1000, n_features=1000,
        n_informative=50, n_redundant=0, random_state=2024
    )
    ```

3. Split the data:

```
X_train, X_test, y_train, y_test = train_test_split(
    X, y, test_size=0.3, random_state=2024)
```

For this example, we generated a synthetic dataset to help illustrate SVM when our training data has numerous features, in this case, 1000, as set by the preceding n_features=1000 argument.

How to do it...

Now, let's implement SVMs for high-dimensional data:

1. Load the model:

```
svm_model = SVC(kernel='linear')
```

2. Train the model:

```
svm_model.fit(X_train, y_train)
```

3. Make predictions:

```
y_pred = svm_model.predict(X_test)
```

4. Evaluate the model:

```
accuracy = accuracy_score(y_test, y_pred)
report_df = pd.DataFrame(classification_report(
    y_test, y_pred, output_dict=True)
).transpose()
```

5. Stylize the DataFrame:

```
styled_report_df = (report_df
    .style
    .background_gradient(
        cmap='Blues',
        subset=['precision', 'recall', 'f1-score']
    )
    .format({
        'precision': '{:.3f}',
        'recall': '{:.3f}',
        'f1-score': '{:.3f}',
        'support': '{:.0f}'
    })
)
```

```
print(f"Accuracy: {accuracy:.2f}")
styled_report_df
```

Just using the SVM's default arguments on this higher-dimensional dataset did not elicit the strongest performance! Good that we know how to address these types of performance issues now.

	precision	recall	f1-score	support
0	0.765	0.765	0.765	162
1	0.725	0.725	0.725	138
accuracy	0.747	0.747	0.747	1
macro avg	0.745	0.745	0.745	300
weighted avg	0.747	0.747	0.747	300

Figure 7.8 – SVM classification report (high-dimensional data)

How it works...

SVMs handle high-dimensional data efficiently by leveraging kernel functions. The choice of kernel depends on the nature of the data and the complexity of the decision boundary:

- **Linear kernel**: Suitable for linearly separable data or when the number of features is large
- **Non-linear kernels (e.g., RBF or polynomial)**: Useful for non-linearly separable data, allowing SVMs to find complex decision boundaries

Visualizing high-dimensional data

Visualizing high-dimensional data directly is challenging, but we can use dimensionality reduction techniques such as **Principal Component Analysis (PCA)** to project the data onto a lower-dimensional space for visualization.

To visualize the data using PCA, follow these steps:

1. Import PCA from `sklearn.decomposition`:

   ```
   from sklearn.decomposition import PCA
   ```

2. Apply PCA to reduce dimensionality:

   ```
   pca = PCA(n_components=2)
   X_pca = pca.fit_transform(X)
   ```

3. Plot the reduced data:

```
plt.figure(figsize=(8, 6))
plt.scatter(
    X_pca[:, 0], X_pca[:, 1], c=y,
    edgecolors='k', marker='o'
)
plt.title("High-Dimensional Data in 2D Space Using PCA")
plt.xlabel("Principal Component 1")
plt.ylabel("Principal Component 2")
plt.show()
```

As you can see, even after applying PCA to the dataset and color coding by class, the separability for our classes in these two dimensions (PC1 and PC2) would be very challenging for a standard linear classifier.

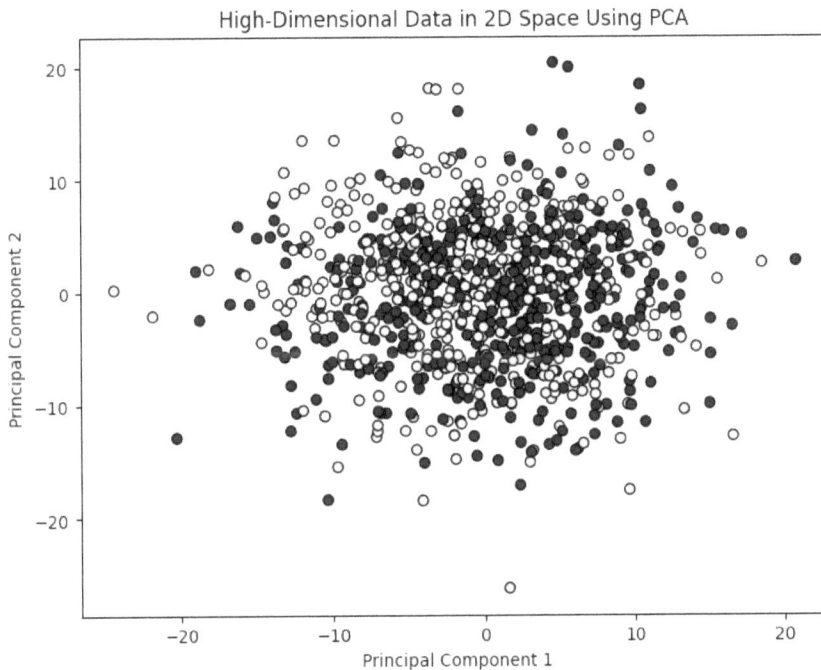

Figure 7.9 – Two-dimensional representation of PCA-transformed data

This visualization shows how high-dimensional data looks when projected onto a two-dimensional space, providing insights into the structure of the data. In this case, the data is quite messy.

There's more...

In high-dimensional spaces, regularization techniques such as L1 and L2 regularization can be crucial in preventing overfitting by reducing the impact of irrelevant features.

Hands-on exercises

To illustrate these techniques, please refer to the GitHub repository (`https://github.com/PacktPublishing/scikit-learn-Cookbook-Third-Edition`). We will engage in hands-on exercises focused on applying SVMs to high-dimensional datasets. Although we've included code examples, we encourage you to explore on your own and try using these tools with different arguments to see what results. The following steps outline a general workflow:

1. Clone the GitHub repository and ensure that all the necessary libraries are installed.
2. Create a synthetic high-dimensional dataset using `make_classification()` from `sklearn.datasets`.
3. Clean your dataset by handling missing values if necessary.
4. Load SVC from `sklearn.svm`.
5. Implement SVM models using different kernels (e.g., linear or RBF).
6. Evaluate model performance using metrics such as accuracy score and classification report.
7. Use PCA to reduce dimensionality and visualize the data in a lower-dimensional space.
8. Experiment with different kernel parameters to observe their effects on model performance in high-dimensional spaces.

Evaluating SVM models

Evaluating the performance of SVM models is crucial for understanding how well they generalize to new data. In this recipe, we will explore key metrics for evaluating SVM models, including accuracy, precision, recall, and **Receiver Operating Characteristic** (**ROC**) curves (defined in the next section). By applying these metrics, we can assess the strengths and weaknesses of our SVM models and make informed decisions about their deployment.

Getting ready

Before evaluating SVM models, let's ensure that we have the necessary Python libraries installed and the dataset loaded:

1. Load the libraries:

    ```
    from sklearn.model_selection import train_test_split
    from sklearn.svm import SVC
    from sklearn.datasets import load_breast_cancer
    from sklearn.metrics import (
        classification_report, roc_curve, auc)
    import pandas as pd
    import matplotlib.pyplot as plt
    ```

2. Load the dataset:

    ```
    data = load_breast_cancer()
    X = data.data
    y = data.target
    feature_names = data.feature_names
    df = pd.DataFrame(X, columns=feature_names)
    df['target'] = y
    ```

3. Split the data:

    ```
    X_train, X_test, y_train, y_test = train_test_split(
        X, y, test_size=0.3, random_state=2024)
    ```

We do not need to prepare our data any differently to utilize ROC curves. We are also using a different dataset this time.

How to do it...

Now, let's implement the SVM and evaluate its performance using various metrics:

1. Load the model:

    ```
    svm_model = SVC(kernel='linear', probability=True)
    ```

2. Train the model:

    ```
    svm_model.fit(X_train, y_train)
    ```

3. Make predictions:

```
y_pred = svm_model.predict(X_test)
y_prob = svm_model.predict_proba(X_test)[:, 1]
```

4. Evaluate the model:

```
report = classification_report(
    y_test, y_pred, output_dict=True)
report_df = pd.DataFrame(report).transpose()
```

5. Stylize the DataFrame:

```
styled_report_df = (report_df
    .style
    .background_gradient(
        cmap='Blues',
        subset=['precision', 'recall', 'f1-score']
    )
    .format({
        'precision': '{:.3f}',
        'recall': '{:.3f}',
        'f1-score': '{:.3f}',
        'support': '{:.0f}'
    })
)
print(f"Accuracy: {accuracy:.2f}")
styled_report_df
```

The classification report shows substantial performance over our previous applications, but this is partially due to using a different dataset from before, with classes that are easier to separate. Additionally, this is a binary classification problem instead of one with three classes as before with the *Iris* dataset.

	precision	recall	f1-score	support
0	0.926	0.940	0.933	67
1	0.961	0.952	0.957	104
accuracy	0.947	0.947	0.947	1
macro avg	0.944	0.946	0.945	171
weighted avg	0.948	0.947	0.947	171

Figure 7.10 – SVM classification report (ROC curve demonstration)

We've reviewed classification reports before, but let's see how our model performs using the ROC curve we used in *Chapter 6*.

6. Plot the ROC curve:

```
fpr, tpr, thresholds = roc_curve(y_test, y_prob)
roc_auc = auc(fpr, tpr)
plt.figure(figsize=(8, 6))
plt.plot(
    fpr, tpr, color='darkorange', lw=2,
    label=f'ROC curve (area = {roc_auc:.2f})'
)
plt.plot([0, 1], [0, 1], color='navy', lw=2, linestyle='--')
plt.xlabel('False Positive Rate')
plt.ylabel('True Positive Rate')
plt.title('Receiver Operating Characteristic (ROC)')
plt.legend(loc="lower right")
plt.show()
```

Running the code should produce the following ROC graph:

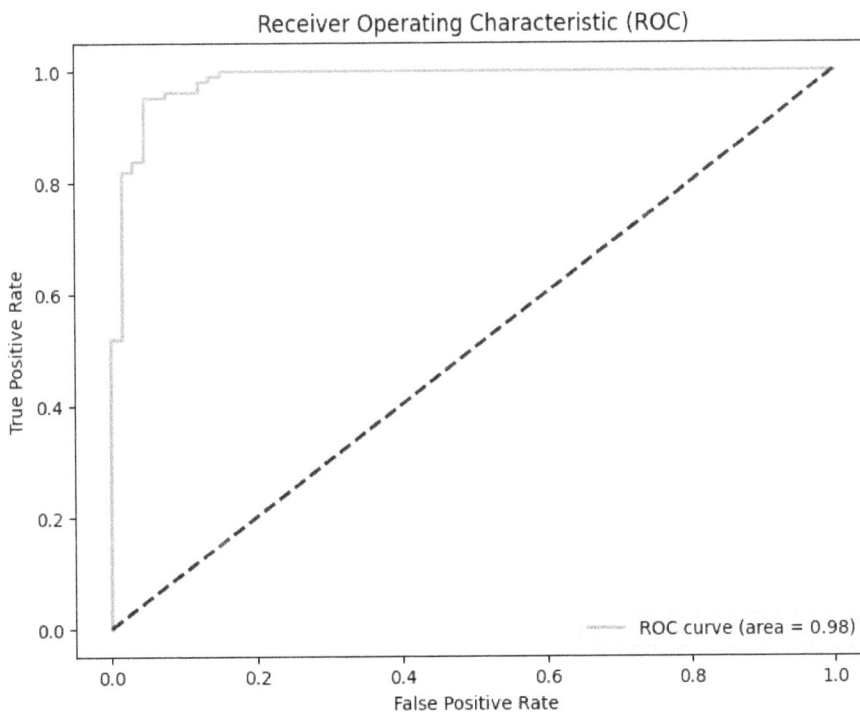

Figure 7.11 – SVM ROC curve

Remember, ROC curves visualize the true positive rate (i.e., how frequently our model predicts the *positive* class) against the false positive rate (i.e., how frequently the model misclassifies a *negative* class data point as *positive*). The dotted line indicates a model that performs no better than guessing between the two classes. The yellow line, ideally, moves toward the upper-left corner, indicating a high true positive rate and a low false positive rate. Furthermore, we can measure the **area under the curve** (**AUC**) to quantify this metric as a percentage. In this instance, it is 98%.

How it works...

Evaluating SVM models involves assessing their performance using various metrics:

- **Accuracy**: Measures the proportion of correctly classified instances
- **Precision**: Measures the proportion of true positives among all predicted positive instances
- **Recall**: Measures the proportion of true positives among all actual positive instances
- **F1-score**: The harmonic mean of precision and recall, providing a balanced measure of both
- **ROC curve**: Plots the true positive rate against the false positive rate at different thresholds, providing a comprehensive view of the model's performance across all possible thresholds
- **AUC**: Quantifies the overall ability of the model to distinguish between positive and negative classes

Visualizing model performance

The ROC curve visualizes the trade-off between the true positive rate and the false positive rate. The AUC provides a single scalar value that summarizes the performance of the classifier across all possible threshold settings. A higher AUC indicates better performance.

There's more...

The choice of evaluation metric depends on the specific goals of the classification task and the characteristics of the dataset. For example, in situations where false positives are costly, precision may be more important than recall. In situations where it is important to capture as many positive instances as possible, recall may be more important than precision.

Hands-on exercises

To illustrate these techniques, please refer to the GitHub repository (`https://github.com/PacktPublishing/scikit-learn-Cookbook-Third-Edition`). We will engage in hands-on exercises focused on evaluating SVM models using various metrics. Although we've included code examples, we encourage you to explore on your own and try using these tools with different arguments to see what results.

The following steps outline a general workflow:

1. Clone the GitHub repository and ensure that all the necessary libraries are installed.

2. Load the *Breast Cancer* dataset using `load_breast_cancer()` from `sklearn.datasets`.

3. Clean your dataset by handling missing values and encoding categorical variables if necessary.

4. Load SVC from `sklearn.svm`.

5. Fit your model using training data with the `fit` method.

6. Use the `predict` method on your test data to generate predictions.

7. Calculate metrics such as accuracy score, precision, recall, F1-score, and ROC AUC to assess how well your model performs.

8. Generate plots to visualize ROC curves to visually assess model performance across different thresholds.

Practical exercises with SVMs

In this final section, we will engage in practical exercises that involve building, tuning, and evaluating SVM models on various datasets. These exercises are designed to reinforce the concepts learned throughout the chapter and demonstrate how to effectively apply SVMs in different scenarios. By the end of this section, we will have hands-on experience that can be leveraged in our own ML projects.

Exercise 1: Building a simple SVM classifier

In this exercise, we will build a simple SVM classifier using the *Iris* dataset.

These are the implementation steps:

1. Load the libraries.

2. Load the dataset.

3. Split the data.

4. Create and train an SVM classifier.

5. Make predictions.

6. Evaluate performance.

Exercise 2: Tuning SVM parameters with grid search

In this exercise, we will tune SVM parameters using grid search on the *Breast Cancer* dataset.

These are the implementation steps:

1. Load the libraries.
2. Load the dataset.
3. Split the data.
4. Define a hyperparameter for grid search.
5. Perform grid search with cross-validation.
6. Train a new model with the best hyperparameters.
7. Make predictions with the best model.
8. Evaluate the best model.

Exercise 3: Visualizing SVM decision boundaries

In this exercise, we will visualize the decision boundaries of an SVM model trained on a synthetic dataset.

These are the implementation steps:

1. Load the libraries for visualization and dataset creation.
2. Create a synthetic dataset for binary classification.
3. Split the data.
4. Create and train an SVM model.
5. Create a mesh grid for plotting decision boundaries.
6. Predict class probabilities across the grid.
7. Plot decision boundaries.

## 8

Tree-Based Algorithms and Ensemble Methods

While many **machine learning** (**ML**) algorithms are complex and oftentimes challenging to wrap your head around (for instance, **support vector machines** (**SVMs**) and their kernel trick explored in *Chapter 7*), not every ML approach requires an advanced understanding of mathematics to truly comprehend its methodology. Tree-based algorithms are the case in point. These algorithms utilize a recursive stepwise data splitting process for training and performing classification and regression predictions. Furthermore, in real-world applications, tree-based approaches are often combined using a technique called **ensembles**, which combines the predictions of several models for additional predictive performance. In this chapter, we'll learn about decision trees, random forests, and gradient boosting, focusing on ensemble techniques for improving model performance. Exercises involve implementing these models, tuning hyperparameters, and comparing ensemble methods. By the end of this chapter, you'll have learned about decision trees, random forests, and gradient boosting, focusing on ensemble techniques for improving model performance.

In this chapter, we're going to cover the following recipes:

- Introduction to decision trees
- Random forests and bagging
- Gradient boosting machines
- Hyperparameter tuning for trees and ensembles
- Comparing ensemble methods

Technical requirements

It is advisable to create a Python environment for safely isolating your work from other Python installations/libraries. See the GitHub repository for more details (`https://github.com/PacktPublishing/scikit-learn-Cookbook-Third-Edition`). You will need the following for this chapter:

- Git >=2.46.x

- Python >=3.9.x

- Cloned GitHub repository and Python environment built from the `requirements.txt` file

Introduction to decision trees

Decision trees are powerful and, compared to other ML techniques, intuitive models used for classification and regression tasks. They work by recursively splitting data based on feature values, creating a tree-like structure composed of nodes and branches. Each internal node represents a *decision* based on a feature, while *leaf nodes* represent the predicted outcome. Decision trees are popular due to their interpretability and effectiveness in handling both numerical and categorical data. Even though they are relatively easy to understand, they are still powerful and can often outperform more complex models, so don't dismiss them from your ML arsenal! To get started, let's get comfortable with the base implementation of scikit-learn's decision trees using default values.

Getting ready

First, we need to prepare our environment and dataset:

1. Load the libraries:

    ```
    import numpy as np
    import pandas as pd
    from sklearn.datasets import load_iris
    from sklearn.model_selection import train_test_split
    from sklearn.tree import DecisionTreeClassifier
    from sklearn.metrics import classification_report
    from sklearn.metrics import accuracy_score
    ```

2. Load the *Iris* dataset:

    ```
    iris = load_iris()
    X = iris.data
    y = iris.target
    ```

3. Split the data:

```
X_train, X_test, y_train, y_test = train_test_split(
    X, y, test_size=0.3, random_state=2024)
```

Now, we are all set to train our model!

How to do it...

We can now build our decision tree classifier, train it, and evaluate its performance:

1. Instantiate the model:

```
clf = DecisionTreeClassifier(random_state=2024)
```

2. Fit the model to the training data:

```
clf.fit(X_train, y_train)
```

3. Generate predictions:

```
y_pred = clf.predict(X_test)
```

4. Evaluate the model:

```
accuracy = accuracy_score(y_test, y_pred)
```

5. Create a classification report:

```
report = classification_report(
    y_test, y_pred, output_dict=True)
report_df = pd.DataFrame(report).transpose()
```

6. Stylize the DataFrame:

```
styled_df = (report_df
    .style
    .background_gradient(
        cmap='Blues',
        subset=['precision', 'recall', 'f1-score']
    )
    .format({
        'precision': '{:.3f}',
        'recall': '{:.3f}',
        'f1-score': '{:.3f}',
        'support': '{:.0f}'
    })
)
```

```
styled_df
```

Let's see the results of our classification report in the following screenshot:

	precision	recall	f1-score	support
0	1.000	1.000	1.000	18
1	0.714	0.833	0.769	12
2	0.846	0.733	0.786	15
accuracy	0.867	0.867	0.867	1
macro avg	0.853	0.856	0.852	45
weighted avg	0.873	0.867	0.867	45

Figure 8.1 – Decision tree classification report

Our model performs generally well, even with the default hyperparameters.

How it works...

Decision trees work by splitting the dataset based on feature values. The goal at each split is to increase homogeneity, or *sameness*, within each subgroup. The decision to split is typically determined by criteria such as Gini impurity (used by default in scikit-learn) or entropy.

We can visualize the decision tree to better understand how splits were made:

1. Load the libraries:

    ```
    from sklearn.tree import plot_tree
    import matplotlib.pyplot as plt
    ```

2. Plot the figure:

    ```
    plt.figure(figsize=(15,10))
    plot_tree(clf, feature_names=iris.feature_names,
              class_names=iris.target_names, filled=True)
    plt.title("Decision Tree for Iris Dataset")
    plt.show()
    ```

The displayed decision tree output provides a lot of valuable information to help us understand the structure of our model and its decision-making process.

Decision Tree for Iris Dataset

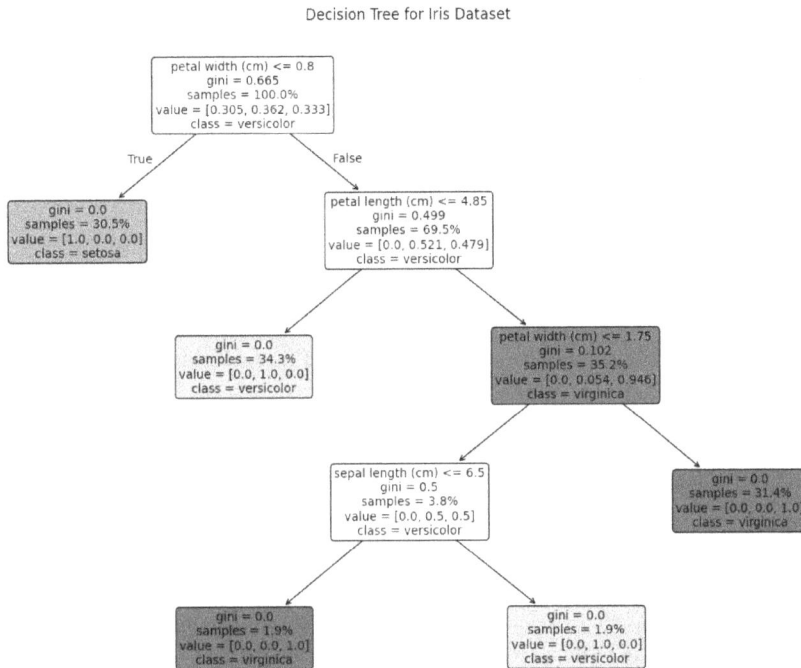

Figure 8.2 – Decision tree for the Iris dataset

You'll notice that each *leaf* or *node* in our tree gives us insight into how the model used the training dataset features to build a classifier.

- **Feature name**: Features, for example, `petal width (cm)` and `petal length (cm)`, are training features. The top node, or *root node*, displays `petal width (cm) <=0.8`, which indicates the decision criteria and what arrow, or *edge*, to move along as we continue to work through the classification process. In this instance, if a record in our dataset (e.g., an iris) has a petal width measuring 0.8 cm or less, we'd move along the *True* path to the left; otherwise, we'd move along the *False* path to the right. Once we've reached a node with no further path, we call this a *terminal* or *classification node* and apply the class prediction to the record corresponding to the class with the greatest proportion represented in that node. So, in this example, if we are trying to classify a new iris using this model and its petal width is less than or equal to 0.8 cm, we'd move to the left along the decision tree. Since there are no more splits, we'd classify the iris as *setosa*.

- **Gini impurity**: The Gini value indicates the *purity* of that node, or the proportion that a single class is represented. Remember, a decision tree works by trying to split our dataset to create the best partition between our classes, so ideally, each node tries to be composed of a single class. However, unless our classes are perfectly separable, this rarely happens early in the splitting process. Gini values range from 0.0 to 1.0, with 0.0 indicating a perfectly *pure* node that contains only a single class, and 1.0 indicating an even balance of all classes.

- **Samples**: This indicates the proportion of training data records contained in that node. At the root node, we start with all the data (100%), and as we split the data, that proportion drops the further down the tree we progress.

- **Value**: This shows the proportion of each class represented in the node. Once a single class occupies that node (i.e., 1.0), the Gini impurity becomes 0.0, indicating maximum purity.

- **Class**: This indicates the class that is the highest in that node. If this is a terminal node, we'd assign our record to that prediction.

The visualization shows each split and how the decision tree classifies data points based on feature values.

There's more...

We can control the complexity of a decision tree to prevent overfitting by tuning parameters such as max_depth, min_samples_split, and min_samples_leaf. scikit-learn provides a straightforward interface for these hyperparameter adjustments.

Let's look at what these and other hyperparameters do more closely, since you will come across them in most tree-based classification models:

- max_depth: This hyperparameter controls the number of levels of splits your tree algorithm is allowed to make. For example, when you begin training, all training data samples are part of the same cluster of data. Each time a feature is used to create a split, the tree has added one level of depth. Each consecutive split built from a previous one adds another level. In *Figure 8.2*, for example, not counting the initial node that contains all our training samples, the tree has a depth of four. max_depth creates a trade-off between tree complexity and node purity.

- min_samples_split: This hyperparameter limits additional node splitting based on how many samples exist in a node. If the number of samples is below the set value, the algorithm will not split the node any further.

- min_samples_leaf: Similar to min_samples_split, this hyperparameter sets a minimum number of samples for each leaf node of a split. If a given feature used to create a split would leave a resulting node with fewer than the threshold value set here, then the split will not be performed.

- `max_features`: When creating splits, `max_features` sets a maximum threshold on the number of features to consider in the training set; however, the algorithm will still continue if a split isn't found among the features it searches through. The default value for this hyperparameter is `None`, meaning all features will be considered at every split decision point.

- `min_impurity_decrease`: This hyperparameter sets a value that is used to determine whether a split will reduce the impurity to a certain level if a split were made. If yes, the split will be created; if no, the algorithm will halt additional splitting of the node.

Hands-on exercises

To explore decision trees practically, please refer to the GitHub repository (`https://github.com/PacktPublishing/scikit-learn-Cookbook-Third-Edition`). You will engage in hands-on exercises with decision tree classifiers. We encourage experimentation with different datasets and hyperparameters. Follow these steps:

1. Clone the GitHub repository and install the necessary libraries.
2. Choose a dataset suitable for classification tasks.
3. Prepare your dataset by splitting it into training and testing subsets.
4. Instantiate `DecisionTreeClassifier()` from `sklearn.tree`.
5. Train your model on the training subset using the `fit` method.
6. Predict outcomes on the test set using the trained model.
7. Evaluate the classifier using accuracy and confusion matrices.
8. Experiment with visualizing the decision tree and interpreting the splits.

Random forests and bagging

While building a single decision tree model is intuitive, most real-world applications will only use them as part of an ensemble method due to some of their shortcomings, especially in overfitting. As the saying goes, "Two heads (or trees in this case) are better than one!"

Cleverly named **random forests** are robust ensemble models that combine multiple decision trees to improve accuracy and reduce overfitting. They achieve this by employing a method known as **bootstrap aggregating** (**bagging**), where multiple trees are trained on different subsets of the data sampled with replacement. Each tree contributes a prediction vote, and the final prediction is based on the majority vote or the average of predictions from all trees. Random forests excel in handling large datasets and complex feature interactions better than a single decision tree alone. This recipe will introduce you to ensemble methods.

Getting ready

We will utilize scikit-learn to demonstrate building a random forest classifier:

1. Load the libraries:

```
import numpy as np
import pandas as pd
from sklearn.datasets import load_iris
from sklearn.model_selection import train_test_split
from sklearn.ensemble import RandomForestClassifier
from sklearn.metrics import accuracy_score
```

2. Load the dataset:

```
iris = load_iris()
X = iris.data
y = iris.target
```

3. Split the data:

```
X_train, X_test, y_train, y_test = train_test_split(
    X, y, test_size=0.3, random_state=2024)
```

We split our training data the same way as always when using random forest models.

How to do it...

We will now build, train, and evaluate our random forest classifier:

1. Instantiate the model:

```
rf_clf = RandomForestClassifier(
    n_estimators=100, random_state=2024)
```

2. Fit the model to the training data:

```
rf_clf.fit(X_train, y_train)
```

3. Generate predictions:

```
y_pred = rf_clf.predict(X_test)
```

4. Evaluate the model:

```
accuracy = accuracy_score(y_test, y_pred)
report = classification_report(
    y_test, y_pred, output_dict=True)
report_df = pd.DataFrame(report).transpose()
```

5. Stylize the DataFrame:

```
styled_df = (report_df
    .style
    .background_gradient(
        cmap='Blues',
        subset=['precision', 'recall', 'f1-score']
    )
    .format({
        'precision': '{:.3f}',
        'recall': '{:.3f}',
        'f1-score': '{:.3f}',
        'support': '{:.0f}'
    })
)
styled_df
```

Now that we have the power of several classification models working for us together, we should see an improvement in our performance.

	precision	recall	f1-score	support
0	1.000	1.000	1.000	18
1	0.833	0.833	0.833	12
2	0.867	0.867	0.867	15
accuracy	0.911	0.911	0.911	1
macro avg	0.900	0.900	0.900	45
weighted avg	0.911	0.911	0.911	45

Figure 8.3 – Random forest classification report

We improved quite a bit in the overall performance of our predictions. Our single decision tree reported an accuracy of 0.867, while our random forest's accuracy is 0.911.

How it works...

Random forests construct multiple decision trees, each trained on *bootstrapped* samples of the dataset. Additionally, at each split in a tree, a random subset of features is considered, introducing further diversity. This approach reduces variance and increases model stability and generalization, which is designed to allow it to work with unseen data it might encounter in a production application.

Let's visualize feature importance to understand which features contributed most to the decision-making process:

1. Load the libraries:

    ```
    import matplotlib.pyplot as plt
    ```

2. Calculate feature importance:

    ```
    importances = rf_clf.feature_importances_
    indices = np.argsort(importances)[::-1]
    ```

3. Plot the feature importance:

    ```
    plt.figure(figsize=(10,6))
    plt.title("Feature Importances in Random Forest")
    plt.bar(range(X.shape[1]),
            importances[indices], align="center")
    plt.xticks(range(X.shape[1]),
               [iris.feature_names[i] for i in indices],
               rotation=45)
    plt.ylabel("Importance")
    plt.show()
    ```

Let's display our results:

Feature Importances in Random Forest

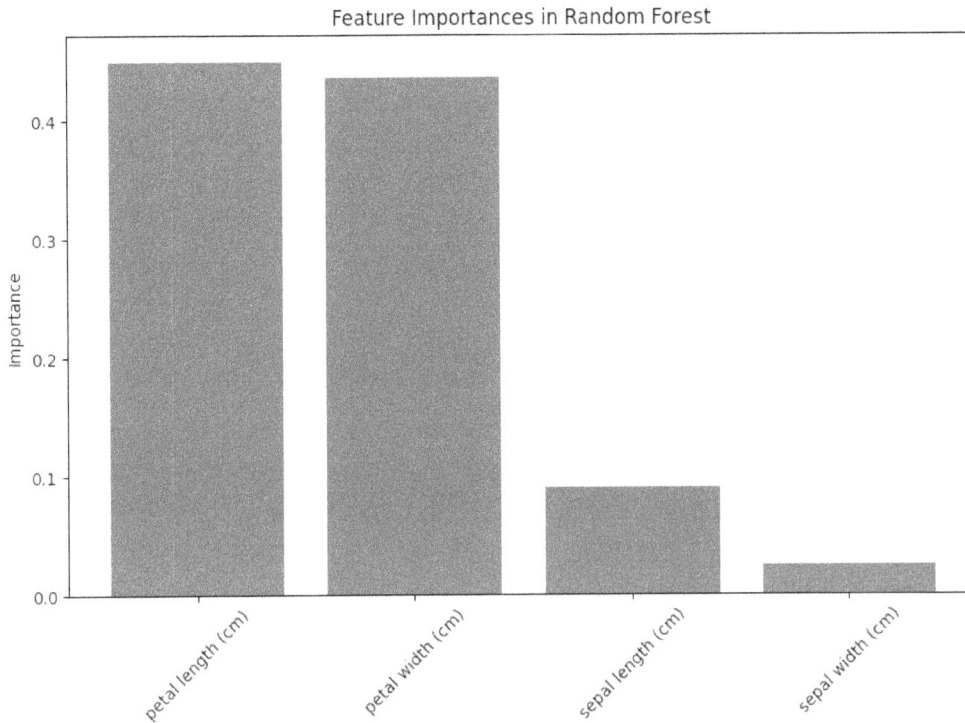

Figure 8.4 – Feature importance in random forest

This plot shows the relative importance of each feature, helping us interpret the model—in this case, `petal length (cm)` and `petal width (cm)`. Sometimes, random forest models are used *only* for feature selection, where the most important features are selected using this technique, then passed along for modeling with a different ML algorithm.

There's more...

Random forest hyperparameters such as `max_features`, `max_depth`, and `n_estimators` can be tuned to optimize performance. Additionally, bagging can be applied to other models in scikit-learn using `BaggingClassifier()` and `BaggingRegressor()`.

Hands-on exercises

To practically apply random forests, please refer to the GitHub repository (`https://github.com/PacktPublishing/scikit-learn-Cookbook-Third-Edition`). You will explore ensemble methods with random forest classifiers. We encourage experimentation with datasets and parameter tuning. Follow these steps:

1. Clone the GitHub repository and install the necessary libraries.

2. Select a dataset appropriate for classification tasks.

3. Split your dataset into training and test subsets.

4. Instantiate `RandomForestClassifier()` from `sklearn.ensemble`.

5. Train your model using the `fit` method on the training data.

6. Predict outcomes on the test set with your trained model.

7. Evaluate the model using metrics such as accuracy, precision, and recall.

8. Visualize and analyze feature importances to interpret model decisions.

Gradient boosting machines

Gradient boosting machines (**GBMs**) are advanced ensemble techniques that sequentially build and combine weak prediction models, typically decision trees, to produce a stronger predictive performance. Unlike random forests, GBMs construct trees one at a time, each aiming to minimize errors from previous models. Another way to think about this is that while random forests build a collection of decision trees *in parallel*, GBMs build them *sequentially*. This is where the term *boosting* comes from: we try to boost the predictive performance of each successive tree. This iterative approach can significantly enhance accuracy, making GBMs highly effective for various ML tasks. This recipe will introduce GBMs as another ensemble approach for ML modeling.

Getting ready

We will use scikit-learn to illustrate how to create a gradient boosting classifier:

1. Load the libraries:

    ```
    import numpy as np
    import pandas as pd
    from sklearn.datasets import load_iris
    from sklearn.model_selection import train_test_split
    from sklearn.ensemble import GradientBoostingClassifier
    from sklearn.metrics import accuracy_score
    ```

2. Load the dataset:

```
iris = load_iris()
X = iris.data
y = iris.target
```

3. Split the data:

```
X_train, X_test, y_train, y_test = train_test_split(
    X, y, test_size=0.3, random_state=2024)
```

Our data is split, so let's begin training.

How to do it...

Now, let's build and evaluate our gradient boosting model:

1. Instantiate the model:

```
gbm_clf = GradientBoostingClassifier(
    n_estimators=1000,
    learning_rate=0.2,
    random_state=2024
)
```

2. Fit the model to the training data:

```
gbm_clf.fit(X_train, y_train)
```

3. Generate predictions:

```
y_pred = gbm_clf.predict(X_test)
```

4. Evaluate the model:

```
report = pd.DataFrame(classification_report(
    y_test, y_pred, output_dict=True)).transpose()
```

5. Stylize the DataFrame:

```
styled_df = (report
    .style
    .background_gradient(
        cmap='Blues',
        subset=['precision', 'recall', 'f1-score']
    )
    .format({
        'precision': '{:.3f}',
```

```
        'recall': '{:.3f}',
        'f1-score': '{:.3f}',
        'support': '{:.0f}'
    })
)
styled_df
```

Let's review our classification report:

	precision	recall	f1-score	support
0	1.000	1.000	1.000	18
1	0.714	0.833	0.769	12
2	0.846	0.733	0.786	15
accuracy	0.867	0.867	0.867	1
macro avg	0.853	0.856	0.852	45
weighted avg	0.873	0.867	0.867	45

Figure 8.5 – GBM classification report

You'll notice that the results are the same as our single decision tree model. This could mean that both the decision tree and GBM approaches are overfitting our data and have reached a local maximum with their predictive performance. In the next section on hyperparameter tuning, we'll address issues like these.

How it works...

GBMs work by iteratively building new models that predict the residuals (errors) of previous models. Each new model aims to minimize these residuals, gradually refining the overall prediction accuracy. The process begins with an initial simple prediction, and subsequent trees are added to model the residuals—the differences between the actual outcomes and the predictions. At each iteration, the model attempts to minimize prediction error. This iterative refinement helps the model learn complex patterns and improves its accuracy over time.

There's more...

Fine-tuning hyperparameters such as `learning_rate`, `max_depth`, and `n_estimators` can significantly enhance gradient boosting performance. Techniques such as **early stopping** and **validation curves** further aid in optimizing model efficiency and avoiding overfitting:

- **Early stopping**: This refers to setting a limitation on the iterative fitting process of a training algorithm to avoid overfitting. In our decision trees, for example, if we don't constrain the training process using hyperparameters, the tree will be built until all individual training samples are bucketed into terminal nodes. This obviously would create a highly overfit model not conducive to generalization, so adjusting the hyperparameters in such a way effectively stops the fitting process early for a model, which, while it may include more erroneous predictions in a test environment, will allow the model to be useful.

- **Validation curves**: These allow us to visually inspect the influence of hyperparameter changes on the quality of model predictions. Typically, we measure the influence using both the training and testing datasets to compare the resulting impact on whatever metric we are trying to optimize (e.g., accuracy). For example, if the accuracy of a model is low for both the training and testing data, we'd assume our model is underfitting and can be further improved. However, if we see that our accuracy for training is high and validation is low, we'd suspect model overfitting since it performs well on the data it was trained on, but worse on unseen testing data.

Hands-on exercises

To practice gradient boosting models, refer to the GitHub repository (`https://github.com/PacktPublishing/scikit-learn-Cookbook-Third-Edition`). Experimentation with gradient boosting classifiers and hyperparameter tuning is recommended. Follow these steps:

1. Clone the GitHub repository and install the necessary libraries.
2. Select an appropriate classification dataset.
3. Prepare your dataset by splitting it into training and testing subsets.
4. Instantiate `GradientBoostingClassifier()` from `sklearn.ensemble`.
5. Train your model using the training data and the `fit` method.
6. Generate predictions on your test dataset.
7. Evaluate model performance using accuracy and other relevant metrics.
8. Visualize model training progress and explore the effects of tuning hyperparameters.

Hyperparameter tuning for trees and ensembles

As we've learned by now, hyperparameter tuning is essential for optimizing the performance of models and ensembles, including decision trees, random forests, and GBMs. By carefully selecting hyperparameters such as maximum tree depth, number of estimators, and learning rates, we can significantly enhance model performance and prevent overfitting. We will utilize the same tools (only the hyperparameters themselves will be specific to these model types) we used previously in scikit-learn, such as grid search and cross-validation, to systematically tune our models. This recipe will show how we can apply hyperparameter optimization to tree-based models.

Getting ready

We'll demonstrate hyperparameter tuning using `GridSearchCV()` from scikit-learn with a gradient boosting classifier:

1. Load the libraries:

    ```
    import numpy as np
    import pandas as pd
    from sklearn.datasets import load_iris
    from sklearn.model_selection import (
        train_test_split, GridSearchCV)
    from sklearn.ensemble import GradientBoostingClassifier
    from sklearn.metrics import accuracy_score
    ```

2. Load the dataset:

    ```
    iris = load_iris()
    X = iris.data
    y = iris.target
    ```

3. Split the data:

    ```
    X_train, X_test, y_train, y_test = train_test_split(
        X, y, test_size=0.3, random_state=2024)
    ```

Now, let's train the model.

How to do it...

We'll now use grid search combined with cross-validation to find the best hyperparameters for our gradient boosting model:

1. Define the hyperparameter grid:

    ```python
    param_grid = {
        'n_estimators': [50, 100, 150],
        'max_depth': [3, 4, 5],
        'learning_rate': [0.01, 0.1, 0.2]
    }
    ```

2. Set up `GridSearchCV()`:

    ```python
    grid_search = GridSearchCV(
        GradientBoostingClassifier(random_state=2024),
        param_grid,
        cv=5,
        scoring='accuracy'
    )
    ```

3. Fit `GridSearchCV()` to the training data:

    ```python
    grid_search.fit(X_train, y_train)
    ```

4. Identify the best parameters:

    ```python
    print(f'Best Parameters: {grid_search.best_params_}')
    ```

5. Evaluate the best model:

    ```python
    best_model = grid_search.best_estimator_
    y_pred = best_model.predict(X_test)
    ```

6. Generate the classification report:

    ```python
    report = pd.DataFrame(classification_report(
        y_test, y_pred, output_dict=True)).transpose()
    ```

7. Stylize the DataFrame:

    ```python
    styled_df = (report
        .style
        .background_gradient(
            cmap='Blues',
            subset=['precision', 'recall', 'f1-score']
        )
    ```

```
      .format({
          'precision': '{:.3f}',
          'recall': '{:.3f}',
          'f1-score': '{:.3f}',
          'support': '{:.0f}'
      })
  )
  styled_df
```

When displaying our classification table, this time, we are also shown the best-performing parameters from our hyperparameter tuning process.

```
Best Parameters: {'learning_rate': 0.01, 'max_depth': 4, 'n_estimators': 50}
```

	precision	recall	f1-score	support
0	1.000	1.000	1.000	18
1	0.714	0.833	0.769	12
2	0.846	0.733	0.786	15
accuracy	0.867	0.867	0.867	1
macro avg	0.853	0.856	0.852	45
weighted avg	0.873	0.867	0.867	45

Figure 8.6 – Hyperparameter tuning classification report

When executing the code, we can see how grid search identifies the best set of parameters for our model.

How it works...

Grid search exhaustively tests combinations of specified hyperparameters, using cross-validation to evaluate each set's performance. The model achieving the best cross-validation score is then selected as the *optimal* configuration.

Another cross-validation technique, called `RandomizedSearchCV()` in scikit-learn, performs cross-validation but uses a randomized set of hyperparameters at the first iteration and adjusts those hyperparameters with each additional iteration for a given number in order to find the optimal set. Sometimes, this technique, maybe counterintuitively, produces faster and better results than `GridSearchCV()`.

Cross-validation ensures reliable performance estimates by evaluating each hyperparameter configuration across multiple subsets of the dataset, which is our way of trying to simulate the nuances our model might see when performing *in the wild.*

We can visualize the results to better understand the effect of different hyperparameters:

1. Load the libraries:

```
import matplotlib.pyplot as plt
import seaborn as sns
```

2. Create a pivot table:

```
results = pd.DataFrame(grid_search.cv_results_)
pivot_table = results.pivot_table(
    values='mean_test_score',
    index='param_max_depth',
    columns='param_n_estimators'
)
```

3. Plot the heatmap:

```
plt.figure(figsize=(8,6))
sns.heatmap(pivot_table, annot=True,
            fmt='.3f', cmap='viridis')
plt.title(
    'Grid Search Accuracy by Max Depth and Number of
    Estimators')
plt.xlabel('Number of Estimators')
plt.ylabel('Max Depth')
plt.show()
```

Let's display the heatmap:

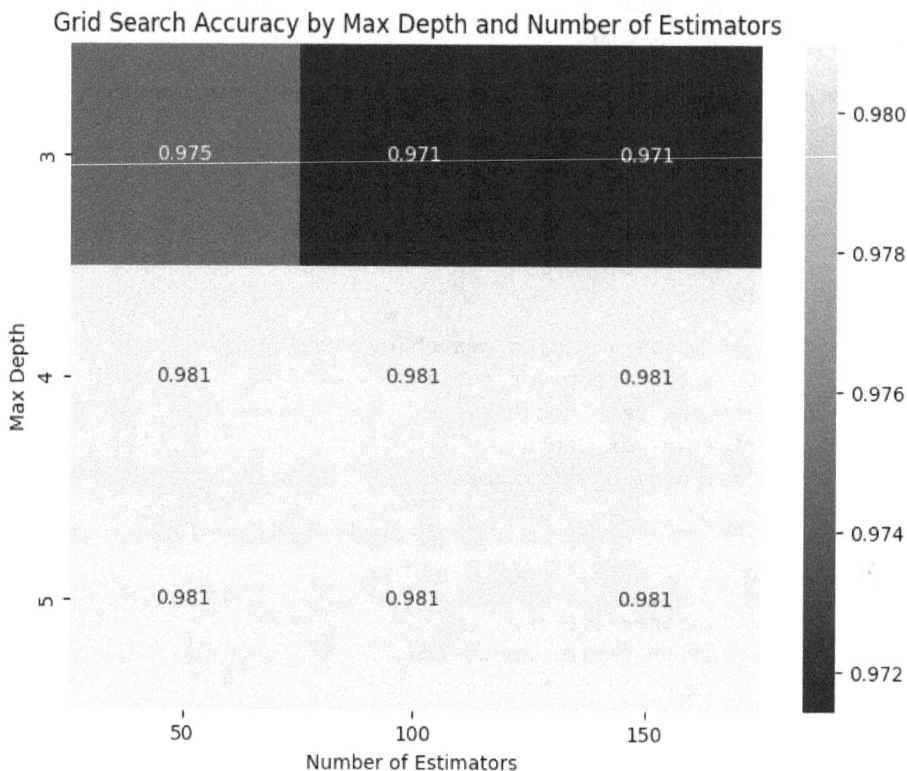

Figure 8.7 – Hyperparameter heatmap

This heatmap helps visualize how accuracy changes across combinations of hyperparameters. We see that after setting `max_depth` and `n_estimators` above 4 and 50, respectively, our accuracy does not improve.

Hands-on exercises

Explore hyperparameter tuning techniques further by referring to the GitHub repository (`https://github.com/PacktPublishing/scikit-learn-Cookbook-Third-Edition`). Experimentation with grid search and other optimization methods is encouraged. Follow these steps:

1. Clone the GitHub repository and install the necessary libraries.

2. Choose a dataset suitable for classification tasks.

3. Split your data into training and testing subsets.

4. Define a hyperparameter grid relevant to your chosen model.

5. Apply `GridSearchCV()` or `RandomizedSearchCV()` with your chosen classifier.

6. Evaluate the optimized model on the test dataset.

7. Visualize your tuning results to interpret the effects of different hyperparameters.

Comparing ensemble methods

Comparing ensemble methods helps us recognize the relative strengths and weaknesses of approaches such as bagging, boosting, and stacking (which we'll look at next). Each method has unique characteristics—bagging reduces variance, boosting reduces bias, and stacking leverages multiple algorithms to enhance predictive performance. Through comparative experiments on various datasets, we can determine which ensemble strategy works best for specific problems. This recipe will allow you to compare different methods for ensemble training.

Getting ready

We'll demonstrate comparing different ensemble methods using scikit-learn with a classification dataset:

1. Load the libraries:

    ```
    import numpy as np
    import pandas as pd
    from sklearn.datasets import load_iris
    from sklearn.model_selection import train_test_split
    from sklearn.ensemble import (
        RandomForestClassifier, GradientBoostingClassifier)
    from sklearn.ensemble import StackingClassifier
    from sklearn.linear_model import LogisticRegression
    from sklearn.metrics import accuracy_score
    ```

2. Load the dataset:

    ```
    iris = load_iris()
    X = iris.data
    y = iris.target
    ```

3. Split the data:

    ```
    X_train, X_test, y_train, y_test = train_test_split(
        X, y, test_size=0.3, random_state=2024)
    ```

Let's train both a random forest model and a GBM model to compare.

How to do it...

We'll build and evaluate bagging (random forests), boosting (gradient boosting), and stacking classifiers:

1. Instantiate models:

    ```
    rf_clf = RandomForestClassifier(
        n_estimators=100, random_state=2024
    )
    gb_clf = GradientBoostingClassifier(
        n_estimators=100, random_state=2024
    )
    stacking_clf = StackingClassifier(
        estimators=[('rf', rf_clf), ('gb', gb_clf)],
        final_estimator=LogisticRegression(),
        cv=5
    )
    ```

2. Fit the models:

    ```
    rf_clf.fit(X_train, y_train)
    gb_clf.fit(X_train, y_train)
    stacking_clf.fit(X_train, y_train)
    ```

3. Generate predictions:

    ```
    rf_pred = rf_clf.predict(X_test)
    gb_pred = gb_clf.predict(X_test)
    stacking_pred = stacking_clf.predict(X_test)
    ```

4. Evaluate the models

    ```
    rf_accuracy = accuracy_score(y_test, rf_pred)
    gb_accuracy = accuracy_score(y_test, gb_pred)
    stacking_accuracy = accuracy_score(y_test, stacking_pred)
    ```

5. Print the accuracy scores:

    ```
    print(f'Random Forest Accuracy: {rf_accuracy:.2f}')
    print(f'Gradient Boosting Accuracy: {gb_accuracy:.2f}')
    print(f'Stacking Accuracy: {stacking_accuracy:.2f}')

    # Output:
    Random Forest Accuracy: 0.91
    Gradient Boosting Accuracy: 0.87
    Stacking Accuracy: 0.87
    ```

Our random forest model outperforms both GBM and the stacked model.

How it works...

Bagging (with random forests) averages predictions from multiple trees built on bootstrapped datasets, reducing variance. Boosting (with GBMs) sequentially builds trees to correct errors from previous models, focusing on reducing bias. Stacking, on the other hand, combines multiple base models using a *meta-model* to enhance predictive performance further.

We can visualize the comparative results clearly:

1. Load the libraries:

    ```
    import matplotlib.pyplot as plt
    ```

2. Create a bar plot:

    ```
    methods = [
        'Random Forest', 'Gradient Boosting', 'Stacking'
    ]
    accuracies = [
        rf_accuracy, gb_accuracy, stacking_accuracy
    ]
    ```

3. Plot the bar plot:

    ```
    plt.figure(figsize=(8, 6))
    plt.bar(methods, accuracies, color=['skyblue',
            'salmon', 'lightgreen'])
    plt.title('Accuracy Comparison of Ensemble Methods')
    plt.ylabel('Accuracy')
    plt.ylim(0, 1)
    plt.show()
    ```

Let's compare our ensemble methods:

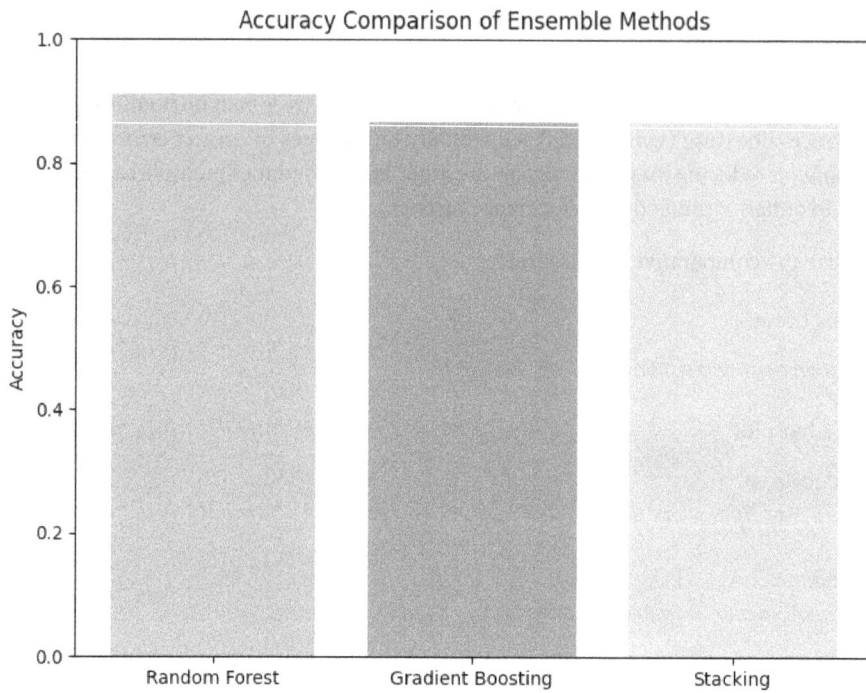

Figure 8.8 – Comparing accuracy

This bar chart clearly illustrates the relative performance of each ensemble method.

There's more...

To deepen our understanding, we can compare ensemble methods on more diverse datasets or consider additional metrics such as precision, recall, F1-score, or ROC curves.

Hands-on exercises

To practice comparing ensemble methods further, refer to the GitHub repository (`https://github.com/PacktPublishing/scikit-learn-Cookbook-Third-Edition`). We encourage experimentation with ensemble methods on various datasets. Follow these steps:

1. Clone the GitHub repository and install the necessary libraries.

2. Select multiple classification datasets.

3. Split the datasets into training and testing subsets.

4. Train bagging, boosting, and stacking classifiers.

5. Generate predictions and evaluate each method using multiple performance metrics.

6. Visualize comparative results to clearly understand the strengths and weaknesses of each method.

Practical exercises with tree-based models

In this final section, we will engage in practical exercises that involve building, tuning, and evaluating tree-based and ensemble models on real-world datasets. These exercises are designed to reinforce the concepts learned throughout the chapter and demonstrate how to effectively apply these models in complex ML scenarios. By the end of this section, we will have hands-on experience that we can leverage in our own ML projects.

Exercise 1: Building and evaluating a decision tree classifier

In this exercise, we'll build and evaluate a basic decision tree classifier.

These are the implementation steps:

1. Load the libraries.

2. Load the dataset.

3. Split the data.

4. Create and train the classifier.

5. Make predictions.

6. Evaluate the performance.

Exercise 2: Hyperparameter tuning with random forests

We'll fine-tune a random forest classifier using grid search to find the optimal parameters.

These are the implementation steps:

1. Load the libraries.

2. Load the dataset.

3. Split the data.

4. Define a hyperparameter grid and perform grid search.

5. Evaluate the best model.

Exercise 3: Comparing gradient boosting and random forest

We'll compare the performance of gradient boosting and random forest classifiers on a classification dataset.

These are the implementation steps:

1. Load the libraries.
2. Load the dataset.
3. Split the data.
4. Create and train the models.
5. Make predictions and evaluate.

9

Text Processing and Multiclass Classification

Most of the data stored in the world is not in the form of numerical data. Just think of the vast information stores in corporate wikis and knowledge bases – not to mention things many of us use every day, such as email and online message boards. The common connection between all these is that this data is stored as text…and the *problem* with text-based data is that computers do not inherently understand how to *read* text. This means that in order to unlock this potential treasure trove of data (which we are already doing a very good job of in the development and utilization of **large language models** or **LLMs** such as GPT, Llama, and Claude), we need methods to process text into a format digestible by computers. In this chapter, we will cover natural language processing techniques using scikit-learn, including text vectorization, feature extraction, and multiclass classification strategies. By the end, we expect you to begin seeing that data comes in many forms, including text!

In this chapter, we're going to cover the following recipes:

- Introduction to text processing
- Text vectorization techniques
- Feature extraction from text
- Implementing text classification models
- Multiclass classification strategies
- Evaluating text models

Technical requirements

It is advisable to create a Python environment for safely isolating your work from other Python installations/libraries. See the GitHub repository for more details (`https://github.com/PacktPublishing/scikit-learn-Cookbook-Third-Edition`). You will need the following:

- Git >=2.46.x

- Python >=3.9.x

- Cloned GitHub repository and Python environment built from the `requirements.txt` file

Introduction to text processing

Text processing is a fundamental step in ML, especially crucial when dealing with natural language data. It is estimated that somewhere between 80% to 90% of data is unstructured data, which includes text as well as other non-traditional data sources such as images, video, audio, and so on. Like structured data, textual data often contains noise, irrelevant information, and varying formatting that can pose challenges for **effective** modeling. Effective preprocessing converts raw text into structured numerical data, enabling the application of ML algorithms. Let's start by learning some of the basic scikit-learn tools for working with this type of data. We will also incorporate a few other Python libraries, including pandas and NumPy.

Getting ready

We'll prepare our environment by loading essential libraries and text data. Now that we are using text data rather than numeric data, we will utilize a built-in dataset from Python's **Natural Language Tool Kit (NLTK)** library. Typically, we call a collection of text used in the context of modeling a **corpus**. This particular corpus is the `movie_reviews` dataset, which contains 2,000 reviews categorized as either positive or negative:

1. Load the libraries:

```
import numpy as np
from sklearn.feature_extraction.text import CountVectorizer
from sklearn.model_selection import train_test_split
import nltk
from nltk.corpus import movie_reviews
```

2. Download NLTK data if not already present (specifically, the `movie_reviews` corpus):

```
try:
    movie_reviews.sents()
except LookupError:
    nltk.download('movie_reviews')
```

3. Load the dataset from the NLTK `movie_reviews` corpus:

```
documents = []
labels = []
for category in movie_reviews.categories():
    for fileid in movie_reviews.fileids(category):
        documents.append(movie_reviews.raw(fileid))
        labels.append(category)
```

4. Convert labels to numerical (0 for 'neg', and 1 for 'pos'):

```
label_map = {
    label: i for i,
    label in enumerate(sorted(list(set(labels))))
}
numerical_labels = [
    label_map[label] for label in labels
]
```

5. Split the data:

```
# Using a smaller subset for demonstration purposes
# to speed up processing
# and reduce memory usage,
# as the full movie_reviews corpus is quite large.
# You can adjust subset_size or
# remove this sampling for full dataset usage.
subset_size = 500 # Using 500 samples for quicker demonstration
if len(documents) > subset_size:
    # Stratified sampling to maintain class proportions
    texts_subset, _, labels_subset, _ = train_test_split(
        documents, numerical_labels,
        train_size=subset_size,
        stratify=numerical_labels,
        random_state=2024
    )
else:
    texts_subset = documents
    labels_subset = numerical_labels
X_train, X_test, y_train, y_test = train_test_split(
    texts_subset, labels_subset,
    test_size=0.3, random_state=2024,
    stratify=labels_subset
)
```

Now, let's explore some text-oriented functions in scikit-learn.

How to do it...

First, we will transform raw text into a numerical representation using scikit-learn's `CountVectorizer()`:

1. Instantiate and fit `CountVectorizer()` with stopword removal:

> **Note**
>
> **Stopwords** are words that are of little value in regard to some text-based ML problems, such as classification. These include frequent words such as *the*, *a*, *an*, and so on.

```
vectorizer = CountVectorizer(stop_words='english')
X_train_vect = vectorizer.fit_transform(X_train)
```

2. Transform the test data:

```
X_test_vect = vectorizer.transform(X_test)
```

We will utilize `CountVectorizer()` frequently in this chapter since it's a valuable function for text preprocessing.

How it works...

`CountVectorizer()` converts text data into a sparse matrix of token counts, where each row represents a document, and each column represents a unique token. In the context of text processing, a **token** can refer to a fundamental unit of text – a word, a sentence, a paragraph, or even an individual letter can all be treated as a token depending on the application. This numerical representation is suitable for training various ML models. The `CountVectorizer()` function counts the occurrences of all words (the default token unit in this case) within each document.

Let's visualize this numerical representation:

1. Visualizing the token counts:

```
feature_names = vectorizer.get_feature_names_out()
counts = X_train_vect.toarray().sum(axis=0)
plt.figure(figsize=(10,6))
plt.barh(feature_names, counts, color='skyblue')
plt.xlabel('Count')
plt.title('Token Frequency in Training Data')
plt.show()
```

This bar chart clearly shows the frequency of the top 20 tokens within our training dataset:

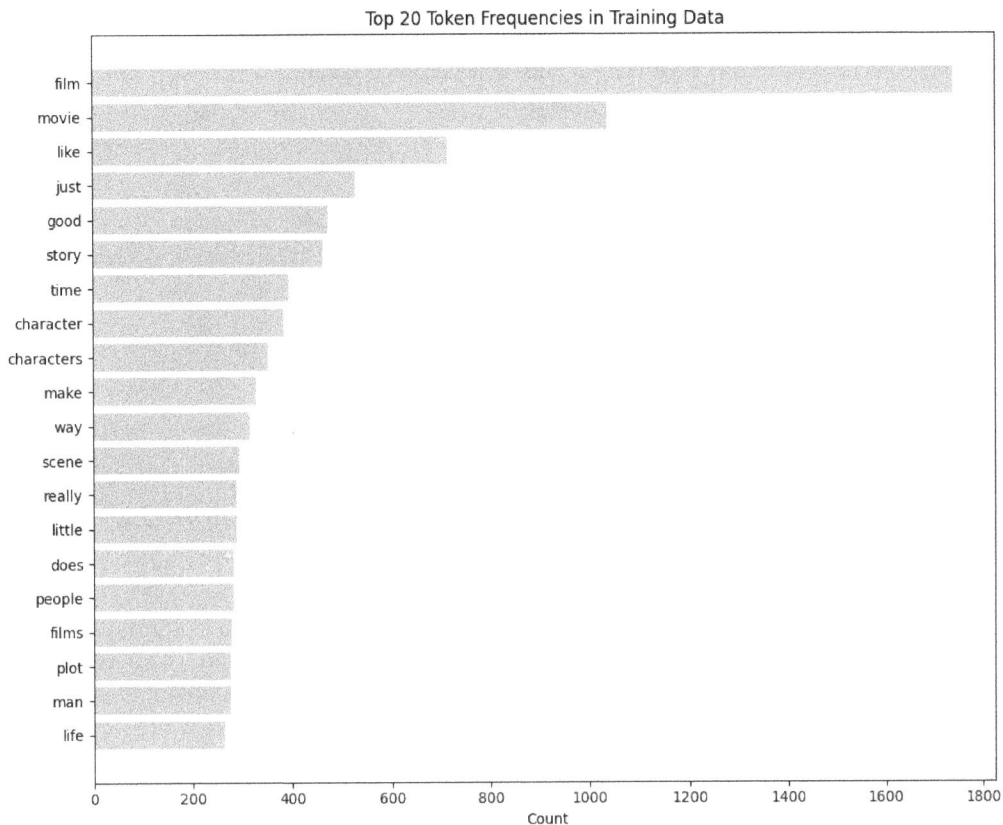

Figure 9.1 – CountVectorizer() frequency of common words in the movie_reviews corpus

With stopwords removed, we can see some of the most commonly occurring words in our corpus. It should come as no surprise that tokens such as `film` and `movie` occur most frequently.

There's more...

Additional text processing techniques include **Term Frequency-Inverse Document Frequency (TF-IDF)** transformation, stemming, lemmatization, removing stop words, and handling groupings of sequential words (n-grams). These approaches further enhance the text preprocessing pipeline, improving model performance.

Hands-on exercises

To explore text processing further, reference the GitHub repository (`https://github.com/PacktPublishing/scikit-learn-Cookbook-Third-Edition`). Engage with practical text-processing tasks by following these steps:

1. Clone the GitHub repository and install the necessary libraries.

2. Choose a suitable textual dataset or create your own.

3. Clean and preprocess your text data, handling punctuation, case normalization, and tokenization.

4. Apply `CountVectorizer()` or `TfidfVectorizer()` from scikit-learn to transform your text into numerical data.

5. Split the dataset into training and testing subsets.

6. Train an ML model (e.g., logistic regression, Naive Bayes, etc.) using processed data.

7. Evaluate the model using appropriate metrics such as accuracy or F1-score.

8. Visualize token frequencies or other meaningful aspects of your processed data.

Text vectorization techniques

Text vectorization techniques transform raw text into numerical representations, enabling ML algorithms to effectively analyze textual data. Techniques such as **Bag of Words** (**BoW**), TF-IDF, and word embeddings offer different approaches for capturing textual features and semantic meaning. Keep in mind, however, that even before text vectorization begins, a computer still must have a way to represent a letter in the first place. This is typically done using ASCII or Unicode encodings as an initial way to represent and store text in computer memory. This recipe will provide examples of different methodologies for text vectorization.

Getting ready

We'll load the necessary libraries and prepare textual data for vectorization. This time, we will use the `reuters` corpus from NLTK. It contains 10,788 news documents and approximately 1.3 million words with over 90 possible topics for classification. We will just classify based on the first category for simplicity:

1. Load the libraries:

    ```
    import numpy as np
    from sklearn.feature_extraction.text import (
        CountVectorizer, TfidfVectorizer)
    from sklearn.model_selection import train_test_split
    import nltk
    from nltk.corpus import reuters
    ```

2. Download the `reuters` corpus if not already downloaded:

```
try:
    reuters.fileids()
except LookupError:
    nltk.download('reuters')
```

3. Load the dataset from the NLTK `reuters` corpus:

```
documents = reuters.fileids()
# Using the first category as the label for simplicity:
texts = [reuters.raw(doc_id) for doc_id in documents]
labels = [reuters.categories(doc_id)[0] for doc_id in documents]
```

4. Split the data:

```
X_train, X_test, y_train, y_test = train_test_split(
    texts, labels, test_size=0.5, random_state=2024)
```

With our dataset prepared, let's explore these vectorization techniques.

How to do it...

We'll demonstrate text vectorization using two common techniques (BoW and TF-IDF), and briefly discuss word embeddings.

For BoW, instantiate and fit `CountVectorizer()`:

```
bow_vectorizer = CountVectorizer()
X_train_bow = bow_vectorizer.fit_transform(X_train)
X_test_bow = bow_vectorizer.transform(X_test)
```

For TF-IDF vectorization, instantiate and fit `TfidfVectorizer()`:

```
tfidf_vectorizer = TfidfVectorizer()
X_train_tfidf = tfidf_vectorizer.fit_transform(X_train)
X_test_tfidf = tfidf_vectorizer.transform(X_test)
```

Now that we've applied these techniques, let's take a close look at their use cases.

How it works...

Text vectorization comes in a variety of *flavors*, including the two approaches we just looked at. How do they compare?

- **BoW** represents texts as frequency counts of individual words, disregarding word order and grammar.

- **TF-IDF** adjusts word frequencies by considering their rarity across all documents, assigning higher weights to distinctive terms. This technique is a little more involved than BoW and allows the classification of documents based on the occurrence of words much more efficiently.

Let's visualize TF-IDF weights:

1. Create a `TfidfVectorizer` instance with English stop words removed:

   ```
   vis_tfidf_vectorizer = TfidfVectorizer(stop_words='english')
   vis_X_train_tfidf = (
       vis_tfidf_vectorizer.fit_transform(X_train))
   ```

2. Get feature names and their mean TF-IDF weights from this new vectorization:

   ```
   feature_names = vis_tfidf_vectorizer.get_feature_names_out()
   tfidf_means = vis_X_train_tfidf.toarray().mean(axis=0)
   ```

3. Set the number of top terms to display:

   ```
   N = 20
   ```

4. Ensure that N is not greater than the number of available features:

   ```
   if len(feature_names) < N:
       N = len(feature_names)
   ```

5. Get indices of the N-largest TF-IDF means:

   ```
   # np.argsort sorts in ascending order,
   # so we take the last N indices.
   # These indices will correspond to the N features
   # with the highest TF-IDF scores,
   # sorted from the Nth highest to the 1st highest
   # (suitable for plt.barh to plot highest at top).
   if N > 0 :
   # Proceed only if there are features to plot
       sorted_indices_ascending = np.argsort(tfidf_means)
       top_n_plotting_indices = sorted_indices_ascending[-N:]
   ```

6. Select the top N feature names and their TF-IDF means using these indices:

```
plot_feature_names = feature_names[
    top_n_plotting_indices]
plot_tfidf_means = tfidf_means[
    top_n_plotting_indices]
```

7. Create the plot:

```
plt.figure(
    figsize=(10, 8)
) # Adjusted figsize for better readability with 20 items
plt.barh(
    plot_feature_names,
    plot_tfidf_means, color='salmon'
)
plt.xlabel('Mean TF-IDF Weight (Stopwords Removed)')
plt.title(
    f'Top {N} TF-IDF Feature Weights '
    '(Stopwords Removed)')
else:
# Handle case with no features
# (e.g., if all features were stopwords or N=0)
    plt.figure(
        figsize=(10, 6)
    ) # Original figsize for empty or minimal plot
    plt.barh([], []) # Plot empty data
    plt.xlabel('Mean TF-IDF Weight (Stopwords Removed)')
    plt.title(
        'TF-IDF Feature Weights '
        '(No non-stopword features to display)'
    )
plt.show()
```

This visualization highlights the most significant TF-IDF scores, indicating their importance across documents:

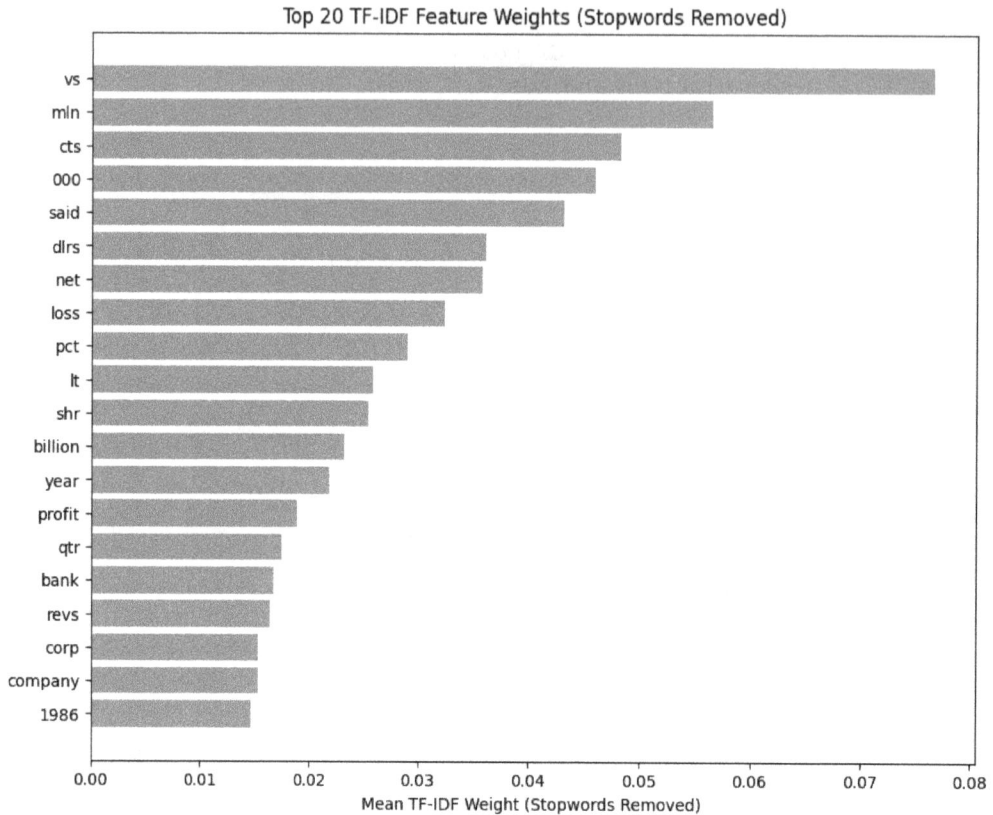

Figure 9.2 – Top 20 TF-IDF feature weights

Although the top 20 tokens (sorted by their weight calculated as a formula of their distinctiveness within and among documents in the `reuters` corpus) might look a bit odd, they can be highly valuable for our ML classification model to learn from.

There's more...

Word embeddings, such as Word2Vec and GloVe, represent words as dense vectors capturing semantic relationships. Although scikit-learn does not provide direct implementations for generating embeddings, embeddings created externally can be integrated into ML models for improved performance. Embeddings are also a significant preprocessing step in modern LLMs.

Hands-on exercises

To explore these text vectorization techniques further, reference the GitHub repository (https://github.com/PacktPublishing/scikit-learn-Cookbook-Third-Edition). Follow these steps:

1. Clone the GitHub repository and ensure that all the necessary libraries are installed.

2. Select a textual dataset suitable for vectorization.

3. Clean and preprocess the dataset, addressing punctuation, case normalization, and tokenization.

4. Apply CountVectorizer() and TfidfVectorizer() to convert your text into numerical features.

5. Split your dataset into training and testing subsets.

6. Train and evaluate ML models using these vectorized features.

7. Optionally, experiment with integrating pretrained word embeddings.

8. Visualize and analyze the feature weights from TF-IDF to interpret model inputs.

Feature extraction from text

Feature extraction from text is central for enhancing the performance of text classification models by identifying meaningful patterns and attributes within textual data. Techniques such as n-grams, **part-of-speech** (**POS**) tagging, and **named entity recognition** (**NER**) provide structured insights into textual content, significantly improving model accuracy and interpretability. This recipe will teach you how to extract meaningful elements (or *features*) from a given corpus of text.

Getting ready

We'll load the essential libraries and prepare the dataset for feature extraction. Here, we will use the brown corpus, also built into the NLTK library. It contains 500 sources categorized by genre:

1. Load the libraries:

```
from sklearn.feature_extraction.text import CountVectorizer
from sklearn.model_selection import train_test_split
import nltk
from nltk.corpus import brown
from nltk.util import ngrams as nltk_ngrams
import matplotlib.pyplot as plt
from collections import Counter
import nltk
from nltk.corpus import stopwords
```

2. Download the necessary NLTK data (if not already present):

```
nltk.download('brown', quiet=True)
nltk.download('punkt', quiet=True)
```

3. Load the dataset using the brown corpus:

```
texts = []
labels = []
```

4. Define the categories to use and the number of sentences per category:

```
# We'll use the first two categories from
# the Brown corpus for this example
# and take a small number of sentences from each.
# This will create a small dataset suitable for demonstration.
categories_to_use = brown.categories()[:2] # Example:
                                          # ['adventure',
                                          #  'belles_lettres']
num_sents_per_category = 2 # Number of sentences to extract
                           # from each category
for i, category in enumerate(categories_to_use):
    # Get sentences for the current category
    # brown.sents() returns a list of sentences,
    # where each sentence is a list of tokens.
    category_sents = brown.sents(categories=category)
    # Take the specified number of sentences
    # from the beginning of the list
    for sent_tokens in category_sents[
        :num_sents_per_category
    ]:
        # Join tokens to form a single string sentence:
        texts.append(" ".join(sent_tokens))
        # Assign a numerical label based on the category index:
        labels.append(i)
# At this point, 'texts' will contain :
# 2*num_sents_per_category sentences,
# and 'labels' will contain corresponding integer labels
# (e.g., [0, 0, 1, 1] if num_sents_per_category=2)
```

5. Split the data:

```
# The dataset will have 4 samples if
# num_sents_per_category=2.
# test_size=0.5 will result in :
# 2 training samples and 2 testing samples.
X_train, X_test, y_train, y_test = train_test_split(
    texts, labels, test_size=0.5, random_state=2024)
```

With our dataset prepared, let's move on.

How to do it...

We'll demonstrate extracting meaningful text features using n-grams, POS tagging, and NER:

1. N-gram extraction:

```
# Instantiate and fit CountVectorizer() with n-grams
ngram_vectorizer = CountVectorizer(ngram_range=(1,2))
X_train_ngram = ngram_vectorizer.fit_transform(X_train)
X_test_ngram = ngram_vectorizer.transform(X_test)
```

2. POS tagging using NLTK:

```
nltk.download('punkt_tab', quiet=True)
nltk.download('averaged_perceptron_tagger_eng', quiet=True)
```

3. POS tagging example:

```
print("--- POS Tagging of Tokens and N-grams in Training
Sentences ---")
for i, text in enumerate(X_train):
    print(f"\nOriginal Sentence {i+1}: \"{text}\"")
    tokens = nltk.word_tokenize(text)
    pos_tags = nltk.pos_tag(tokens)
    # This returns a list of (token, TAG) tuples
```

4. Display tagged unigrams (individual tokens with their tags):

```
print("  Tagged Tokens (Unigrams):")
if pos_tags: # Check if list is not empty
    # Format as: token1/TAG1 token2/TAG2 ...
    unigram_str = " ".join([
        f"{token}/{tag}"
        for token, tag in pos_tags
    ])
    print(f"    {unigram_str}")
else:
    print("    (No tokens to tag)")
```

5. Display tagged bigrams:

```
# A bigram here means two consecutive (token, TAG) pairs
if len(pos_tags) >= 2:
    print("  Tagged Bigrams:")
    # nltk_ngrams on pos_tags will yield tuples
    # like ( (token1, TAG1), (token2, TAG2) )
    tagged_bigrams = list(nltk_ngrams(pos_tags, 2))
    for bigram_tuple in tagged_bigrams:
        # bigram_tuple is, e.g.,
        # (('The', 'DT'), ('quick', 'JJ'))
        # item1 is ('The', 'DT'),
        # item2 is ('quick', 'JJ')
        item1, item2 = bigram_tuple
        # Format as: token1/TAG1 token2/TAG2
        bigram_display_str = (
            f"{item1[0]}/{item1[1]} "
            f"{item2[0]}/{item2[1]}"
        )
        print(f"    {bigram_display_str}")
    else:
        print("(Not enough tagged tokens for bigrams)")
print("\n--- End of POS Tagging Display ---")

# Output:
--- POS Tagging of Tokens and N-grams in Training Sentences ---
Original Sentence 1: "Northern liberals are the chief supporters
of civil rights and of integration ."
Tagged Tokens (Unigrams): Northern/NNP liberals/NNS are/VBP the/
DT chief/JJ supporters/NNS of/IN civil/JJ rights/NNS and/CC of/
IN integration/NN
Tagged Bigrams:
Northern/NNP liberals/NNS
```

```
liberals/NNS are/VBP
are/VBP the/DT
the/DT chief/JJ
chief/JJ supporters/NNS
supporters/NNS of/IN
of/IN civil/JJ
civil/JJ rights/NNS
rights/NNS and/CC
and/CC of/IN
of/IN integration/NN
integration/NN
Original Sentence 2: "Dan Morgan told himself he would forget
Ann Turner ."
Tagged Tokens (Unigrams): Dan/NNP Morgan/NNP told/VBD himself/
PRP he/PRP would/MD forget/VB Ann/NNP Turner/NNP
Tagged Bigrams:
Dan/NNP Morgan/NNP
Morgan/NNP told/VBD
told/VBD himself/PRP
himself/PRP he/PRP
he/PRP would/MD
would/MD forget/VB
forget/VB Ann/NNP
Ann/NNP Turner/NNP
Turner/NNP
--- End of POS Tagging Display ---
```

The resulting output displays two sentences *tagged*, word-for-word, by their POS. Different taggers sometimes assign different tag labels. Please refer to the following list to identify the tags used in the output:

- NN: Noun (singular or mass)

- NNS: Noun (plural)

- JJ: Adjective

- VB: Verb (base form)

- RB: Adverb

- PRP: Pronoun

- CC: Coordinating conjunction

- DT: Determiner

- IN: Preposition or subordinating conjunction

- CD: Cardinal number

- FW: Foreign word

- NNP: Proper noun (singular)

- NNPS: Proper noun (plural)

- VBZ: Verb, third-person singular present

- VBD: Verb, past tense

- VBG: Verb, gerund or present participle

- VBN: Verb, past participle

- VBP: Verb, non-third-person singular present

How it works...

Each of the three elements we just extracted plays a vital role in text processing, depending on the use case:

- **N-grams** capture sequences of words, providing context that individual words might miss. The *n* in n-gram references the number of words considered collectively. For example, in the output of `Original Sentence 1` from our Python output, we have *bigrams* (i.e., two words). N-grams are also collected with overlap between each other, so in `Original Sentence 2`, the bigrams are `Dan Morgan`, `Morgan told`, and so on.

- **POS tagging** categorizes words into grammatical types, enabling models to leverage syntactic structure.

- **NER** identifies and classifies named entities such as persons, organizations, and locations, enriching textual data analysis.

Let's visualize the most frequent n-grams:

1. Visualize POS tag frequencies:

```
nltk.download('stopwords', quiet=True)
```

2. Get the set of English stop words for efficient lookup:

```
stop_words_set = set(stopwords.words('english'))
all_individual_pos_tags = []
```

3. Iterate through each text in X_train to extract POS tags:

```
# X_train is assumed to be a list of strings
# (sentences) from previous cells.
for text_content in X_train:
    # Split text into words
    tokens = nltk.word_tokenize(text_content)
    # Filter out stop words. Comparison is case-insensitive.
    filtered_tokens = [
        token for token in tokens
        if token.lower() not in stop_words_set
    ]
    # If the sentence becomes empty after stop word removal
    # (e.g., all tokens were stop words),
    # or if the original sentence was empty,
    # skip to the next sentence.
    if not filtered_tokens:
        continue
    # Perform Part-of-Speech tagging on the filtered tokens.
    # This returns a list of (token, TAG) tuples,
    # e.g., [('cat', 'NN'), ('sat', 'VBD')]
    pos_tagged_tokens = nltk.pos_tag(filtered_tokens)
    # Extract and store only the POS tags (the TAG part)
    for _, tag in pos_tagged_tokens:
        # We only need the tag,
        # not the token itself for this visualization
        all_individual_pos_tags.append(tag)
```

4. Count the frequencies of all collected individual POS tags:

```
pos_tag_counter = Counter(all_individual_pos_tags)
```

5. Get the 10 most common POS tags and their counts (or all if fewer than 10):

```
top_10_pos_tags = pos_tag_counter.most_common(10)
```

6. Check whether any POS tags were found before attempting to plot:

```
if top_10_pos_tags:
    # Unzip the list of (tag, count) tuples in two separate lists
    tags, counts = zip(*top_10_pos_tags)
    # plt is assumed to be imported as matplotlib.pyplot:
    plt.figure(figsize=(10,6))
    # Create a horizontal bar chart;
    # convert tuples from zip to lists for plotting
    plt.barh(list(tags), list(counts), color='lightcoral')
```

```
            plt.xlabel('Frequency')
            plt.ylabel('POS Tag')
            plt.title(
                'Top 10 Most Frequent POS Tags in '
                'Training Data (Stop Words Removed)'
            )
            # Invert y-axis to show the most frequent item at the top
            plt.gca().invert_yaxis()
            plt.show()
        else:
            # This message is displayed if X_train was empty,
            # all tokens were stop words,
            # or no tokens remained after filtering to be tagged.
            print(
                "No POS tags found to display. "
                "Check X_train data and stop word filtering process."
            )
```

This visualization highlights the most common POS tags (minus stopwords) in the dataset, which is useful for understanding key textual patterns. As you might expect, proper nouns, nouns, and adjectives make up the majority:

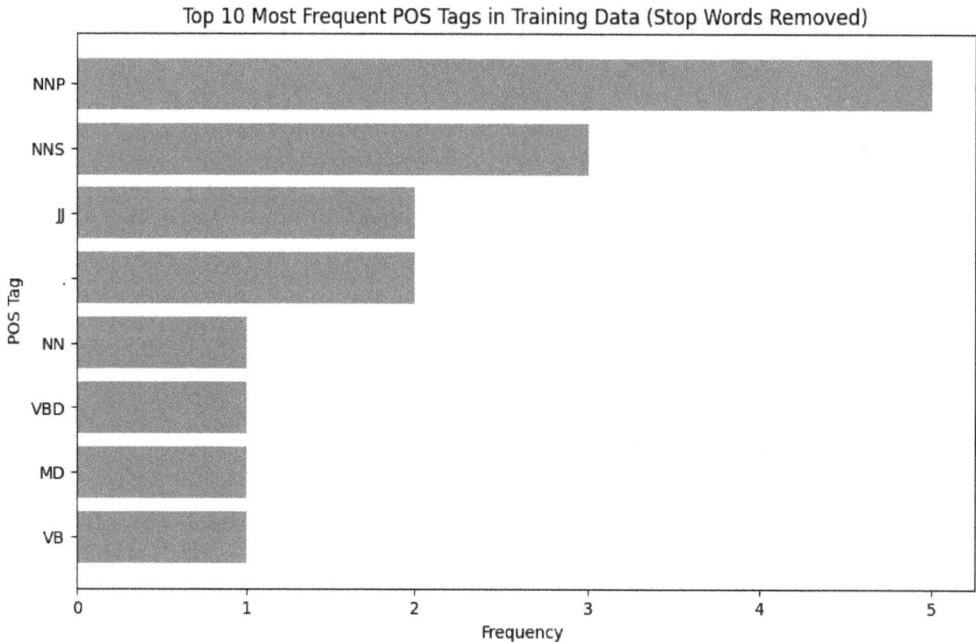

Figure 9.3 – Frequency of POS tags

While out of scope for this book, other techniques exist for text preprocessing.

There's more...

Advanced feature extraction methods also include dependency parsing and sentiment analysis, which further enrich text data and enhance predictive modeling capabilities.

Hands-on exercises

Explore these feature extraction techniques further by referencing the GitHub repository (`https://github.com/PacktPublishing/scikit-learn-Cookbook-Third-Edition`). Follow these steps:

1. Clone the GitHub repository and ensure that all the necessary libraries, including spaCy, are installed.
2. Choose a textual dataset appropriate for feature extraction.
3. Preprocess and clean your dataset, ensuring optimal quality.
4. Extract n-grams using `CountVectorizer()` with various n-gram ranges.
5. Apply POS tagging and NER using spaCy to enrich your dataset.
6. Train text classification models using the extracted features.
7. Evaluate your models with metrics such as accuracy, precision, recall, and F1-score.
8. Visualize feature extraction results, such as n-gram frequencies or named entity distributions, to interpret your model's performance.

Implementing text classification models

Implementing text classification models allows us to categorize textual data effectively, such as sentiment analysis or topic classification. Using scikit-learn, we can employ popular algorithms, including Naive Bayes, **support vector machines** (**SVM**), and logistic regression, to accurately predict categories based on textual input. Now, let's look at a recipe for applying classification techniques to text-based datasets.

Getting ready

We'll begin by preparing our environment and data for classification modeling. We will use the brown corpus again:

> **Note**
>
> You may need to run nltk.download('punkt_tab') if you run into issues using the following Punkt tokenizer. This code snippet will download the tokenizer to your scikit-learn session.

1. Load the libraries:

```
import pandas as pd
from sklearn.feature_extraction.text import TfidfVectorizer
from sklearn.model_selection import train_test_split
from sklearn.naive_bayes import MultinomialNB
from sklearn.svm import SVC
from sklearn.linear_model import LogisticRegression
from sklearn.metrics import classification_report
import nltk
from nltk.corpus import brown
import matplotlib.pyplot as plt
from sklearn.metrics import classification_report
```

2. Download the NLTK resources (if not already downloaded):

```
# It's good practice to include this, though in a real notebook,
# it might be run once in a separate cell.
try:
    nltk.data.find('corpora/brown.zip')
except nltk.downloader.DownloadError:
    nltk.download('brown', quiet=True)
try:
    # Punkt is a tokenizer dependency
    # for some NLTK corpus operations.
    nltk.data.find('tokenizers/punkt')
except nltk.downloader.DownloadError:
    nltk.download('punkt', quiet=True)
```

3. Load the dataset from the NLTK brown corpus:

```
document_ids = brown.fileids()
texts = [
    ' '.join(brown.words(file_id))
    for file_id in document_ids
]
# Each document in Brown corpus is assigned to a category
(genre).
# We use the first category as the label.
raw_labels = [
    brown.categories(file_id)[0]
    for file_id in document_ids
]
```

4. Convert string labels (categories) to numerical labels for scikit-learn:

```
unique_raw_labels = sorted(list(set(raw_labels)))
label_to_int_mapping = {
    label: i
    for i, label in enumerate(unique_raw_labels)
}
labels = [
    label_to_int_mapping[label]
    for label in raw_labels
]
```

5. Split the data:

```
# The Brown corpus has 500 documents and 15 categories.
# The minimum number of samples per category is >20,
# so stratify will work fine.
X_train, X_test, y_train, y_test = train_test_split(
    texts, labels, test_size=0.5,
    stratify=labels, random_state=2024
)
```

Now, let's train the models and compare performance.

How to do it...

We'll transform the textual data and train three different classification models:

1. Vectorize text using TF-IDF:

```
vectorizer = TfidfVectorizer()
X_train_vect = vectorizer.fit_transform(X_train)
X_test_vect = vectorizer.transform(X_test)
```

2. Train a Naive Bayes model:

```
nb_clf = MultinomialNB()
nb_clf.fit(X_train_vect, y_train)
```

3. Train an SVM model:

```
svm_clf = SVC(random_state=2024)
svm_clf.fit(X_train_vect, y_train)
```

4. Train a logistic regression model:

```
lr_clf = LogisticRegression(random_state=2024, max_iter=1000)
lr_clf.fit(X_train_vect, y_train)
```

5. Evaluate the models:

```
models = {
    'Naive Bayes': nb_clf, 'SVM': svm_clf,
    'Logistic Regression': lr_clf
}
for name, model in models.items():
    y_pred = model.predict(X_test_vect)
    print(f'{name} Classification Report:')
    # Generate classification report as a dictionary
    # Utilize unique_raw_labels for
    # target_names to show actual class names
    report_dict = classification_report(
        y_test, y_pred,
        target_names=unique_raw_labels,
        output_dict=True, zero_division=0
    )
    # Convert to DataFrame
    report_df = pd.DataFrame(report_dict).transpose()
    # Stylize the DataFrame
    styled_df = (report_df
        .style
```

```
        .background_gradient(
            cmap='Blues',
            subset=['precision', 'recall', 'f1-score']
        )
        .format({
            'precision': '{:.3f}',
            'recall': '{:.3f}',
            'f1-score': '{:.3f}',
            'support': '{:.0f}'
        })
    )
    display(styled_df)
    print("\n")
```

Each classification table shows the result of each model's fit, but do keep in mind that we are using a very small dataset (with very simple labeling), so our models will appear to perform better/worse than they might on real-world data.

	precision	recall	f1-score	support
adventure	0.000	0.000	0.000	15
belles_lettres	0.173	1.000	0.295	37
editorial	0.000	0.000	0.000	14
fiction	0.000	0.000	0.000	14
government	0.000	0.000	0.000	15
hobbies	0.000	0.000	0.000	18
humor	0.000	0.000	0.000	4
learned	0.556	0.500	0.526	40
lore	0.000	0.000	0.000	24
mystery	0.000	0.000	0.000	12
news	0.000	0.000	0.000	22
religion	0.000	0.000	0.000	9
reviews	0.000	0.000	0.000	8
romance	0.000	0.000	0.000	15
science_fiction	0.000	0.000	0.000	3
accuracy	0.228	0.228	0.228	0
macro avg	0.049	0.100	0.055	250
weighted avg	0.114	0.228	0.128	250

Figure 9.4 – Naive Bayes classification report

Naive Bayes is a simple model and, in this case, doesn't perform all that well.

	precision	recall	f1-score	support
adventure	0.400	0.133	0.200	15
belles_lettres	0.236	0.946	0.378	37
editorial	0.000	0.000	0.000	14
fiction	0.312	0.357	0.333	14
government	0.000	0.000	0.000	15
hobbies	0.000	0.000	0.000	18
humor	0.000	0.000	0.000	4
learned	0.424	0.700	0.528	40
lore	0.000	0.000	0.000	24
mystery	0.000	0.000	0.000	12
news	1.000	0.409	0.581	22
religion	0.000	0.000	0.000	9
reviews	0.000	0.000	0.000	8
romance	0.667	0.267	0.381	15
science_fiction	0.000	0.000	0.000	3
accuracy	0.332	0.332	0.332	0
macro avg	0.203	0.187	0.160	250
weighted avg	0.272	0.332	0.245	250

Figure 9.5 – SVM classification report

When comparing SVM with logistic regression, while the two techniques are relatively similar in performance, we can see that they operate differently on certain text elements in our corpus.

	precision	recall	f1-score	support
adventure	1.000	0.067	0.125	15
belles_lettres	0.231	0.919	0.370	37
editorial	0.000	0.000	0.000	14
fiction	0.000	0.000	0.000	14
government	0.000	0.000	0.000	15
hobbies	1.000	0.056	0.105	18
humor	0.000	0.000	0.000	4
learned	0.377	0.725	0.496	40
lore	0.000	0.000	0.000	24
mystery	0.000	0.000	0.000	12
news	0.875	0.318	0.467	22
religion	0.000	0.000	0.000	9
reviews	0.000	0.000	0.000	8
romance	0.643	0.600	0.621	15
science_fiction	0.000	0.000	0.000	3
accuracy	0.324	0.324	0.324	0
macro avg	0.275	0.179	0.146	250
weighted avg	0.342	0.324	0.227	250

Figure 9.6 – Logistic regression classification report

Each model's performance is highly differentiated from one another, with Naive Bayes performing quite poorly. However, across all models, we can see that tokens with a higher frequency help improve inferences.

How it works...

We've explored some of these models previously, and as you can see, once our text is preprocessed, they work well in this context, too:

- Naive Bayes performs well on text data due to its probabilistic nature and efficiency in handling large feature spaces
- SVM excels at capturing complex relationships by finding optimal hyperplanes to separate classes
- Logistic regression provides robust predictions and interpretable probabilities, making it useful for binary classification tasks

Let's visualize the classification accuracy of these models:

1. Visualize classification accuracies:

```
model_accuracies = {}
for model_name, model_instance in models.items():
    y_pred = model_instance.predict(X_test_vect)
    # Using parameters consistent with the
    # report generation in the preceding cells.
    # Assumes unique_raw_labels is defined
    # and available from a previous cell,
    # as it was used in file_context_0
    # for generating classification reports.
    # The target_names parameter does not affect the
    # overall 'accuracy' value but is included
    # for consistency.
    report_dict = classification_report(
        y_test, y_pred,
        target_names=unique_raw_labels,
        output_dict=True, zero_division=0
    )
    model_accuracies[model_name] = report_dict['accuracy']
plt.figure(figsize=(8,6))
```

2. Plot using the calculated accuracies:

```
# .keys() and .values() from the same dictionary will be in
# corresponding orders.
plt.bar(
    model_accuracies.keys(),
    model_accuracies.values(),
    color=['blue', 'orange', 'green']
)
plt.ylabel('Accuracy')
plt.title('Model Accuracy Comparison')
plt.ylim(0, 1)
plt.show()
```

This bar chart clearly demonstrates the accuracy of each text classification model:

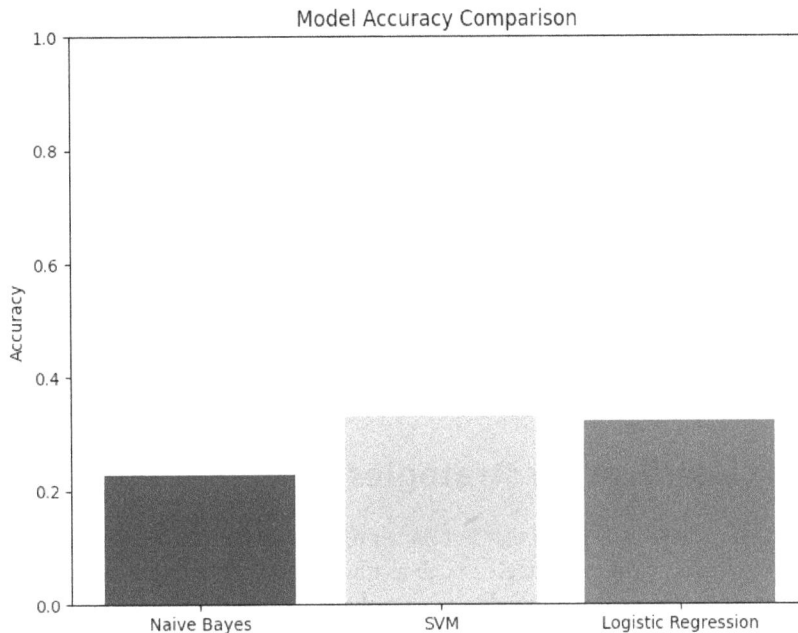

Figure 9.7 – Classification model accuracy

This is just a sample of approaches we can use for text classification. Entire Python libraries outside of scikit-learn exist for building predictive models for text. This has become especially relevant in today's world when LLM-based models have become extremely valuable.

There's more...

Additional techniques such as ensemble models, deep learning-based methods, and hyperparameter tuning can further enhance text classification performance. Experimenting with feature extraction methods such as embeddings can also boost model efficacy.

Hands-on exercises

Explore text classification further by referencing the GitHub repository (`https://github.com/PacktPublishing/scikit-learn-Cookbook-Third-Edition`). Follow these steps:

1. Clone the GitHub repository and install the required libraries.

2. Choose a dataset appropriate for text classification tasks.

3. Clean and preprocess your dataset, ensuring text quality.

4. Vectorize the text data using TF-IDF or other relevant vectorization methods.

5. Train multiple classification models (Naive Bayes, SVM, and logistic regression).

6. Evaluate the models using comprehensive metrics such as accuracy, precision, recall, and F1-score.

7. Visualize the model performance and interpret the classification results.

Multiclass classification strategies

Multiclass classification, as we saw previously in *Chapter 6*, involves predicting categories when there are more than two classes. Various strategies, such as **one-vs-rest** (**OvR**), **one-vs-one** (**OvO**), and hierarchical classification, help effectively tackle these problems. Using scikit-learn, we can implement and explore these approaches for text classification tasks. Here, we will apply techniques for when our classification model can have multiple labels or multiple labels per inference. Here, we will apply techniques for when our classification model can have multiple labels or multiple labels per inference.

Getting ready

We'll set up our environment and dataset to implement multiclass classification strategies. This time, we'll use the `brown` corpus, which, according to NLTK, *"includes content from a Firefox discussion forum, conversations overheard in New York, the movie script of Pirates of the Caribbean, personal advertisements, and wine reviews."* Follow these steps:

1. Load the libraries:

    ```
    import nltk
    from nltk.corpus import brown
    ```

2. Download the NLTK brown corpus if not already present:

    ```
    # Using quiet=True to suppress verbose download output in the
    notebook
    try:
        # Check if already downloaded and accessible
        _ = brown.fileids()
    except LookupError:
    ```

```
        nltk.download('brown', quiet=True)
    except Exception:
        # Catch other potential NLTK setup issues
        nltk.download('brown', quiet=True)
```

3. Load the dataset from the NLTK brown corpus:

```
file_ids = brown.fileids()
texts = [brown.raw(file_id) for file_id in file_ids]
# Use the filename (without .txt extension) as the label
labels = [brown.categories(file_id)[0] for file_id in file_ids]
```

4. Split the data:

```
# With 6 documents in brown,
# test_size=0.5 gives 3 train and 3 test samples.
X_train, X_test, y_train, y_test = train_test_split(
    texts, labels, test_size=0.5, random_state=2024)
```

Now, let's look at how to apply multiclass techniques.

How to do it...

We will demonstrate two primary strategies, OvR and OvO classification:

1. Vectorize the text using TF-IDF:

```
from sklearn.multiclass import (
    OneVsOneClassifier, OneVsRestClassifier)
vectorizer = TfidfVectorizer()
X_train_vect = vectorizer.fit_transform(X_train)
X_test_vect = vectorizer.transform(X_test)
```

2. Implement OvR classification:

```
ovr_clf = OneVsRestClassifier(LogisticRegression(
    random_state=2024, solver='liblinear'))
ovr_clf.fit(X_train_vect, y_train)
y_pred_ovr = ovr_clf.predict(X_test_vect)
```

3. Implement OvO classification:

```
ovo_clf = OneVsOneClassifier(LogisticRegression(
    random_state=2024, solver='liblinear'))
ovo_clf.fit(X_train_vect, y_train)
y_pred_ovo = ovo_clf.predict(X_test_vect)
```

4. Evaluate the classifiers:

```python
# Added zero_division=0 to handle cases where
# precision/recall might be ill-defined
# due to no predicted samples or no true samples for a class.
print('One-vs-Rest Classification Report:')
report_ovr_dict = classification_report(
    y_test, y_pred_ovr,
    zero_division=0, output_dict=True
)
report_ovr_df = pd.DataFrame(
    report_ovr_dict
).transpose()
styled_ovr_df = (report_ovr_df
    .style
    .background_gradient(
        cmap='Blues',
        subset=['precision', 'recall', 'f1-score']
    )
    .format({
        'precision': '{:.3f}',
        'recall': '{:.3f}',
        'f1-score': '{:.3f}',
        'support': '{:.0f}'
    })
)
display(styled_ovr_df)
print("\n")
print('One-vs-One Classification Report:')
report_ovo_dict = classification_report(
    y_test, y_pred_ovo,
    zero_division=0, output_dict=True
)
report_ovo_df = pd.DataFrame(
    report_ovo_dict
).transpose()
styled_ovo_df = (report_ovo_df
    .style
    .background_gradient(
        cmap='Blues',
        subset=['precision', 'recall', 'f1-score']
    )
    .format({
        'precision': '{:.3f}',
```

```
        'recall': '{:.3f}',
        'f1-score': '{:.3f}',
        'support': '{:.0f}'
    })
)
display(styled_ovo_df)
print("\n")
```

Let's see our classification results:

	precision	recall	f1-score	support
adventure	0.000	0.000	0.000	9
belles_lettres	0.224	0.773	0.347	22
editorial	0.000	0.000	0.000	8
fiction	0.000	0.000	0.000	9
government	0.000	0.000	0.000	9
hobbies	0.000	0.000	0.000	11
humor	0.000	0.000	0.000	3
learned	0.345	0.792	0.481	24
lore	0.000	0.000	0.000	14
mystery	0.000	0.000	0.000	7
news	0.875	0.538	0.667	13
religion	0.000	0.000	0.000	5
reviews	0.000	0.000	0.000	5
romance	0.300	0.333	0.316	9
science_fiction	0.000	0.000	0.000	2
accuracy	0.307	0.307	0.307	0
macro avg	0.116	0.162	0.121	150
weighted avg	0.182	0.307	0.205	150

Figure 9.8 – OvR classification report

An interesting note: the term `romance` did not elicit any predictive performance compared to OvO.

	precision	recall	f1-score	support
adventure	0.000	0.000	0.000	9
belles_lettres	0.185	0.773	0.298	22
editorial	0.000	0.000	0.000	8
fiction	0.000	0.000	0.000	9
government	0.000	0.000	0.000	9
hobbies	0.000	0.000	0.000	11
humor	0.000	0.000	0.000	3
learned	0.373	0.792	0.507	24
lore	0.000	0.000	0.000	14
mystery	0.000	0.000	0.000	7
news	0.833	0.385	0.526	13
religion	0.000	0.000	0.000	5
reviews	0.000	0.000	0.000	5
romance	0.000	0.000	0.000	9
science_fiction	0.000	0.000	0.000	2
accuracy	0.273	0.273	0.273	0
macro avg	0.093	0.130	0.089	150
weighted avg	0.159	0.273	0.170	150

Figure 9.9 – OvO classification report

While neither approach elicits great results, OvR slightly edges out OvO.

How it works...

As a refresher from *Chapter 6*, here are two of the techniques we utilized for classification problems featuring more than one class:

- **OvR**: Builds one classifier per class, distinguishing one class from all other classes. This strategy is computationally efficient and straightforward.

- **OvO**: Constructs classifiers for every pair of classes, resulting in a higher number of models, but often providing better performance on balanced datasets.

There's more...

Hierarchical classification structures the classification task into levels, creating multiple classifiers in a tree-like hierarchy. It helps manage complex classification scenarios and improves prediction accuracy.

Hands-on exercises

Explore multiclass classification strategies further by referencing the GitHub repository (https://github.com/PacktPublishing/scikit-learn-Cookbook-Third-Edition). Follow these steps:

1. Clone the GitHub repository and install the necessary libraries.
2. Choose a multiclass text dataset suitable for classification.
3. Preprocess and clean your dataset thoroughly.
4. Convert textual data into numerical features using vectorization techniques such as TF-IDF.
5. Implement and compare multiclass classification strategies (OvR and OvO).
6. Evaluate classifiers using metrics such as accuracy, precision, recall, and F1-score.
7. Visualize and interpret the classification results to better understand model performance.

Evaluating text models

Evaluating text models involves using metrics specifically tailored to assess the performance of text classification tasks. Metrics such as precision, recall, F1-score, and confusion matrices provide detailed insights into how accurately and effectively our models classify textual data, allowing us to interpret and improve model outcomes. However, although it falls outside the scope of this book, LLMs require far more complex techniques to evaluate their performance, especially when generating text rather than using it in more simplistic ML problems such as classification. This recipe applies some of the evaluation techniques we've used earlier to text classification.

Getting ready

Let's set up the necessary libraries and dataset for evaluating text classification models:

1. Load the libraries:

```
from sklearn.feature_extraction.text import TfidfVectorizer
from sklearn.model_selection import train_test_split
from sklearn.linear_model import LogisticRegression
from sklearn.metrics import (
    precision_score, recall_score, f1_score,
    confusion_matrix, classification_report
```

```
)
import matplotlib.pyplot as plt
import seaborn as sns
import nltk
from nltk.corpus import movie_reviews
import random
```

2. Download the NLTK data (the `movie_reviews` corpus) if not already downloaded:

```
try:
    # Check if the corpus is accessible
    movie_reviews.categories()
except LookupError:
    nltk.download('movie_reviews')
```

3. Load the dataset from the NLTK `movie_reviews` corpus:

```
documents = []
for category in movie_reviews.categories():
    for fileid in movie_reviews.fileids(category):
        documents.append((
            list(movie_reviews.words(fileid)),
            category
        ))
```

4. Shuffle the documents for better splitting.

```
# Using a fixed seed for reproducibility,
# consistent with random_state in train_test_split.
random.seed(2024)
random.shuffle(documents)
```

5. Prepare texts (joining words into strings) and labels:

```
texts = [" ".join(words) for words, category in documents]
labels = [category for words, category in documents]
```

6. Split the data:

```
# Kept test_size and random_state as in the original selection
X_train, X_test, y_train, y_test = train_test_split(
    texts, labels, test_size=0.5, random_state=2024)
```

With our dataset created, let's move on.

How to do it...

We'll use logistic regression as an example to demonstrate evaluating text models:

1. Vectorize the text using TF-IDF:

    ```
    vectorizer = TfidfVectorizer()
    X_train_vect = vectorizer.fit_transform(X_train)
    X_test_vect = vectorizer.transform(X_test)
    ```

2. Train a logistic regression classifier:

    ```
    clf = LogisticRegression(random_state=2024)
    clf.fit(X_train_vect, y_train)
    ```

3. Make predictions:

    ```
    y_pred = clf.predict(X_test_vect)
    ```

4. Evaluate the model:

    ```
    print("Precision:", precision_score(
        y_test, y_pred, average='weighted', zero_division=0))
    print("Recall:", recall_score(
        y_test, y_pred, average='weighted', zero_division=0))
    print("F1 Score:", f1_score(
        y_test, y_pred, average='weighted', zero_division=0))
    ```

5. Generate a classification report as a styled DataFrame:

    ```
    report_dict = classification_report(
        y_test, y_pred, labels=clf.classes_,
        target_names=clf.classes_,
        output_dict=True, zero_division=0
    )
    report_df = pd.DataFrame(report_dict).transpose()
    print("\nClassification Report:")
    display(report_df.style.set_caption("Classification Report"))
    ```

6. Generate and visualize a confusion matrix:

    ```
    cm = confusion_matrix(y_test, y_pred, labels=clf.classes_)
    sns.heatmap(
        cm, annot=True, fmt='d',
        xticklabels=clf.classes_,
        yticklabels=clf.classes_, cmap='Blues'
    )
    plt.xlabel('Predicted Labels')
    ```

```
plt.ylabel('True Labels')
plt.title('Confusion Matrix')
plt.show()
```

This confusion matrix visualization clearly displays how well the model is performing across different classes:

	precision	recall	f1-score	support
neg	0.791016	0.818182	0.804369	495.000000
pos	0.815574	0.788119	0.801611	505.000000
accuracy	0.803000	0.803000	0.803000	0.803000
macro avg	0.803295	0.803150	0.802990	1000.000000
weighted avg	0.803417	0.803000	0.802977	1000.000000

Figure 9.10 – Classification report

The model performs well (again, what is considered *well* should be based on the use case). Both positive and negative reviews were identified with similar levels of accuracy:

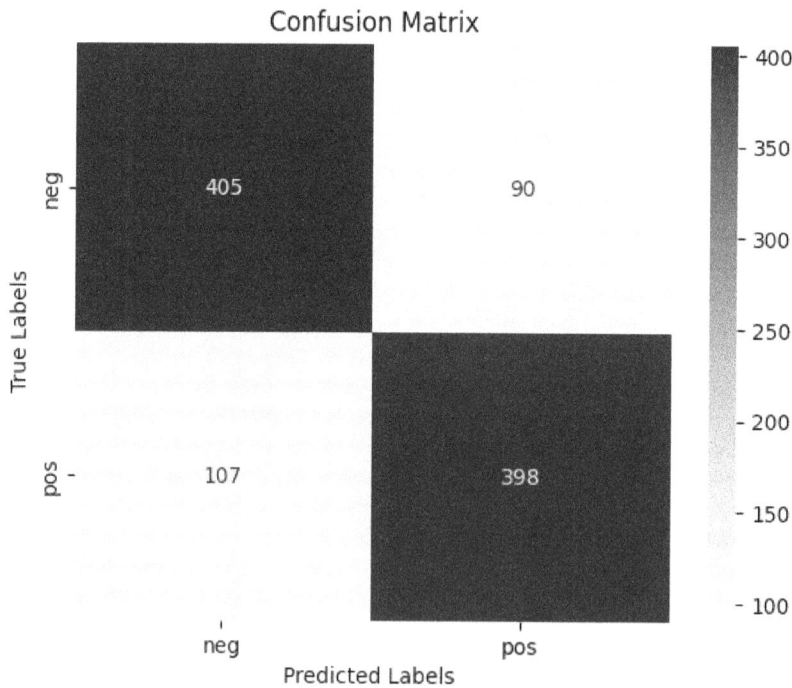

Figure 9.11 – Confusion matrix

Both the classification report and confusion matrix reveal solid performance from our modeling.

How it works...

These terms should already be familiar, but let's recap:

- **Precision** measures the accuracy of positive predictions
- **Recall** (sensitivity) assesses the ability to identify positive instances
- **F1-score** provides a balanced measure by combining precision and recall
- **Confusion matrices** visually represent the accuracy of predictions for each class, helping us easily identify misclassifications

There's more...

Evaluating models using additional metrics such as ROC curves and AUC can provide further insights, especially for binary classification tasks. Cross-validation can also help in obtaining robust evaluations by mitigating variance in performance estimates.

Hands-on exercises

Explore model evaluation metrics further by referencing the GitHub repository (`https://github.com/PacktPublishing/scikit-learn-Cookbook-Third-Edition`). Follow these steps:

1. Clone the GitHub repository and install the necessary libraries.
2. Select an appropriate textual dataset for classification.
3. Preprocess and clean your textual dataset.
4. Train a text classification model, such as logistic regression.
5. Evaluate your model using precision, recall, F1-score, and confusion matrices.
6. Visualize these metrics to interpret and enhance your model's performance.
7. Experiment with additional metrics and cross-validation to thoroughly assess your model.

Practical exercises in text processing

In this final section, we will engage in practical exercises involving preprocessing text data, vectorizing it, extracting meaningful features, and building multiclass classification models. These exercises are designed to reinforce the concepts learned throughout the chapter and demonstrate how to effectively apply text processing and classification techniques in various scenarios. By the end of this section, we will have hands-on experience to apply to our own ML projects.

Exercise 1: Preprocessing and vectorizing text

In this exercise, we'll preprocess raw text data and transform it into numerical features using vectorization techniques.

Here are the implementation steps:

1. Load the libraries.

2. Load the dataset.

3. Preprocess the data (basic cleaning).

4. Vectorize the text.

Exercise 2: Feature extraction with n-grams

In this exercise, we'll extract n-gram features from text to capture context better for classification tasks.

Here are the implementation steps:

1. Load the libraries.

2. Load the dataset.

3. Extract n-gram features.

Exercise 3: Building and evaluating a multiclass classifier

Here, we will build, train, and evaluate a multiclass classifier using logistic regression.

Here are the implementation steps:

1. Load the libraries.

2. Load the dataset.

3. Vectorize the text.

4. Split the data.

5. Train the classifier.

6. Make predictions and evaluate.

Get This Book's PDF Version and Exclusive Extras

UNLOCK NOW

Scan the QR code (or go to packtpub.com/unlock). Search for this book by name, confirm the edition, and then follow the steps on the page.

Note: Keep your invoice handy. Purchases made directly from Packt don't require an invoice.

10
Clustering Techniques

Up to this point, our **machine learning** (**ML**) models have been trained to uncover patterns in data that elicit a specific response or responses from our models' inferences. In other words, "given these input values, can we train a model that can predict an output value when given new inputs that lack the desired output target?" This is supervised learning in a nutshell: our training data contains both inputs and outputs. Yet, we don't always have data with outputs, and sometimes, rather than making predictions, we are more concerned with understanding underlying patterns in our data for the sake of just that. In this final section, we will look at unsupervised learning techniques where our data doesn't have an output we're trying to predict. As we'll see, some of these techniques are precursors for building supervised learning models, so the two are intimately related.

This chapter will explore various clustering techniques, including K-means, hierarchical clustering, and **Density-Based Spatial Clustering of Applications with Noise** (**DBSCAN**), focusing on how to group data points into clusters based on their features. Your goal will be to implement these algorithms using scikit-learn, working through exercises with real-world datasets to understand the strengths and limitations of each method, as well as techniques for evaluating clustering performance.

In this chapter, we're going to cover the following recipes:

- Introduction to clustering
- K-means clustering
- Hierarchical clustering
- Density-based clustering with DBSCAN
- Cluster evaluation metrics
- Choosing the right clustering algorithm
- Advanced clustering techniques

Technical requirements

It is advisable to create a Python environment to safely isolate your work from other Python installations/ libraries. See the GitHub repository for more details (`https://github.com/PacktPublishing/ scikit-learn-Cookbook-Third-Edition`).

- Git >=2.46.x

- Python >=3.9.x

- Cloned GitHub repository and Python environment built from the `requirements.txt` file

Introduction to clustering

Clustering is an unsupervised learning technique used to group similar data points based on their intrinsic structure – a structure that might not be readily apparent just by eyeballing a table of data. It's useful for tasks like market segmentation, anomaly detection, and organizing unlabeled data. Some common challenges include determining the number of clusters, handling noise, and choosing appropriate algorithms for different data types and scales. Just keep in mind that clustering, like most unsupervised learning techniques, is a bit more of an art than a science!

As an example of clustering applied to the real world, let's consider market segmentation. Businesses realize that not all of their customers are the same and typically interact with them in a variety of ways. Therefore, it doesn't make sense to treat all customers the same way. But how do we uncover these subpopulations of our customers so we can customize their user experience? Clustering, applied to market segmentation, is just such an approach. Given a set of customer data – say, recent sales, purchase frequency, product categories purchased together, and so on – with clustering, we can find these subgroups and market to them more effectively than just a single blanket campaign where we treat them all the same.

Let's start by creating some sample data, then we'll jump into our first technique, K-means clustering.

Getting ready

We'll start by creating some dummy data with scikit-learn's `make_blobs()` function (which is very appropriately named).

1. Load the libraries:

    ```
    import numpy as np
    import pandas as pd
    import matplotlib.pyplot as plt
    from sklearn.datasets import make_blobs
    from sklearn.preprocessing import StandardScaler
    ```

2. Create the dataset:

```
X, _ = make_blobs(
    n_samples=300, centers=4,
    cluster_std=0.60, random_state=2024
)
X = StandardScaler().fit_transform(X)
```

With this code, we've generated 300 sample datapoints around 4 centroids.

How to do it...

Let's have a look at what we generated. You'll also notice that we applied `StandardScaler()` in order to transform our values using z-scores. This will make our clusters easier to visualize.

1. Visualize the raw data:

```
plt.figure(figsize=(8, 6))
plt.scatter(X[:, 0], X[:, 1], s=50)
plt.title("Sample Dataset for Clustering")
plt.xlabel("Feature 1")
plt.ylabel("Feature 2")
plt.show()
```

Let's see what our generated data looks like.

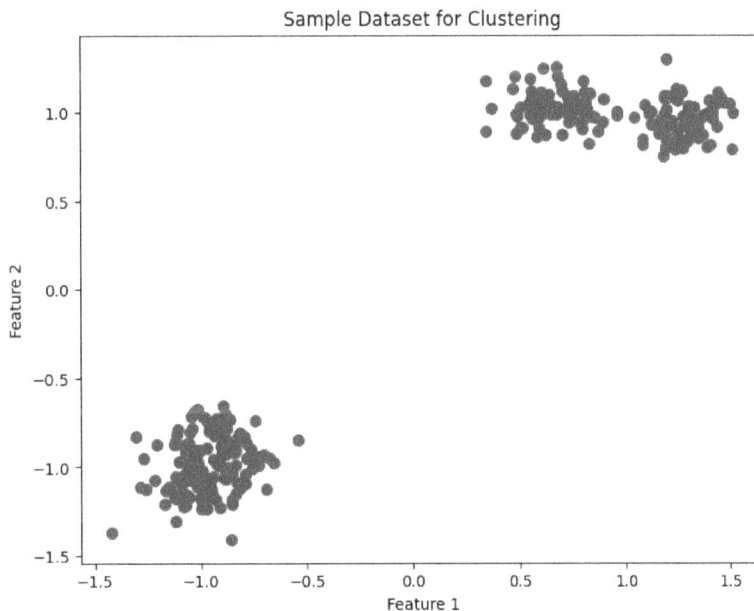

Figure 10.1 – scikit-learn generated "blob" data

This scatter plot shows the raw dataset that we'll use for demonstrating clustering methods. The clusters are currently unlabeled and serve as the input for the algorithms we'll explore.

How it works...

Clustering works by calculating the similarity between data points based on distance metrics or density measures. Depending on the algorithm, the approach to determining clusters can vary significantly:

- **Centroid-based**: Forms clusters around a central point (e.g., K-means)
- **Connectivity-based**: Builds clusters using hierarchical linkages (e.g., hierarchical/agglomerative clustering)
- **Density-based**: Detects clusters of varying shape and identifies noise (e.g., DBSCAN)

These differences impact the suitability of each technique based on data shape, noise, and scale.

Hands-on exercises

To illustrate these techniques, please reference the GitHub repository (`https://github.com/PacktPublishing/scikit-learn-Cookbook-Third-Edition`). You will engage in hands-on exercises using clustering algorithms in scikit-learn. Although we've included the preceding code examples, we encourage you to explore on your own and try using these tools with different arguments to see what results. The following steps outline a general workflow:

1. Clone the GitHub repository and ensure all necessary libraries are installed.
2. Generate synthetic data using `make_blobs()` or load a real-world unlabeled dataset.
3. Visualize the data to understand its structure.
4. Apply different clustering algorithms (e.g., KMeans, AgglomerativeClustering, DBSCAN).
5. Visualize the resulting clusters to compare algorithm effectiveness.
6. Experiment with different parameters and observe how the clusters change.

K-means clustering

K-means is a *centroid-based* clustering algorithm that partitions data into a predefined number of clusters, which is perfect considering our data is quite *blobby* from the *Introduction to clustering* section. First, K-means randomly creates centroids in our feature space. Next, it iteratively assigns each data point to the nearest cluster centroid and then recalculates the cluster centroids and moves them in the feature space so that they are positioned approximately within the average distance among the data points currently assigned to them in the current iteration. This process continues until *convergence*, where the centroids don't move much and data points are not reassigned to other cluster centroids. K-means is efficient and works best when clusters are convex, isotropic, and roughly equal in size... which also can be its greatest weakness. This recipe will walk you through this process.

Getting ready

Here, we'll use the previous dummy data and just load in the KMeans() function from scikit-learn.

1. Load the libraries:

```
from sklearn.cluster import KMeans
```

2. Reuse the dataset from the previous recipe:

```
# Dataset already loaded and scaled as X
```

Now, let's generate the model for K-means clustering to assign our datapoints to a given cluster.

How to do it...

To apply K-means, we have to simply provide n_clusters as our only required argument (the *k* in *K-means* is a reference to this cluster number). This initializes the same number of centroids when we begin the iterative process described in the *Introduction to clustering* section. This also implies that we know, or at least can estimate, the number of clusters beforehand. This could also be a potential limitation of K-means if we don't have an estimate to begin with. However, typically we take steps to refine this value, as we'll see here.

1. Apply K-means clustering:

```
kmeans = KMeans(n_clusters=4, random_state=2024)
y_kmeans = kmeans.fit_predict(X)
```

2. Plot the clustered data:

```
plt.figure(figsize=(8, 6))
plt.scatter(
    X[:, 0], X[:, 1],
    c=y_kmeans, s=50, cmap='viridis'
)
centers = kmeans.cluster_centers_
plt.scatter(
    centers[:, 0], centers[:, 1],
    c='black', s=200, alpha=0.75, marker='X'
)
plt.title("K-Means Clustering Results")
plt.xlabel("Feature 1")
plt.ylabel("Feature 2")
plt.show()
```

The visualization of the final solution is color-coded for easier cluster identification.

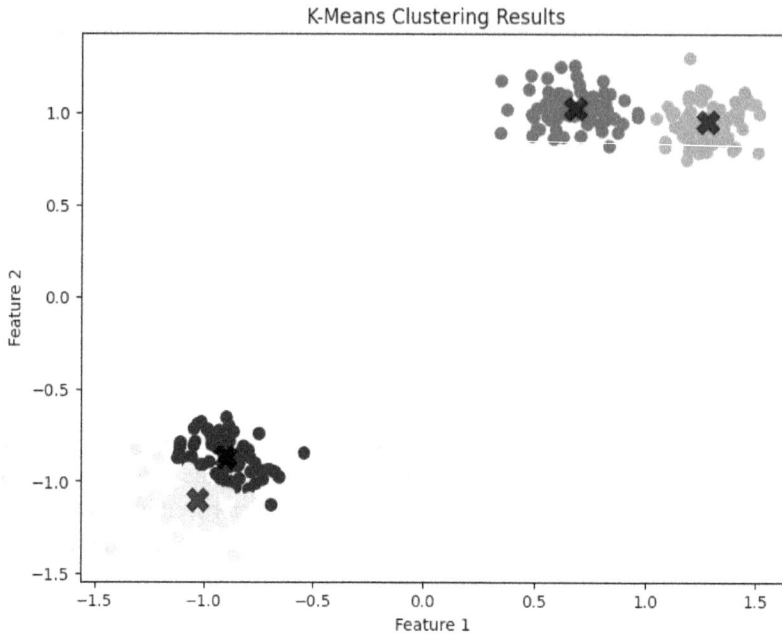

Figure 10.2 – K-means clustering results

This plot displays the four clusters found by K-means, along with their respective centroids marked by black Xs.

How it works...

K-means follows an iterative refinement approach:

- **Initialization**: The centroids of k clusters are initialized randomly or using methods such as *K-means++*

- **Assignment step**: Each data point is assigned to the nearest centroid based on a distance metric (typically, Euclidean distance, which uses the common straight-line distance described using x/y coordinates)

- **Update step**: The centroid of each cluster is recalculated as the mean of all assigned points

This process continues until the assignments no longer change (convergence) or a maximum number of iterations is reached. K-means minimizes within-cluster variance (inertia).

There's more...

How do you choose the optimal number of clusters? One popular method to determine the best value of k is the elbow method. It involves plotting the sum of squared distances (inertia) for a range of k values and looking for the point where adding more clusters yields diminishing returns.

1. Calculate and plot clustering inertia:

```
inertia = []
k_values = range(1, 10)
for k in k_values:
    km = KMeans(n_clusters=k, random_state=2024)
    km.fit(X)
    inertia.append(km.inertia_)
plt.plot(k_values, inertia, 'bo-')
plt.xlabel("Number of Clusters (k)")
plt.ylabel("Inertia")
plt.title("Elbow Method for Optimal k")
plt.show()
```

According to the chart, two to three clusters are the optimal choices for **k**.

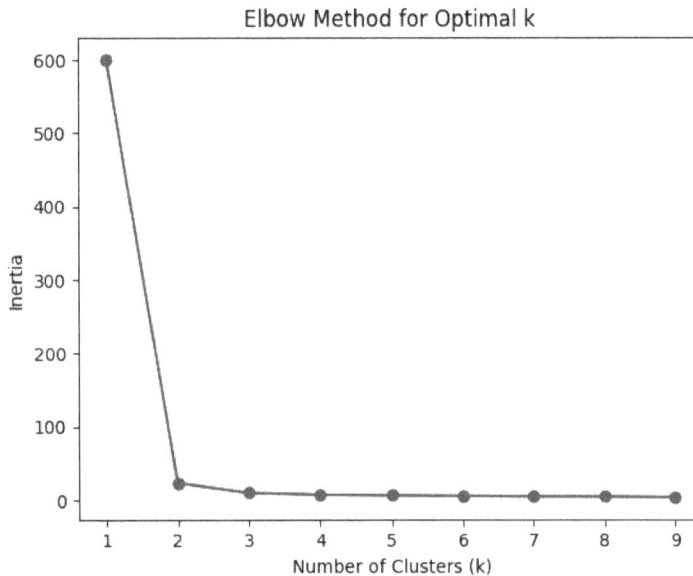

Figure 10.3 – Elbow method for optimal K

This elbow plot helps us visually identify the optimal number of clusters by locating the *elbow point* where the rate of decrease in inertia sharply slows.

Hands-on exercises

To illustrate these techniques, please reference the GitHub repository (`https://github.com/PacktPublishing/scikit-learn-Cookbook-Third-Edition`). You will engage in hands-on exercises using K-means clustering. Although we've included the preceding code examples, we encourage you to explore on your own and try using these tools with different arguments to see what results. The following steps outline a general workflow:

1. Clone the GitHub repository and ensure all necessary libraries are installed.

2. Generate or load an unlabeled dataset (e.g., using `make_blobs()`).

3. Use KMeans from `sklearn.cluster` to fit and predict cluster assignments.

4. Visualize the results using a scatter plot and cluster centroids.

5. Apply the elbow method to determine the optimal number of clusters.

6. Try changing the initialization method or using different values of "k" to observe the impact on clustering.

Hierarchical clustering

Hierarchical clustering builds nested clusters by either merging or splitting them successively. It is especially useful when the number of clusters is not known in advance, and it provides a tree-like structure (dendrogram) that visually conveys relationships among the data. There are two main approaches: agglomerative (bottom-up) and divisive (top-down). In practice, agglomerative clustering is more commonly used and supported directly in scikit-learn. This recipe will utilize that approach for hierarchical clustering.

Getting ready

As before, we can use the same dataset we created earlier and simply apply the new technique to it by importing the scikit-learn class and helper functions.

1. Load the libraries:

    ```
    from sklearn.cluster import AgglomerativeClustering
    from scipy.cluster.hierarchy import dendrogram, linkage
    ```

2. Reuse the dataset from the *Introduction to clustering* section.

    ```
    # Dataset already loaded and scaled as X
    ```

Now, let's apply the clustering technique.

How to do it...

In the following steps, we apply agglomerative clustering. We can specify a number of clusters, or we can specify a distance metric threshold to create a cutoff point for the number of clusters returned – one or the other, but in its purest form, no set number of clusters is required.

1. Apply agglomerative clustering:

```
agg = AgglomerativeClustering(n_clusters=4)
y_agg = agg.fit_predict(X)
```

2. Plot the clustered data:

```
plt.figure(figsize=(8, 6))
plt.scatter(X[:, 0], X[:, 1], c=y_agg, cmap='viridis', s=50)
plt.title("Agglomerative Clustering Results")
plt.xlabel("Feature 1")
plt.ylabel("Feature 2")
plt.show()
```

Since our data is a bit *messy*, it will be interesting to see how our algorithm clusters it.

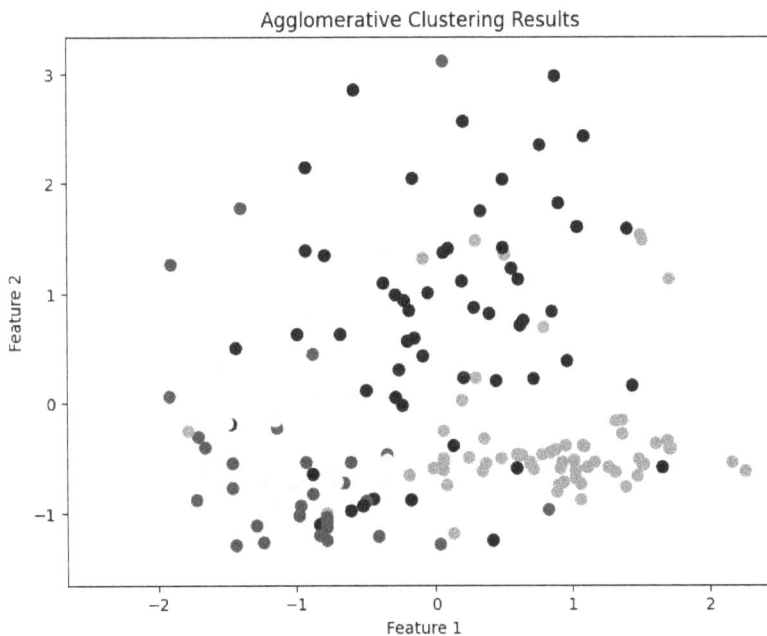

Figure 10.4 – Agglomerative clustering results

3. Generate the dendrogram using SciPy:

```
linked = linkage(X, method='ward')
plt.figure(figsize=(12, 6))
dendrogram(linked, leaf_rotation=90, leaf_font_size=8)
plt.title("Dendrogram for Hierarchical Clustering")
plt.xlabel("Sample Index")
plt.ylabel("Distance")
plt.xticks(rotation=45)
plt.tight_layout()
plt.show()
```

Let's see what our plot looks like.

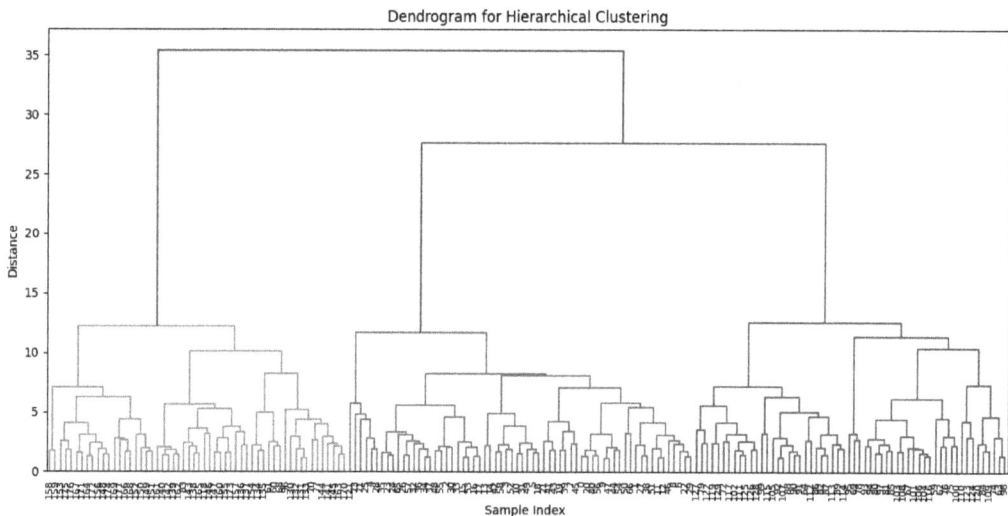

Figure 10.5 — Dendrogram for hierarchical clustering

The scatter plot shows the clusters found by the agglomerative algorithm, while the dendrogram reveals the full hierarchical structure used to determine these groupings.

> **Note**
>
> Due to the number of data points in the dataset, the *x* axis can be difficult to read as each data point is represented. More important, however, is understanding how the hierarchical process slowly merged data points into clusters as we move from the bottom of the dendrogram to the top.

How it works...

Agglomerative clustering follows a bottom-up approach:

- Each data point starts as its own cluster
- At each step, the two closest clusters are merged based on a linkage criterion
- This continues until all points are merged into a single cluster or until a stopping condition (such as a predefined number of clusters) is met

The linkage method defines how the distance between clusters is calculated:

- **Ward**: Minimizes the variance of the merged clusters (default and most commonly used)
- **Complete**: Maximum distance between points in two clusters
- **Average**: Average distance between all pairs of points
- **Single**: Minimum distance between points

The dendrogram visualizes the clustering process and can guide the selection of the number of clusters by choosing a height to *cut* the tree.

There's more...

Dendrograms are powerful for understanding the structure of the data. If clusters are well-separated, the height of the linkage distances will show clear gaps. This can help in determining whether a natural grouping exists in the data.

While scikit-learn does not provide native support for divisive clustering (top-down), similar approaches can be implemented using other tools or custom algorithms. Divisive clustering starts with all points in one cluster and recursively splits them.

Hands-on exercises

To illustrate these techniques, please reference the GitHub repository (`https://github.com/PacktPublishing/scikit-learn-Cookbook-Third-Edition`). You will engage in hands-on exercises using hierarchical clustering. Although we've included the preceding code examples, we encourage you to explore on your own and try using these tools with different arguments to see what results. The following steps outline a general workflow:

1. Clone the GitHub repository and ensure all necessary libraries are installed.
2. Generate or reuse a dataset suitable for clustering.
3. Apply `AgglomerativeClustering()` from `sklearn.cluster` with different linkage methods.

4. Visualize the clustered results using a scatter plot.

5. Generate a dendrogram using `scipy.cluster.hierarchy` to interpret the hierarchical structure.

6. Explore how the number of clusters changes when cutting the dendrogram at different levels.

Density-based clustering with DBSCAN

DBSCAN is a somewhat unique clustering algorithm capable of identifying clusters of varying shapes and sizes. It differs from K-means and hierarchical clustering by not requiring the number of clusters to be specified in advance and by handling outliers (noise) effectively. This means, unlike K-means, it does not generate centroids a priori. This recipe applies DBSCAN on a rather unconventional dataset.

Getting ready

Here, we are going to use another data generator function in scikit-learn, called `make_moons()`, which, again, like `make_blobs()`, is aptly named!

1. Load the libraries:

    ```
    from sklearn.cluster import DBSCAN
    from sklearn.datasets import make_moons
    ```

2. Create a new one with noise:

    ```
    X, _ = make_moons(n_samples=300, noise=0.1,
                    random_state=2024)
    ```

Another scikit-learn dataset generator (`make_moons`) creates crescent-shaped datasets for exploring clustering algorithms that work better with data not arranged in spherical groupings.

How to do it...

Let's execute DBSCAN. In this example, we are setting the two most important arguments, `eps` and `min_samples`, to `0.2` and 5, respectively. More on these follows.

1. Apply DBSCAN:

    ```
    dbscan = DBSCAN(eps=0.2, min_samples=5)
    y_db = dbscan.fit_predict(X)
    ```

2. Plot the DBSCAN results:

    ```
    plt.figure(figsize=(8, 6))
    plt.scatter(X[:, 0], X[:, 1], c=y_db, cmap='plasma', s=50)
    plt.title("DBSCAN Clustering Results")
    ```

```
plt.xlabel("Feature 1")
plt.ylabel("Feature 2")
plt.show()
```

Next, we'll see how the make_moons algorithm generates data with a unique shape that some clustering techniques, such as K-means, would fail at providing an optimal clustering solution to.

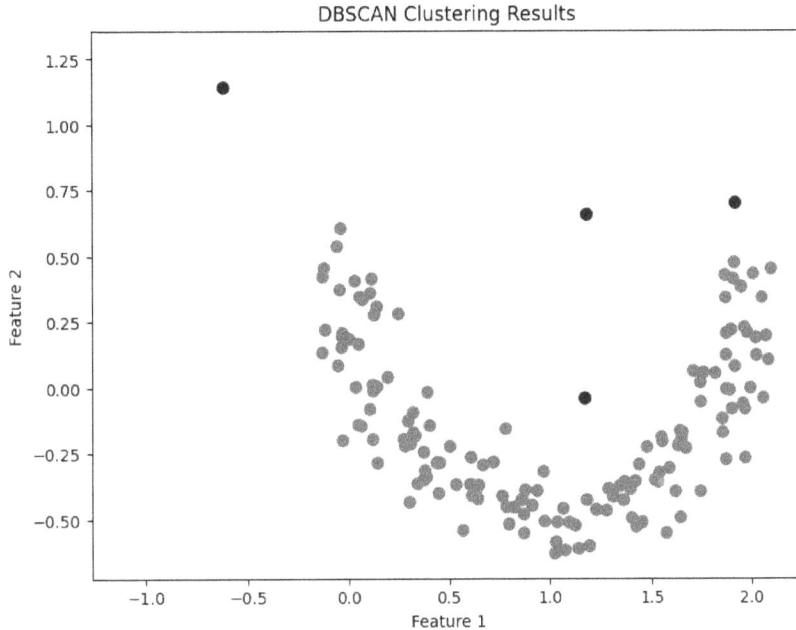

Figure 10.6 – DBSCAN clustering results

This plot shows how DBSCAN groups the crescent-shaped data while identifying noise points (typically labeled as -1) that don't belong to any cluster.

How it works...

DBSCAN groups data points based on two main parameters:

- eps: The radius of the neighborhood around a point
- min_samples: The minimum number of points required to form a dense region

Points are classified into three categories:

- **Core points**: Have at least `min_samples` within eps distance
- **Border points**: Fall within the eps neighborhood of a core point but have fewer than `min_samples` neighbors themselves
- **Noise points**: Neither core nor border points

DBSCAN starts from an unvisited point, checks its *neighborhood*, and forms clusters by recursively including density-connected neighbors. It's particularly good at identifying non-spherical clusters and separating noise, which is highly valuable in real-world applications where data is often *dirty*.

There's more...

How do you choose `eps` and `min_samples`? The performance of DBSCAN is sensitive to the choice of `eps` and `min_samples`. A **k-distance plot** can help determine a good value for `eps`. Plot the distance to the k-th nearest neighbor (where `k` = `min_samples`) for all points and look for a sharp bend (elbow).

1. Load the libraries:

```
from sklearn.neighbors import NearestNeighbors
```

2. Generate the nearest neighbors:

```
neighbors = NearestNeighbors(n_neighbors=5)
neighbors_fit = neighbors.fit(X)
distances, indices = neighbors_fit.kneighbors(X)
distances = np.sort(distances[:, 4])
```

3. Plot k-distance:

```
plt.figure(figsize=(8, 6))
plt.plot(distances)
plt.title("k-Distance Plot (k=5)")
plt.xlabel("Points sorted by distance")
plt.ylabel("5th Nearest Neighbor Distance")
plt.show()
```

Let's review our plot for insights.

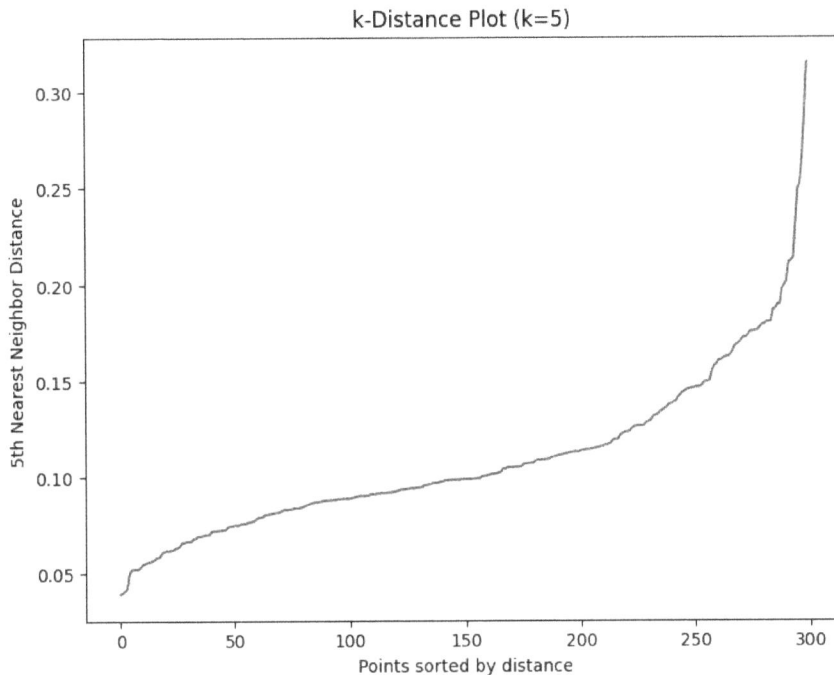

Figure 10.7 – k-distance plot

This elbow in the distance plot helps select a good `eps` parameter.

Hands-on exercises

To illustrate these techniques, please reference the GitHub repository (`https://github.com/PacktPublishing/scikit-learn-Cookbook-Third-Edition`). You will engage in hands-on exercises using DBSCAN. Although we've included the preceding code examples, we encourage you to explore on your own and try using these tools with different arguments to see what results. The following steps outline a general workflow:

1. Clone the GitHub repository and ensure all necessary libraries are installed.
2. Create a noisy dataset using functions such as `make_moons()` or `make_circles()`.
3. Use DBSCAN from `sklearn.cluster` and apply it to the dataset.
4. Visualize the results and identify which points are considered noise.
5. Generate a k-distance plot using `NearestNeighbors` to help choose an appropriate `eps`.
6. Try different combinations of `eps` and `min_samples` to see their effect on the clustering results.

Cluster evaluation metrics

Evaluating the results of clustering is crucial to assessing the quality and relevance of the groupings discovered by unsupervised algorithms. However, unlike supervised learning, clustering lacks true labels or target values we're trying to predict, so we rely on internal and external evaluation metrics such as the **silhouette score**, **Davies-Bouldin index**, and adjusted **Rand index** to determine how well the model has performed. Again, with unsupervised learning techniques, evaluation can be seen as more of an art than a science, but we can still make educated decisions with the right tools. This recipe explores some methods for evaluating your clustering techniques and optimizing your solution.

Getting ready

To begin, we'll load our evaluation metrics, create a dummy dataset, and fit a K-means clustering model.

1. Load the libraries:

```
from sklearn.metrics import (
    silhouette_score,
    davies_bouldin_score,
    adjusted_rand_score
)
from sklearn.datasets import make_blobs
from sklearn.cluster import KMeans
```

2. Generate a labeled dataset for evaluation:

```
X, y_true = make_blobs(
    n_samples=300, centers=4,
    cluster_std=0.60, random_state=2024
)
```

3. Fit KMeans() for use with evaluation metrics:

```
kmeans = KMeans(n_clusters=4, random_state=2024)
y_kmeans = kmeans.fit_predict(X)
```

Now, with our fitted model, let's apply evaluation techniques for deeper insight into how well it fits the data.

How to do it...

Applying the evaluation techniques is straightforward and simply takes the input data and the trained model.

1. Calculate the silhouette score:

```
sil_score = silhouette_score(X, y_kmeans)
print(f"Silhouette Score: {sil_score:.3f}")
```

2. Calculate the Davies-Bouldin index:

```
db_index = davies_bouldin_score(X, y_kmeans)
print(f"Davies-Bouldin Index: {db_index:.3f}")
```

3. (Optional) Calculate the adjusted Rand index if the ground truth is known:

```
ari = adjusted_rand_score(y_true, y_kmeans)
print(f"Adjusted Rand Index: {ari:.3f}")

# Output:
Silhouette Score: 0.534
Davies-Bouldin Index: 0.702
Adjusted Rand Index: 0.814
```

These metrics help us evaluate clustering quality from different perspectives. The silhouette score and Davies-Bouldin index do not require ground truth, while the adjusted Rand index assumes we know the true labels for comparison.

How it works...

Here is a breakdown of how each technique helps us understand our clustering solution.

- **Silhouette score**: Measures how similar a point is to its own cluster compared to other clusters. It ranges from -1 (poor clustering) to 1 (dense and well-separated clusters). A higher value indicates better-defined clusters.

- **Davies-Bouldin index**: Evaluates the average similarity ratio of each cluster with its most similar one. Lower values indicate better clustering. Unlike the silhouette score, this metric penalizes overlapping clusters.

- **Adjusted Rand Index (ARI)**: Compares the clustering result to a known ground truth by examining all pairs of samples and counting pairs assigned to the same or different clusters. It corrects for chance and ranges from -1 to 1, where 1 indicates perfect agreement.

There's more...

Additional metrics to consider include the **Calinski-Harabasz index**. This is also called the variance ratio criterion, and it favors well-separated and dense clusters. Like the Davies-Bouldin index, it is computed using intra-cluster and inter-cluster dispersion.

Hands-on exercises

To illustrate these techniques, please reference the GitHub repository (`https://github.com/PacktPublishing/scikit-learn-Cookbook-Third-Edition`). You will engage in hands-on exercises using scikit-learn's clustering evaluation metrics. Although we've included the preceding code examples, we encourage you to explore on your own and try using these tools with different arguments to see what results. The following steps outline a general workflow:

1. Generate or load a dataset suitable for clustering.
2. Apply `KMeans()` or another clustering algorithm to fit and predict cluster labels.
3. Compute `silhouette_score` and `davies_bouldin_score` to evaluate cluster quality.
4. If the ground truth is available, use `adjusted_rand_score` for external evaluation.
5. Try varying the number of clusters and compare how the evaluation metrics respond.
6. Visualize clustering results alongside metric scores for deeper insight.

Choosing the right clustering algorithm

Selecting the most suitable clustering algorithm depends heavily on the structure and properties of the dataset. There's no one-size-fits-all solution – different algorithms are suited to different types of data distributions, levels of noise, and dimensionality! This recipe compares key characteristics of clustering algorithms and provides guidance for choosing among them.

Getting ready

Let's begin by creating a variety of dummy datasets using scikit-learn functions we've used before.

1. Load the libraries:

    ```
    from sklearn.datasets import (
        make_moons, make_blobs, make_ circles)
    from sklearn.preprocessing import StandardScaler
    ```

2. Create and scale different datasets:

```
X_blobs, _ = make_blobs(
    n_samples=300, centers=3,
    cluster_std=0.6, random_state=2024
)
X_moons, _ = make_moons(
    n_samples=300, noise=0.1,
    random_state=2024
)
X_circles, _ = make_circles(
    n_samples=300, noise=0.05,
    factor=0.5, random_state=2024
)
X_blobs = StandardScaler().fit_transform(X_blobs)
X_moons = StandardScaler().fit_transform(X_moons)
X_circles = StandardScaler().fit_transform(X_circles)
```

Now we have three datasets with a variety of arrangements for our datapoints. Keep in mind: in the real world, you might not see data that looks exactly like this, but these types of datasets are great for exploring optimal use cases for different clustering methods.

How to do it...

Each data structure lends itself to a particular clustering algorithm.

1. Visualize the datasets:

```
fig, axs = plt.subplots(1, 3, figsize=(18, 5))
axs[0].scatter(X_blobs[:, 0], X_blobs[:, 1],
               c='blue', alpha=0.6)
axs[0].set_title("Isotropic Gaussian Blobs")
axs[1].scatter(X_moons[:, 0], X_moons[:, 1],
               c='green', alpha=0.6)
axs[1].set_title("Moons")
axs[2].scatter(X_circles[:, 0], X_circles[:, 1],
               c='purple', alpha=0.6)
axs[2].set_title("Nested Circles")
plt.show()
```

Here are the three datasets we generated.

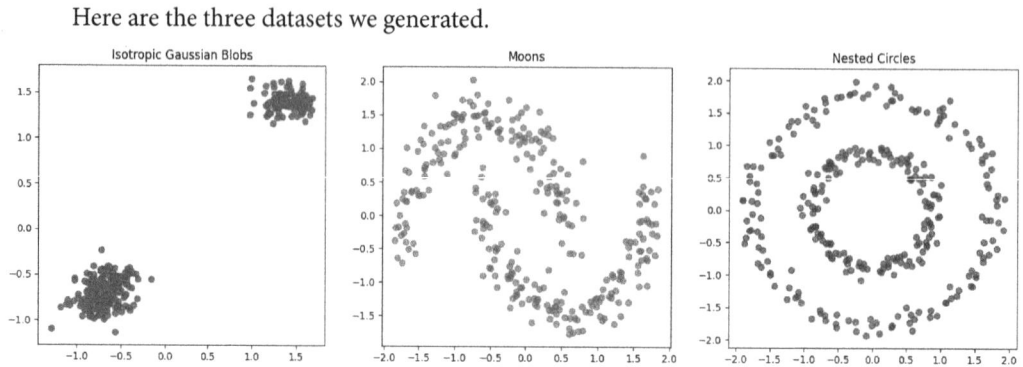

Figure 10.8 – Varieties of data structures

These plots illustrate three types of data distributions: isotropic blobs (ideal for K-means or hierarchical clustering), crescent moons (better suited for DBSCAN), and concentric circles (challenging for many algorithms but handled well by DBSCAN).

How it works...

When selecting a clustering algorithm, consider the following factors:

- **Cluster shape**: K-means performs well with convex clusters. DBSCAN or spectral clustering are better suited for non-convex shapes.

- **Noise handling**: DBSCAN explicitly handles noise by identifying outliers as separate from clusters. K-means and hierarchical clustering assign all points to a cluster.

- **Scalability**: K-means scales well to large datasets. Hierarchical clustering is less scalable due to its time complexity.

- **Parameter sensitivity**:

  - K-means: sensitive to k and initialization.

  - DBSCAN: sensitive to eps and `min_samples`.

  - Agglomerative clustering: affected by linkage method and stopping criteria.

- **Dimensionality**: Clustering in high dimensions often requires dimensionality reduction (e.g., PCA) beforehand due to the curse of dimensionality.

There's more...

Choosing your clustering technique should be based on the characteristics of your data. It's always good to plot your raw dataset beforehand to try to identify any underlying structure that can guide your approach.

Data Characteristic	Recommended Algorithm
Convex clusters	K-means
Non-convex clusters	DBSCAN, spectral clustering
Presence of noise/outliers	DBSCAN
Small datasets	Hierarchical clustering
Large datasets	K-means, MiniBatchKMeans

Table 10.1 – Recommended clustering approaches for certain data characteristics

Another useful approach is combining clustering with dimensionality reduction. When dealing with high-dimensional datasets, reducing dimensionality first can improve clustering results and reduce computation time.

Hands-on exercises

To illustrate these techniques, please reference the GitHub repository (`https://github.com/PacktPublishing/scikit-learn-Cookbook-Third-Edition`). You will engage in hands-on exercises for selecting appropriate clustering algorithms. Although we've included the preceding code examples, we encourage you to explore on your own and try using these tools with different arguments to see what results. The following steps outline a general workflow:

1. Create or load datasets with different spatial characteristics.
2. Visualize data distributions to understand shape and density.
3. Apply `Kmeans`, `DBSCAN`, and `AgglomerativeClustering` to each dataset.
4. Compare results using visualizations and evaluation metrics.
5. Identify which algorithm performs best based on your observations.
6. For high-dimensional data, apply PCA before clustering and compare results.

Advanced clustering techniques

Beyond the *classic* clustering algorithms, scikit-learn offers several advanced techniques such as **spectral clustering** and **Gaussian Mixture Models** (**GMMs**). These methods provide more flexibility in modeling complex cluster shapes and probabilistic cluster assignments, making them useful for more nuanced tasks. This recipe will provide the basic guidelines for generating models with these two techniques.

Getting ready

Let's begin by loading our two new clustering models and generating some dummy data to test them on.

1. Load the libraries:

    ```
    from sklearn.cluster import SpectralClustering
    from sklearn.mixture import GaussianMixture
    ```

2. Create datasets with a complex structure:

    ```
    from sklearn.datasets import make_moons
    from sklearn.preprocessing import StandardScaler
    X, _ = make_moons(n_samples=300, noise=0.05,
                        random_state=2024)
    X = StandardScaler().fit_transform(X)
    ```

Now, let's apply each technique to the generated data.

How to do it...

Each model is fit in a similar fashion to the previous models.

1. Apply spectral clustering:

    ```
    spectral = SpectralClustering(
        n_clusters=2,
        affinity='nearest_neighbors',
        random_state=2024
    )
    y_spectral = spectral.fit_predict(X)
    ```

2. Apply GMM:

    ```
    gmm = GaussianMixture(n_components=2, random_state=2024)
    y_gmm = gmm.fit_predict(X)
    ```

3. Visualize both clustering results:

```
fig, (ax1, ax2) = plt.subplots(1, 2, figsize=(14, 5))
ax1.scatter(
    X[:, 0], X[:, 1], c=y_spectral,
    cmap='plasma', s=50
)
ax1.set_title("Spectral Clustering")
ax2.scatter(
    X[:, 0], X[:, 1], c=y_gmm,
    cmap='viridis', s=50
)
ax2.set_title("Gaussian Mixture Model")
plt.show()
```

Now, let's look at the output of Spectral and Gaussian clustering:

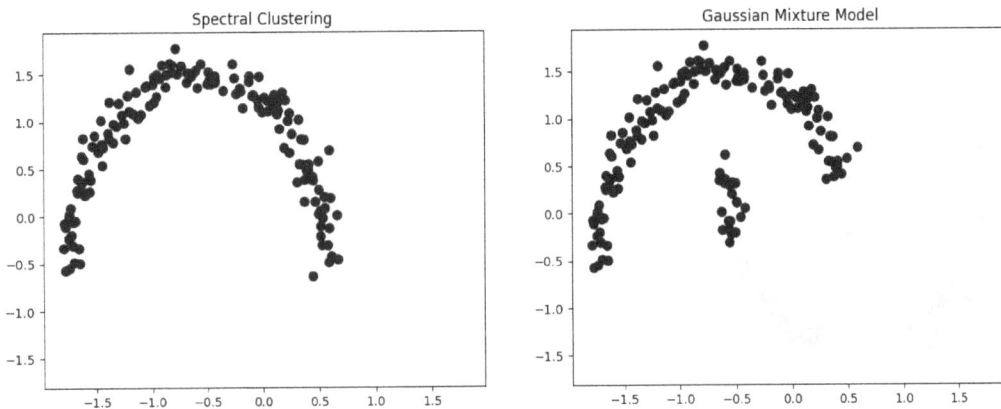

Figure 10.9 – Spectral and Gaussian clustering output

These plots compare two advanced clustering algorithms on the same complex dataset. Spectral clustering handles the curved shape better, while GMM models the underlying probability distributions. In what instances in the real world might you come across data with these types of nuances?

How it works...

Let's take a closer look at each of these techniques to understand how they work.

- **Spectral clustering**:

  - Constructs a similarity graph from the data

  - Constructs a matrix that represents the relationships between the data points

  - Maps this high-dimensional graph to a lower-dimensional feature space

  - Applies K-means on the reduced representation

This method is effective for non-convex clusters and is influenced by the similarity measure (e.g., radial basis, nearest neighbors). It also works well on large datasets with many features.

- **Gaussian Mixture Models (GMMs)**:

  - GMMs are a *soft clustering* method based on the assumption that data is generated from a mixture of several Gaussian (or normal) distributions

  - Each point is assigned a probability of belonging to each cluster

  - The **Expectation-Maximization** (**EM**) algorithm is used to find the parameters that maximize the likelihood of the data

GMMs offer flexibility in capturing elliptical shapes and overlapping clusters and can be used for anomaly detection or probabilistic classification. Because of their reliance on probability estimation, GMMs can fluidly assign data to clusters depending on thresholds, if needed.

There's more...

Visualizing cluster probabilities with GMM provides a `predict_proba` method to show the likelihood of each point belonging to each cluster. This can be useful when uncertainty about data point cluster assignments comes into play. Take note that the probabilities of `predict_proba` can sometimes be over- or under-confident in their class predictions. Although out of scope for this book, review the `CalibratedClassifierCV()` class in the scikit-learn documentation for more information.

Also, one can apply dimensionality reduction with advanced clustering. Advanced clustering methods such as spectral clustering can benefit from prior dimensionality reduction (e.g., PCA or t-SNE), especially with high-dimensional data. This step enhances performance and interpretability.

Hands-on exercises

To illustrate these techniques, please reference the GitHub repository (`https://github.com/PacktPublishing/scikit-learn-Cookbook-Third-Edition`). You will engage in hands-on exercises using spectral clustering and GMMs. Although we've included the preceding code examples, we encourage you to explore on your own and try using these tools with different arguments to see what results. The following steps outline a general workflow:

1. Load or create complex-shaped datasets such as `make_moons()` or `make_circles()`.
2. Apply `SpectralClustering` from `sklearn.cluster` and visualize the results.
3. Apply `GaussianMixture` from `sklearn.mixture` and use both `predict` and `predict_proba`.
4. Compare how these methods handle overlapping, curved, or non-convex clusters.
5. Experiment with varying numbers of components or clusters and observe changes.
6. Try dimensionality reduction before clustering to simplify and accelerate learning.

Practical exercises with clustering models

In this final section, you will engage in practical exercises that involve building, tuning, and evaluating clustering models on real-world datasets. These exercises are designed to reinforce the concepts learned throughout the chapter and demonstrate how to effectively apply clustering techniques in various scenarios. By the end of this section, you will have hands-on experience that you can leverage in your own ML projects.

Exercise 1: Clustering with K-means on the Iris dataset

In this example, we'll apply K-means clustering to the well-known Iris dataset and evaluate the results using multiple metrics.

Here are the implementation steps:

1. Load the libraries.
2. Load the dataset.
3. Create and train the KMeans model.
4. Evaluate the clustering.
5. Visualize the cluster assignments (PCA projection).

Exercise 2: Comparing DBSCAN and K-means on moon data

This exercise demonstrates how DBSCAN can outperform K-means on data with non-convex shapes.

Here are the implementation steps:

1.   Load the libraries.

2.   Create and scale the dataset.

3.   Apply KMeans and DBSCAN.

4.   Visualize the clustering results.

Exercise 3: Clustering high-dimensional data with PCA and GMMs

This exercise combines dimensionality reduction with a probabilistic clustering approach using GMMs.

Here are the implementation steps:

1.   Load the libraries.

2.   Load and preprocess the dataset.

3.   Apply PCA for dimensionality reduction.

4.   Fit the GMM.

5.   Visualize the clustered output.

Get This Book's PDF Version and Exclusive Extras

UNLOCK NOW

Scan the QR code (or go to packtpub.com/unlock). Search for this book by name, confirm the edition, and then follow the steps on the page.

Note: Keep your invoice handy. Purchases made directly from Packt don't require an invoice.

11

Novelty and Outlier Detection

The models we build with scikit-learn can be quite impressive with their predictive capabilities, but they are not infallible. A **machine learning** (**ML**) model is only as good as the data it is trained on, and if that data is messy or not representative of the phenomenon we are trying to model, our predictions will be less than optimal. Today, this has even become a new tactic among the hacker community: data poisoning, or maliciously tampering with data used for training to *break* a model's capabilities. This means that having a robust set of tools for identifying data anomalies is even more important in a world that has become highly reliant on data-based solutions and products.

This chapter will cover techniques for detecting outliers and novel patterns in datasets, focusing on methods such as Isolation Forest, One-Class **support vector machine** (**SVM**), and **Local Outlier Factor** (**LOF**). You will implement these techniques using scikit-learn, working through exercises with datasets containing anomalies to understand how to identify and handle outliers in ML models.

In this chapter, we're going to cover the following recipes:

- Introduction to outlier and novelty detection
- Understanding Isolation Forest
- One-Class SVM for novelty detection
- Detecting outliers with LOF
- Evaluating outlier detection models
- Handling detected outliers
- Choosing the right detection technique

Technical requirements

It is advisable to create a Python environment for safely isolating your work from other Python installations/libraries. See the GitHub repository for more details (`https://github.com/PacktPublishing/scikit-learn-Cookbook-Third-Edition`). You will need the following:

- Git >=2.46.x

- Python >=3.9.x

- Cloned GitHub repository and Python environment built from the `requirements.txt` file

Introduction to outlier and novelty detection

Many practitioners new to ML systems often assume that the data used during training will resemble what the model encounters in production. However, real-world data can contain rare or previously unseen observations (or, as stated previously, malicious data designed to inhibit proper model training). This data is typically categorized as either *outliers* or *novelties*. **Outliers** are data points that deviate significantly from other observations in the training set, while **novelties** are previously unseen data points that occur only at prediction time. Detecting these values is essential for preventing misleading predictions and ensuring robustness, particularly in applications such as fraud detection, industrial monitoring, and medical diagnostics.

In this recipe, we'll explore the purpose and context of outlier and novelty detection within ML pipelines. We'll also introduce scikit-learn tools and algorithms that allow us to identify these anomalous data points before diving into their specific implementations.

Getting ready

To begin, we'll create a synthetic dataset and visualize what outliers might look like:

1. Load the libraries:

    ```
    import numpy as np
    import matplotlib.pyplot as plt
    from sklearn.datasets import make_blobs
    ```

2. Generate a synthetic dataset with intentional outliers:

    ```
    X, _ = make_blobs(
        n_samples=300, centers=1,
        cluster_std=0.60, random_state=2024
    )
    np.random.seed(2024)
    outliers = np.random.uniform(low=-6, high=6, size=(20, 2))
    X_with_outliers = np.vstack([X, outliers])
    ```

3. Visualize the data with outliers:

```
plt.figure(figsize=(8, 6))
plt.scatter(X[:, 0], X[:, 1],
            label="Normal Data", alpha=0.6)
plt.scatter(outliers[:, 0], outliers[:, 1],
            color='red', label="Outliers")
plt.title("Synthetic Data with Outliers")
plt.xlabel("Feature 1")
plt.ylabel("Feature 2")
plt.legend()
plt.grid(True)
plt.show()
```

Let's see our plot:

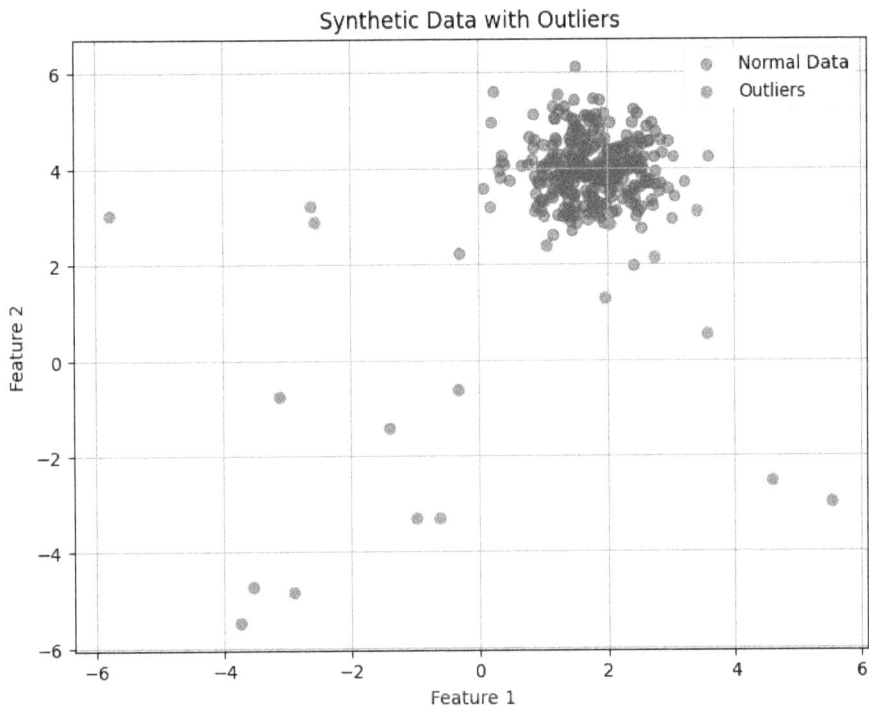

Figure 11.1 – Synthetic data with outliers

This plot shows a dense cluster of normal observations with visibly distant red points representing potential outliers.

How to do it...

To demonstrate outlier and novelty detection techniques, we'll use `LocalOutlierFactor()` (or LOF) from `sklearn.neighbors`. It's an unsupervised method that detects anomalies by comparing local densities of data points. Follow these steps:

1. Load the model:

    ```
    from sklearn.neighbors import LocalOutlierFactor
    ```

2. Fit the model and predict outliers:

    ```
    lof = LocalOutlierFactor(n_neighbors=20, contamination=0.05)
    y_pred = lof.fit_predict(X_with_outliers)
    ```

3. Plot the predictions:

    ```
    plt.figure(figsize=(8, 6))
    plt.scatter(X_with_outliers[y_pred == 1, 0],
                X_with_outliers[y_pred == 1, 1],
                color='blue', label='Inliers', alpha=0.6)
    plt.scatter(X_with_outliers[y_pred == -1, 0],
                X_with_outliers[y_pred == -1, 1],
                color='red', label='Outliers')
    plt.title("Outlier Detection using Local Outlier Factor")
    plt.xlabel("Feature 1")
    plt.ylabel("Feature 2")
    plt.legend()
    plt.grid(True)
    plt.show()
    ```

Now, let's look at our plot:

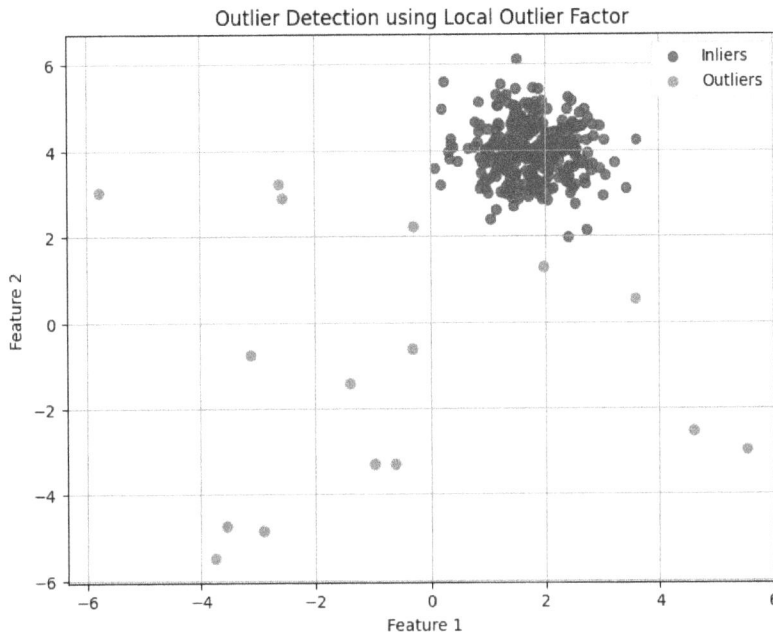

Figure 11.2 – Outlier detection using LOF

This visualization distinguishes inliers from detected outliers, helping us verify model behavior.

How it works...

Outlier and novelty detection methods estimate whether each sample data point significantly deviates from the expected data distribution.

Outliers may exist in training and test data, while novelties appear only in test data. Some models handle one or the other (e.g., `IsolationForest()` supports both; `OneClassSVM()` is typically used for novelty detection). It's important to make this distinction between the two since they each require a different approach for mitigation.

Another factor is *contamination*. This parameter estimates the proportion of outliers in the dataset. Models such as `LocalOutlierFactor()` or `IsolationForest()` use this to calibrate the decision boundary. Finally, consider *density-based detection*. LOF compares the density of each point to that of its neighbors. If a point resides in a much sparser region, it is likely an outlier.

The use of density-based or distance-based methods will depend on the data structure and application context.

There's more...

Here are some alternative applications and detection strategies:

- **Domain-specific knowledge**: Thresholds or rule-based heuristics are often used in combination with statistical models to fine-tune anomaly detection. Sometimes, human experience is a better source of knowledge than a dataset alone!

- **Feature engineering**: Outlier detection is highly sensitive to feature scaling and engineering. Standardizing or normalizing input data can improve detection accuracy.

- **Model monitoring**: In production settings, novelty detection is vital for catching concept drift or unexpected changes in data distributions.

Hands-on exercises

To illustrate these techniques, please reference the GitHub repository (`https://github.com/PacktPublishing/scikit-learn-Cookbook-Third-Edition`). You will engage in hands-on exercises for detecting outliers and novelties using scikit-learn. Although we've included the code examples, we encourage you to explore on your own and try using these tools with different arguments to see what results. The following steps outline a general workflow:

1. Clone the GitHub repository and ensure that all the necessary libraries are installed.

2. Generate synthetic data with built-in noise and outliers using `make_blobs` or `make_moons`.

3. Visualize the dataset using Matplotlib to understand the distribution.

4. Use `LocalOutlierFactor()` or `IsolationForest()` from `sklearn.neighbors` or `sklearn.ensemble`.

5. Train the model using the `fit` method and identify outliers with `predict` or `decision_function`.

6. Plot inliers and outliers in different colors to confirm detection.

7. Try adjusting contamination or distance metric parameters to see how detection boundaries change.

8. Compare outlier detection results across different algorithms, such as LOF, `IsolationForest()`, and `OneClassSVM()`.

Understanding Isolation Forest

Isolation Forest is an efficient and scalable algorithm for detecting outliers in high-dimensional datasets. Rather than profiling normal data points and identifying deviations, it works by isolating anomalies. Outliers are easier to isolate because they tend to differ significantly from most of the data. The algorithm randomly selects a feature and splits the data based on a random threshold; fewer splits are typically needed to isolate anomalies.

This method is particularly well-suited for large datasets and is capable of both outlier and novelty detection, making it a versatile tool in the ML toolkit. This recipe utilizes Isolation Forest to identify both inliers and outliers in datasets.

Getting ready

We'll generate a synthetic dataset that includes visible outliers. This will allow us to compare the performance of Isolation Forest against the known distribution:

1. Load the libraries:

```
import numpy as np
import matplotlib.pyplot as plt
from sklearn.ensemble import IsolationForest
from sklearn.datasets import make_blobs
```

2. Generate synthetic data with outliers:

```
X, _ = make_blobs(
    n_samples=300, centers=1,
    cluster_std=0.6, random_state=2024
)
np.random.seed(2024)
outliers = np.random.uniform(low=-6, high=6, size=(20, 2))
X_combined = np.vstack([X, outliers])
```

3. Visualize the data:

```
plt.figure(figsize=(8, 6))
plt.scatter(X[:, 0], X[:, 1],
            label="Normal Data", alpha=0.6)
plt.scatter(outliers[:, 0], outliers[:, 1],
            color='red', label="Outliers")
plt.title("Synthetic Data with Outliers")
plt.xlabel("Feature 1")
plt.ylabel("Feature 2")
plt.legend()
plt.grid(True)
plt.show()
```

Our synthetic data shows both our normal data and the inliers and outliers we'll try to detect with Isolation Forest:

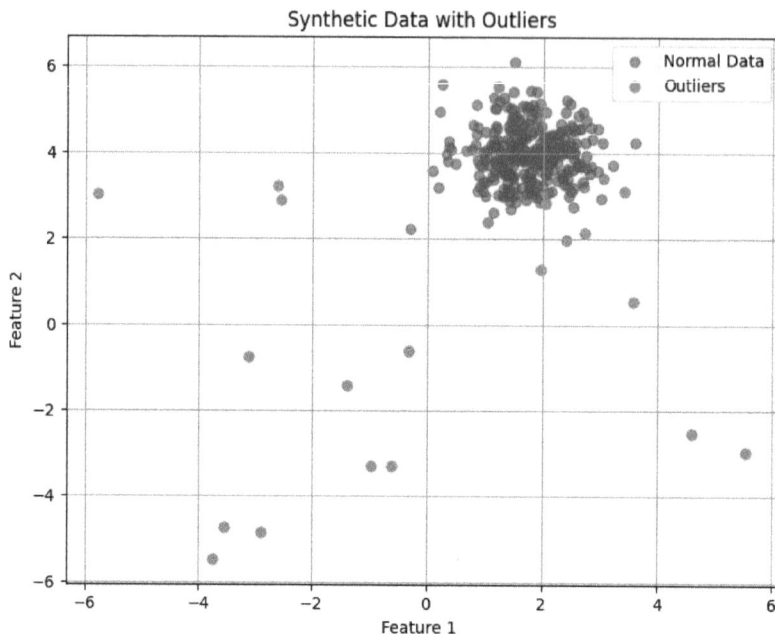

Figure 11.3 – Synthetic data with outliers

The plot shows a dense cluster of *inliers* and a set of scattered red points, visually separating potential anomalies. It's important to note that data does not have to reside *outside* the distribution of your data to be considered anomalous. Inliers can also signal abnormalities in your dataset, even if they are included within the range of values common to your data distribution.

How to do it...

We'll use `IsolationForest()` from `sklearn.ensemble` to identify the anomalies in the dataset:

1. Load and configure the model:

```
model = IsolationForest(
    n_estimators=100,
    contamination=0.05,
    random_state=2024
)
```

2.   Fit the model and make predictions:

```
model.fit(X_combined)
y_pred = model.predict(X_combined)
```

3.   Plot the results:

```
plt.figure(figsize=(8, 6))
plt.scatter(X_combined[y_pred == 1, 0],
            X_combined[y_pred == 1, 1],
            color='blue', label='Inliers', alpha=0.6)
plt.scatter(X_combined[y_pred == -1, 0],
            X_combined[y_pred == -1, 1],
            color='red', label='Outliers')
plt.title("Outlier Detection using Isolation Forest")
plt.xlabel("Feature 1")
plt.ylabel("Feature 2")
plt.legend()
plt.grid(True)
plt.show()
```

Comparing the results of Isolation Forest anomaly detection shows it is fairly accurate for finding outlier data:

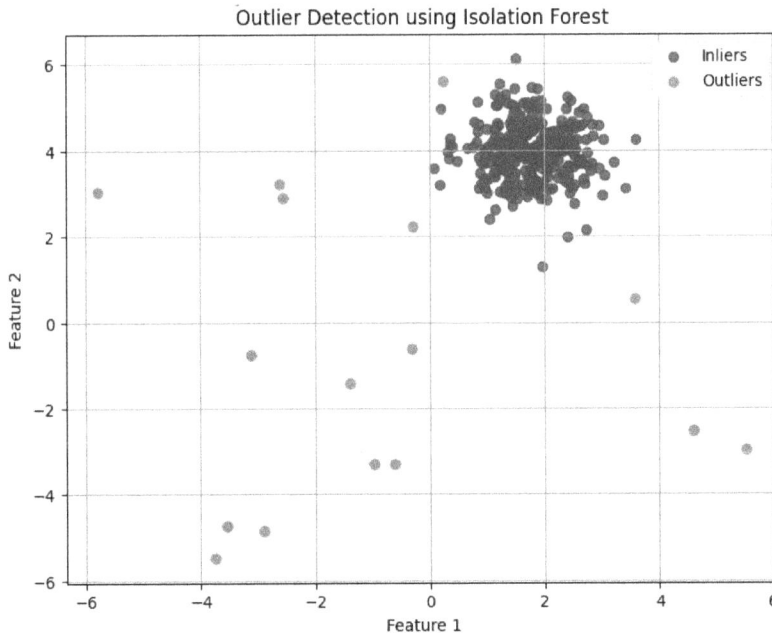

Figure 11.4 – Outlier detection using Isolation Forest

This scatter plot confirms the Isolation Forest's classification of normal points and outliers using blue and red markers, respectively.

How it works...

Isolation Forest isolates anomalies instead of profiling normal observations. The algorithm works as follows:

- **Random splitting**: At each node, the algorithm randomly selects a feature and a split value. This continues recursively, building trees where anomalies are likely to be isolated more quickly.

- **Path length**: Each point's anomaly score is based on the average path length over all trees. Based on the length of the path, it's implied that data points that fall along shorter paths are more likely to be outliers

- **Contamination**: The `contamination` parameter determines the expected proportion of outliers in the dataset and sets a threshold for classification.

Because Isolation Forest does not rely on distance or density metrics, it performs well on high-dimensional datasets and scales efficiently with large samples.

There's more...

Additional information on Isolation Forests includes the following:

- **Feature scaling**: Although less sensitive than distance-based methods, normalizing features may still improve results, especially when features are on vastly different scales

- **Decision function**: Instead of `predict()`, we can use `decision_function()` to get continuous anomaly scores, which can be useful for ranking or threshold tuning

- **Incremental learning**: While Isolation Forest is not incremental, it can be retrained efficiently on batches of new data when used in monitoring scenarios

Hands-on exercises

To illustrate these techniques, please reference the GitHub repository (`https://github.com/PacktPublishing/scikit-learn-Cookbook-Third-Edition`). You will engage in hands-on exercises for detecting anomalies using the Isolation Forest algorithm in scikit-learn. Although we've included the code examples, we encourage you to explore on your own and try using these tools with different arguments to see what results.

The following steps outline a general workflow:

1. Clone the GitHub repository and ensure that all the necessary libraries are installed.

2. Generate or load a dataset containing outliers using `make_blobs()` or a real-world dataset.

3. Visualize the dataset using Matplotlib to observe the data structure.

4. Load and configure `IsolationForest()` from `sklearn.ensemble`.

5. Fit the model and use `predict` to classify points as inliers or outliers.

6. Use Matplotlib to visualize the results, coloring anomalies in red.

7. Adjust the `contamination` parameter to observe its impact on classification.

8. Try using `decision_function()` to rank samples by anomaly score and plot these scores for further interpretation.

One-Class SVM for novelty detection

One-Class SVMs are a prevailing technique for novelty detection, particularly when we only have access to *normal* data during training. Unlike other outlier detection methods, One-Class SVM attempts to learn the boundary of normality and classifies any point lying *outside* this boundary as a novelty. This makes it well-suited for use cases such as fraud detection, equipment failure prediction, or rare disease diagnostics—any situation where anomalous examples are extremely rare or unavailable during training.

One-Class SVM is a **kernel-based method** that can model non-linear boundaries, giving it significant flexibility when separating normal instances from unseen anomalies. This recipe implements the model with a synthetic dataset.

Getting ready

We'll create a dataset with normal training data and include anomalies only at test time to demonstrate novelty detection:

1. Load the libraries:

```
import numpy as np
import matplotlib.pyplot as plt
from sklearn.svm import OneClassSVM
from sklearn.datasets import make_blobs
from sklearn.model_selection import train_test_split
```

2. Generate training data (normal only):

```
X_train, _ = make_blobs(
    n_samples=300, centers=1,
    cluster_std=0.6, random_state=2024
)
```

3. Generate test data (`normal` and `novelty`):

```
X_test_normal, _ = make_blobs(
    n_samples=100, centers=1,
    cluster_std=0.6, center_box=(0, 1),
    random_state=42
)
X_test_novelty = np.random.uniform(low=-6, high=6, size=(20, 2))
X_test = np.vstack([X_test_normal, X_test_novelty])
```

4. Visualize the data:

```
plt.figure(figsize=(8, 6))
plt.scatter(X_train[:, 0], X_train[:, 1],
            label='Training Data', alpha=0.6)
plt.scatter(X_test_novelty[:, 0],
            X_test_novelty[:, 1], color='red',
            label='Novelty Points')
plt.title("Training Data and Novelty Points")
plt.xlabel("Feature 1")
plt.ylabel("Feature 2")
plt.legend()
plt.grid(True)
plt.show()
```

This synthetic dataset is arranged similarly to our previous dataset:

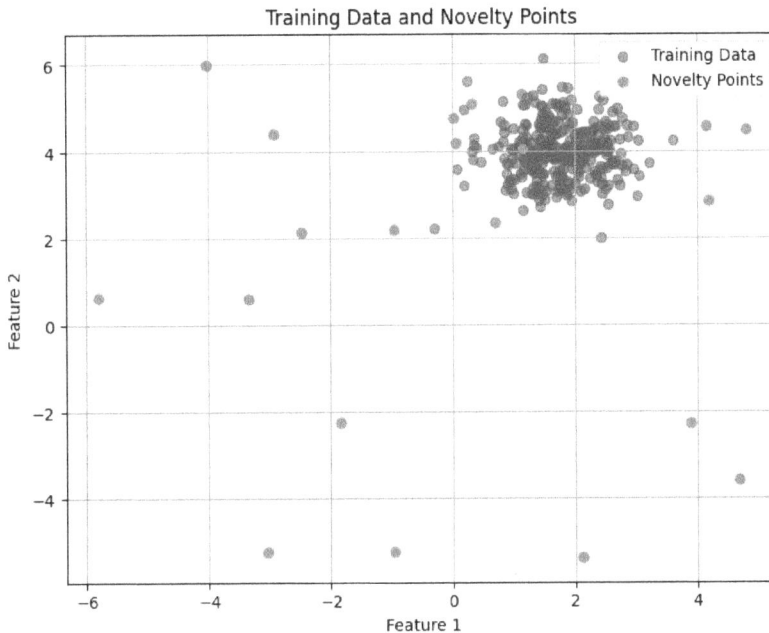

Figure 11.5 – Training data and novelty points

This figure distinguishes the normal training data from the novelty points in the test set.

How to do it...

We'll now use `OneClassSVM()` from `sklearn.svm` to build a novelty detector:

1. Instantiate and fit the model:

```
model = OneClassSVM(kernel='rbf', gamma='scale', nu=0.05)
model.fit(X_train)
```

2. Make predictions on the test data:

```
y_pred = model.predict(X_test)
```

3. Plot the predictions:

```
plt.figure(figsize=(8, 6))
plt.scatter(
    X_test[y_pred == 1, 0], X_test[y_pred == 1, 1],
    color='red', label='Predicted Inliers', alpha=0.6
```

```
    )
    plt.scatter(
        X_test[y_pred == -1, 0], X_test[y_pred == -1, 1],
        color='blue', label='Predicted Novelties'
    )
    plt.title("Novelty Detection using One-Class SVM")
    plt.xlabel("Feature 1")
    plt.ylabel("Feature 2")
    plt.legend()
    plt.grid(True)
    plt.show()
```

Let's see the results:

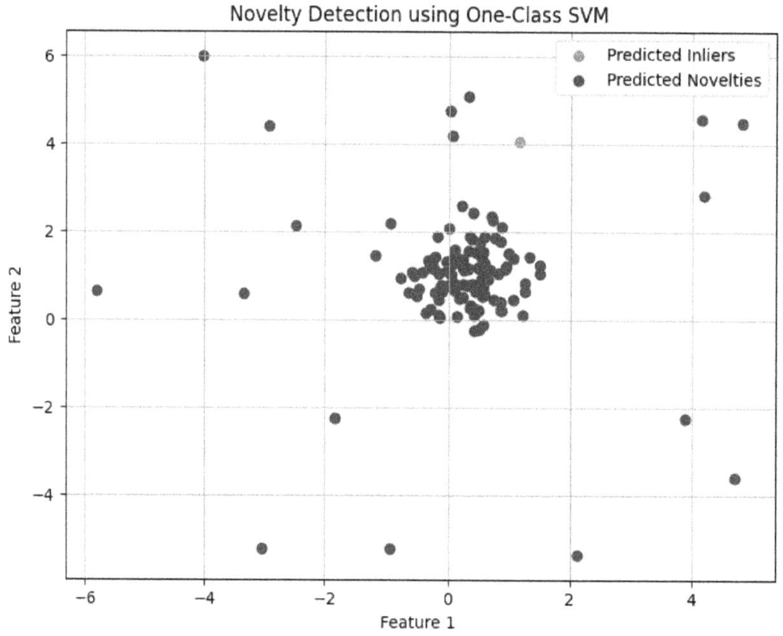

Figure 11.6 – Novelty detection using One-Class SVM

This scatter plot illustrates which test points were identified as normal and which were flagged as novel. While the model's predictions are probably not the best just based on a visual inspection, refining the hyperparameters could yield more positive results.

How it works...

One-Class SVM separates normal data from the origin in a transformed feature space using a decision function. Key parameters include the following:

- **Kernel**: One-Class SVM can use linear, polynomial, or **radial basis function** (**RBF**) kernels. RBF is most common as it can model non-linear boundaries.

- **Gamma**: This defines the *influence* of a single training example. Low values tend to produce smoother decision boundaries while higher values produce more precise, tighter boundaries.

- **Nu**: It controls the trade-off between false positives and model flexibility. Lower values tend to create tighter margins where normal data would lie within a smaller, denser area. Alternatively, a higher value provides more flexibility; however, this could lead to more data points being considered *normal* when they are, in fact, novel.

Unlike outlier detection methods that look at all data (training and test), One-Class SVM learns from normal data only and is evaluated only on new, unseen points.

There's more...

One-Class SVM has a few additional considerations for optimizing its performance:

- **Scaling features**: One-Class SVMs are sensitive to feature scaling. Use `StandardScaler()` or `MinMaxScaler()` before fitting the model.

- **Decision function**: Use `decision_function()` to obtain raw distance scores from the separating hyperplane.

- **High-dimensional data**: One-Class SVM can suffer from high computational cost in large datasets. Consider dimensionality reduction techniques when dealing with many features.

Hands-on exercises

To illustrate these techniques, please reference the GitHub repository (`https://github.com/PacktPublishing/scikit-learn-Cookbook-Third-Edition`). You will engage in hands-on exercises using One-Class SVM for novelty detection. Although we've included the code examples, we encourage you to explore on your own and try using these tools with different arguments to see what results. The following steps outline a general workflow:

1. Clone the GitHub repository and ensure that all the necessary libraries are installed.

2. Generate training data containing only normal instances using `make_blobs()`.

3. Create test data with both normal and anomalous points.

4. Use `OneClassSVM()` from `sklearn.svm` with an RBF kernel.

5. Fit the model using only the training data.

6. Use the `predict` method to classify unseen test points.

7. Plot the results to visually inspect novelty predictions.

8. Adjust the `nu` and `gamma` parameters and observe the effect on decision boundaries.

9. Use `decision_function()` to retrieve confidence scores and interpret anomalies based on thresholds.

Detecting outliers with LOF

LOF is a **density-based** anomaly detection method that identifies outliers by comparing the local density of each data point to that of its neighbors. Rather than using a global threshold, LOF assesses how isolated a data point is with respect to the surrounding neighborhood. If a point lies in a region of significantly lower density than its neighbors, it is flagged as an outlier.

LOF is especially effective in datasets where the density of data points varies across the feature space. It can detect local anomalies that may be overlooked by global methods such as Isolation Forest.

Getting ready

We'll generate a dataset containing clusters with different densities and add noise to simulate outliers:

1. Load the libraries:

```
import numpy as np
import matplotlib.pyplot as plt
from sklearn.datasets import make_blobs
from sklearn.neighbors import LocalOutlierFactor
```

2. Create synthetic data with clusters and noise:

```
X, _ = make_blobs(
    n_samples=400, centers=[[0, 0], [5, 5]],
    cluster_std=[0.5, 1.5], random_state=2024
)
np.random.seed(2024)
outliers = np.random.uniform(low=-6, high=10, size=(20, 2))
X_with_outliers = np.vstack([X, outliers])
```

3. Visualize the data:

```
plt.figure(figsize=(8, 6))
plt.scatter(X[:, 0], X[:, 1],
            label="Clustered Data", alpha=0.6)
plt.scatter(outliers[:, 0], outliers[:, 1],
```

```
                  color='red', label="Outliers")
plt.title("Synthetic Data with LOF-Detectable Outliers")
plt.xlabel("Feature 1")
plt.ylabel("Feature 2")
plt.legend()
plt.grid(True)
plt.show()
```

This dataset will be a little different from the previous examples:

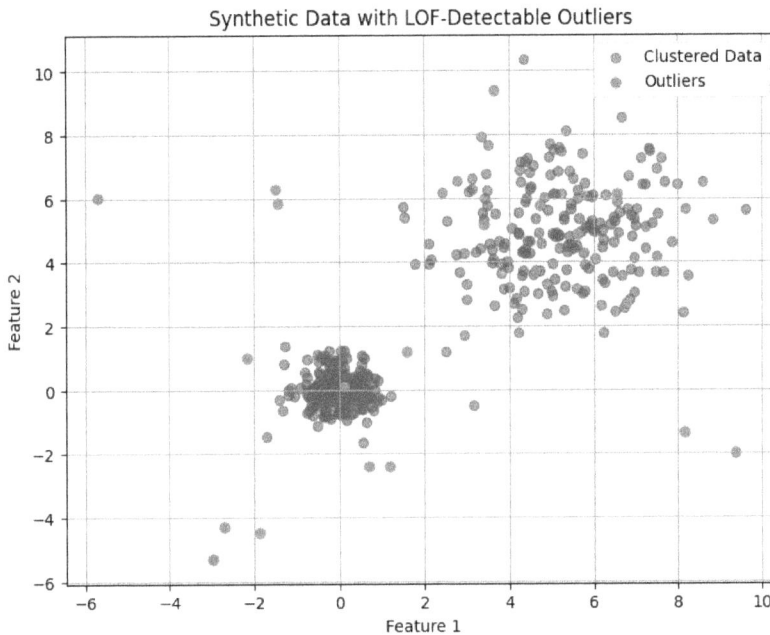

Figure 11.7 – Synthetic data with LOF-detectable outliers

This scatter plot displays clusters of different densities along with uniform outliers.

How to do it...

We'll apply `LocalOutlierFactor()` from `sklearn.neighbors` to identify local anomalies:

1. Initialize and fit the model:

```
lof = LocalOutlierFactor(n_neighbors=20, contamination=0.05)
y_pred = lof.fit_predict(X_with_outliers)
```

2. Plot the predictions:

```
plt.figure(figsize=(8, 6))
plt.scatter(X_with_outliers[y_pred == 1, 0],
            X_with_outliers[y_pred == 1, 1],
            color='blue', label='Inliers', alpha=0.6)
plt.scatter(X_with_outliers[y_pred == -1, 0],
            X_with_outliers[y_pred == -1, 1],
            color='red', label='Outliers')
plt.title("Local Outlier Factor Anomaly Detection")
plt.xlabel("Feature 1")
plt.ylabel("Feature 2")
plt.legend()
plt.grid(True)
plt.show()
```

Let's see how well this technique performs:

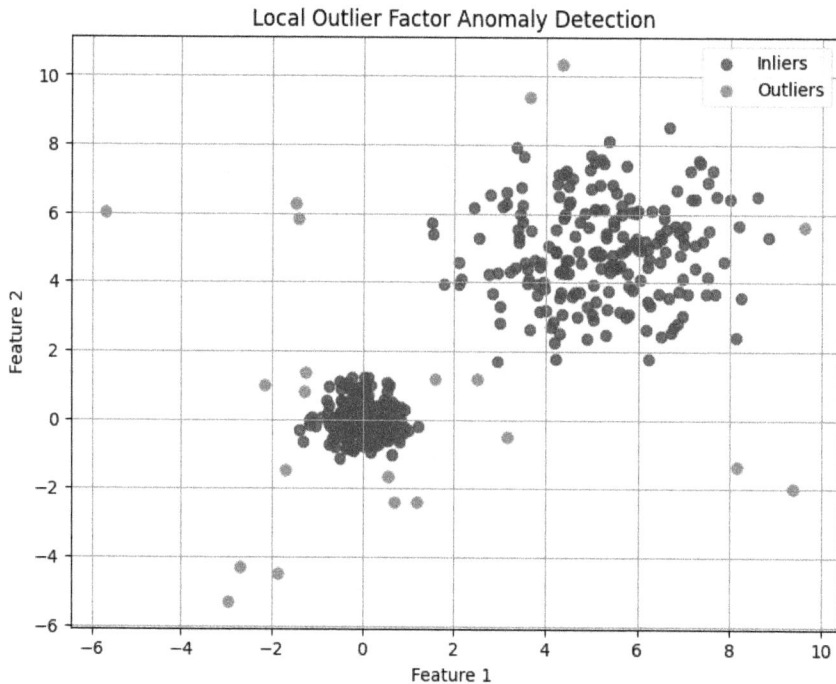

Figure 11.8 – LOF anomaly detection

This scatter plot distinguishes between inliers and outliers using blue and red points, respectively.

How it works...

LOF evaluates the degree of abnormality of a data point as follows:

- **Local density estimation**: It computes the local density around a data point using the distance to its k-nearest neighbors (refer to *Chapter 4* for a refresher).

- **Reachability distance**: The reachability distance smooths distances by considering the maximum between the actual distance and the k-distance of the neighbor.

- **LOF score**: A point's LOF score is the ratio of the average local density of its neighbors to its own local density. Values much greater than 1 suggest *outlierness*.

Unlike other models, LOF does not expose a `.predict()` method for unseen data. It is strictly an unsupervised anomaly detector used at training time.

There's more...

Maximizing the effectiveness of LOF can be optimized with some of the following considerations.

- **Choosing** `n_neighbors`: The value of `n_neighbors()` controls the sensitivity to local variations. Smaller values may overfit noise, while larger values may overlook local anomalies.

- **Performance in varying density**: LOF is more robust than global techniques when working with datasets where density varies across regions.

- **No prediction for new data**: LOF is not suitable for novelty detection because it doesn't support prediction on new unseen samples.

Hands-on exercises

To illustrate these techniques, please reference the GitHub repository (`https://github.com/PacktPublishing/scikit-learn-Cookbook-Third-Edition`). You will engage in hands-on exercises using the LOF algorithm in scikit-learn. Although we've included the code examples, we encourage you to explore on your own and try using these tools with different arguments to see what results. The following steps outline a general workflow:

1. Clone the GitHub repository and ensure that all the necessary libraries are installed.

2. Generate a dataset with clusters of different densities and some added uniform noise.

3. Visualize the dataset using Matplotlib.

4. Load `LocalOutlierFactor()` from `sklearn.neighbors` and configure it with a value for `n_neighbors()`.

5. Use `fit_predict()` to identify inliers and outliers.

6. Plot the results, coloring inliers and outliers differently.

7. Experiment with different values of contamination and `n_neighbors()`.

8. Observe how the LOF score changes based on the local structure of your data.

Evaluating outlier detection models

Evaluating outlier detection models is more nuanced than evaluating traditional supervised models. Outliers are typically rare, and labels may not always be available, which limits the use of standard metrics such as accuracy. Instead, we use metrics suited for imbalanced datasets and binary decisions, such as precision, recall, F1-score, ROC-AUC, and confusion matrices—all of which we've utilized several times up to this point. When *true* labels are available (as in synthetic datasets), we can directly assess how our models identify anomalous points.

In this recipe, we'll walk through evaluation strategies for outlier detection models using labeled data, compare model performance, and visualize the results for interpretability.

Getting ready

We'll generate a labeled dataset with a clear distinction between inliers and outliers:

1. Load the libraries:

```
import numpy as np
import matplotlib.pyplot as plt
from sklearn.datasets import make_blobs
from sklearn.ensemble import IsolationForest
from sklearn.metrics import (
    classification_report, confusion_matrix, roc_auc_score
)
import seaborn as sns
```

2. Generate labeled synthetic data:

```
X_inliers, _ = make_blobs(
    n_samples=300, centers=[[0, 0]],
    cluster_std=0.6, random_state=2024
)
X_outliers = np.random.uniform(low=-6, high=6, size=(30, 2))
X = np.vstack([X_inliers, X_outliers])
y_true = np.array(
    [0] * len(X_inliers) + [1] * len(X_outliers)
)  # 0 = inlier, 1 = outlier
```

3. Visualize the data:

```
plt.figure(figsize=(8, 6))
plt.scatter(X[y_true == 0][:, 0],
            X[y_true == 0][:, 1],
            label='Inliers', alpha=0.6)
plt.scatter(X[y_true == 1][:, 0],
            X[y_true == 1][:, 1],
            color='red', label='True Outliers')
plt.title("Synthetic Labeled Data for Evaluation")
plt.xlabel("Feature 1")
plt.ylabel("Feature 2")
plt.legend()
plt.grid(True)
plt.show()
```

Let's visualize our next synthetic dataset:

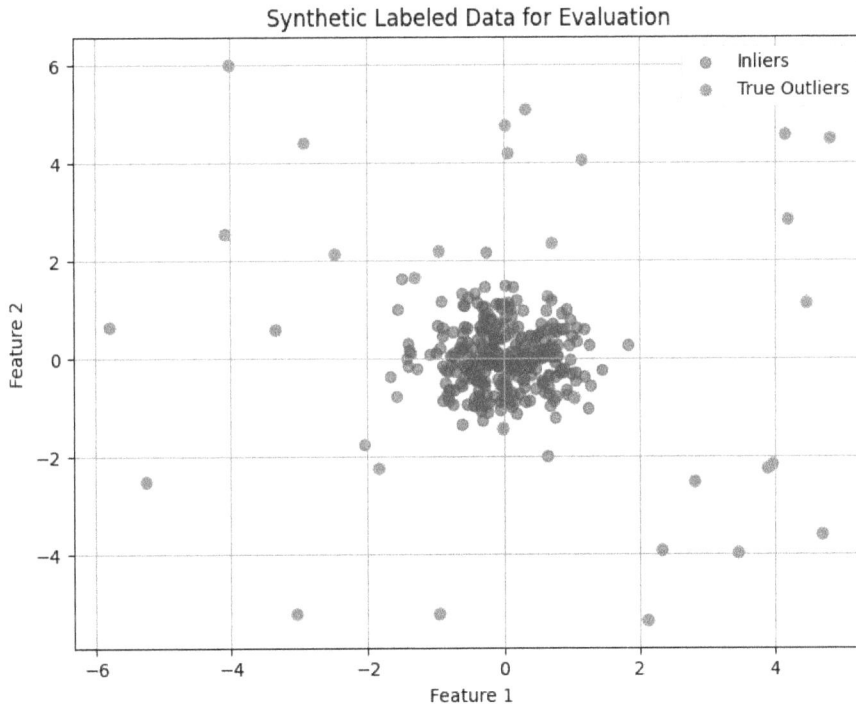

Figure 11.9 – Synthetic labeled data for evaluation

This scatter plot shows both normal data and injected outliers with true labels.

How to do it...

We'll fit an Isolation Forest model and evaluate its predictions using classification metrics:

1. Fit the model and get predictions:

```
model = IsolationForest(contamination=0.09, random_state=2024)
model.fit(X)
y_pred = model.predict(X)
y_pred_binary = np.where(
    y_pred == 1, 0, 1
)  # convert to 0 = inlier, 1 = outlier
```

2. Generate and plot a confusion matrix:

```
cm = confusion_matrix(y_true, y_pred_binary)
plt.figure(figsize=(6, 4))
sns.heatmap(
    cm, annot=True, fmt='d', cmap='Blues', cbar=False,
    xticklabels=['Predicted Inlier', 'Predicted Outlier'],
    yticklabels=['True Inlier', 'True Outlier']
)
plt.xlabel('Prediction')
plt.ylabel('Actual')
plt.title('Confusion Matrix')
plt.show()
```

Let's utilize a confusion matrix for this performance evaluation:

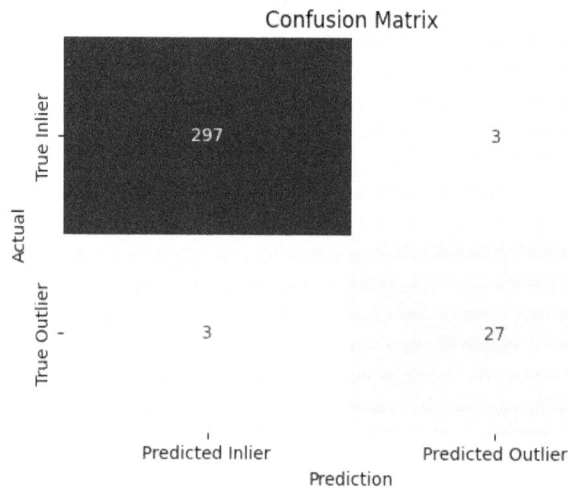

Figure 11.10 – Inlier/outlier confusion matrix

3. Print classification report and AUC:

```
report = classification_report(
    y_true, y_pred_binary, output_dict=True)
report = pd.DataFrame(report).transpose()
styled_report = (report
    .style
    .background_gradient(
        cmap='Blues',
        subset=['precision', 'recall', 'f1-score'])
    .format({
        'precision': '{:.3f}',
        'recall': '{:.3f}',
        'f1-score': '{:.3f}',
        'support': '{:.0f}'
    })
)
display(styled_report)
print("ROC-AUC Score:",
    roc_auc_score(y_true, model.decision_function(X)))
```

We can further break this down with our classification report:

	precision	recall	f1-score	support
0	0.990	0.990	0.990	300
1	0.900	0.900	0.900	30
accuracy	0.982	0.982	0.982	1
macro avg	0.945	0.945	0.945	330
weighted avg	0.982	0.982	0.982	330

```
ROC-AUC Score: 0.005111111111111106
```

Figure 11.11 – Inlier/outlier confusion matrix

The confusion matrix provides a breakdown of true positives, false positives, false negatives, and true negatives. The classification report includes precision, recall, and F1-score. ROC-AUC quantifies the model's ability to distinguish between classes.

How it works...

Each metric offers a unique view of model performance:

- **Precision**: The proportion of predicted outliers that are actually true outliers. High precision indicates fewer false positives.

- **Recall**: The proportion of actual outliers that are correctly identified. High recall means fewer false negatives.

- **F1-score**: The harmonic mean of precision and recall. A balanced measure when dealing with class imbalance.

- **Confusion matrix**: Offers detailed insight into prediction distribution.

- **ROC-AUC score**: Measures the model's ability to rank true outliers above inliers.

When class labels are not available (which is common), model evaluation may rely on expert validation, reconstruction error (e.g., for autoencoders), or proxy metrics such as prediction stability.

There's more...

Use the following tips to help optimize your use of these evaluation techniques:

- **Use case considerations**: In fraud detection, false negatives (missed frauds) may be more costly than false positives. Metric choice should reflect application-specific costs.

- **Threshold tuning**: For models that expose `decision_function()` or anomaly scores, tuning the threshold for classification can balance precision and recall depending on the task.

- **Cross-validation (CV)**: Stratified k-fold CV can be used on labeled anomaly data to ensure robust model comparisons.

Hands-on exercises

To illustrate these techniques, please reference the GitHub repository (`https://github.com/PacktPublishing/scikit-learn-Cookbook-Third-Edition`). You will engage in hands-on exercises to evaluate outlier detection models using labeled datasets. Although we've included the code examples, we encourage you to explore on your own and try using these tools with different arguments to see what results. The following steps outline a general workflow:

1. Clone the GitHub repository and ensure that all the necessary libraries are installed.

2. Generate or load a dataset containing both inliers and known outliers.

3. Fit an `IsolationForest()` model or other outlier detection model to the data.

4. Convert model predictions into binary labels for evaluation.

5. Use `confusion_matrix()` and `classification_report()` from `sklearn.metrics` to evaluate prediction performance.

6. Plot a confusion matrix using Seaborn for visual inspection.

7. Calculate ROC-AUC scores from model `decision_function()` outputs.

8. Explore how different contamination levels or threshold tuning affect metrics.

Handling detected outliers

Once outliers have been identified, we face an important decision: how should we handle them? The appropriate strategy depends on the context of the problem and the nature of the data. Outliers can be informative (e.g., fraud cases) or disruptive (e.g., sensor glitches), and choosing how to treat them affects model performance and interpretability.

This recipe outlines common strategies for handling outliers, including removal, transformation, imputation, and retaining them for specialized modeling. We'll walk through practical code examples to demonstrate each approach.

Getting ready

We'll use a dataset that includes outliers detected via the Isolation Forest method:

1. Load the libraries:

```
import numpy as np
import matplotlib.pyplot as plt
import pandas as pd
from sklearn.ensemble import IsolationForest
from sklearn.datasets import make_blobs
```

2. Generate the dataset:

```
X_inliers, _ = make_blobs(
    n_samples=300, centers=[[0, 0]],
    cluster_std=0.6, random_state=2024
)
X_outliers = np.random.uniform(low=-6, high=6, size=(30, 2))
X = np.vstack([X_inliers, X_outliers])
```

3. Detect outliers using Isolation Forest:

```
model = IsolationForest(contamination=0.09, random_state=2024)
model.fit(X)
outlier_mask = model.predict(X) == -1
```

Now, how do we deal with outlier data?

How to do it...

We'll now explore different strategies for handling the detected outliers:

1. Remove outliers from the dataset:

    ```
    X_cleaned = X[~outlier_mask]
    ```

2. Replace outliers with the feature-wise median:

    ```
    X_replaced = X.copy()
    median_vals = np.median(X[~outlier_mask], axis=0)
    X_replaced[outlier_mask] = median_vals
    ```

3. Cap outliers to specified bounds (winsorization):

    ```
    X_df = pd.DataFrame(X, columns=['feature1', 'feature2'])
    X_capped = X_df.copy()
    for col in X_df.columns:
        lower = X_df[col].quantile(0.05)
        upper = X_df[col].quantile(0.95)
        X_capped[col] = X_df[col].clip(lower=lower, upper=upper)
    ```

4. Visualize original and cleaned datasets:

    ```
    plt.figure(figsize=(12, 5))

    ax1 = plt.subplot(1, 2, 1)
    ax1.scatter(X[:, 0], X[:, 1],
                label='Original Data', alpha=0.6)
    ax1.scatter(X[outlier_mask][:, 0],
                X[outlier_mask][:, 1],
                color='red', label='Detected Outliers')
    ax1.set_title('Original Dataset with Outliers')
    ax1.legend()
    ax1.grid(True)

    ax2 = plt.subplot(1, 2, 2)
    ax2.scatter(X_cleaned[:, 0], X_cleaned[:, 1],
                label='Cleaned Data', alpha=0.6)
    ax2.set_title('Dataset After Outlier Removal')
    ax2.legend()
    ax2.grid(True)
    ```

```
ax2.set_xlim(ax1.get_xlim())
ax2.set_ylim(ax1.get_ylim())

plt.tight_layout()
plt.show()
```

Once the outliers are removed, our data visualization shows a much denser collection of our dataset:

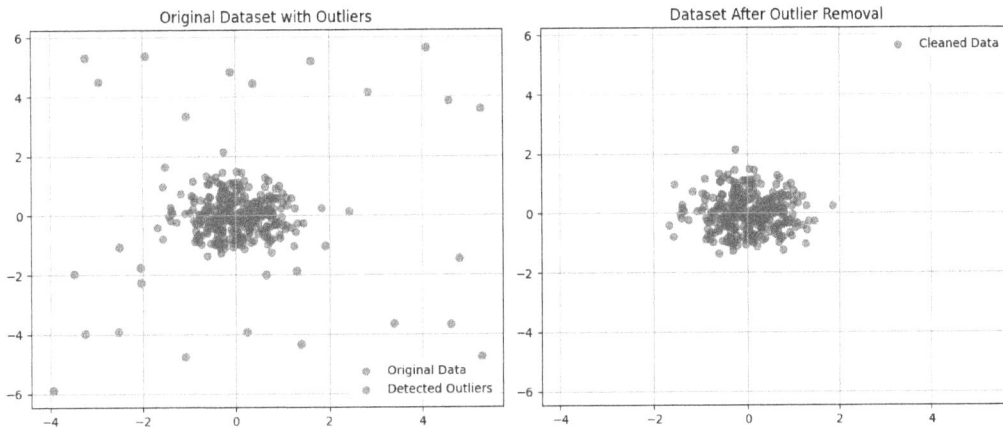

Figure 11.12 – Dataset with outlier removal

This figure compares the full dataset with detected outliers on the left and the cleaned version after outlier removal on the right.

How it works...

The choice of strategy depends on the underlying assumptions and the impact of outliers on model accuracy:

- **Removal**: Appropriate when outliers result from noise, errors, or corrupted records. However, excessive removal may discard a useful signal.

- **Replacement**: Replaces outliers with the mean, median, or another central statistic. This preserves dataset size but may introduce bias.

- **Capping (winsorization)**: Restricts values to a specific range. Useful when values should fall within bounds but still retain ordering.

- **Flagging**: Outliers can also be retained but flagged as a new feature, allowing models to learn behavior differences.

There's more...

Choosing what to do with outliers, inliers, anomalies, and novelties isn't a trivial decision. While the statistical techniques we've explored so far can paint one picture, it's best to approach the decision more holistically:

- **Domain knowledge**: Engage stakeholders or domain experts to validate whether outliers are true anomalies or important edge cases

- **Pipeline integration**: Use scikit-learn's `FunctionTransformer()` or `Pipeline` objects to encapsulate outlier handling as part of model training

- **Imputation vs. deletion**: If outliers are treated as missing values (e.g., imputed), this can retain dataset size without removing structure

Hands-on exercises

To illustrate these techniques, please reference the GitHub repository (`https://github.com/PacktPublishing/scikit-learn-Cookbook-Third-Edition`). You will engage in hands-on exercises that show how to process and handle outliers within an ML workflow. Although we've included the code examples, we encourage you to explore on your own and try using these tools with different arguments to see what results.

The following steps outline a general workflow:

1. Generate a dataset containing injected outliers using `make_blobs()` and uniform noise.
2. Fit `IsolationForest()` to detect outliers and store a binary outlier mask.
3. Remove outliers and compare model performance before and after.
4. Try replacing outliers with median or mean values using NumPy or pandas.
5. Cap outliers to the 5th and 95th percentiles using quantile-based clipping.
6. Visualize the dataset using scatter plots before and after cleaning.
7. Compare the impact of each strategy on downstream model results, such as classification or regression accuracy.
8. Wrap your chosen outlier handling strategy in a scikit-learn pipeline for consistent preprocessing.

Choosing the right detection technique

With multiple approaches to outlier and novelty detection available in scikit-learn, selecting the right method depends on the nature of your dataset, the presence or absence of labels, and the use case. In this section, we'll compare the key characteristics of various detection algorithms covered in this chapter and provide practical guidance to help you determine which approach best suits your needs.

In this recipe, we'll explore decision criteria, including assumptions about the data distribution, scalability, dimensionality, interpretability, and whether the model supports predictions on new, unseen data.

Getting ready

We'll summarize our experimental setup and reuse model evaluation results from earlier sections (note: this part is really optional):

1. Load the libraries:

```
import pandas as pd
from sklearn.ensemble import IsolationForest
from sklearn.neighbors import LocalOutlierFactor
from sklearn.svm import OneClassSVM
```

2. Create a comparison table of methods:

```
data = {
    "Algorithm": ["Isolation Forest",
                  "Local Outlier Factor",
                  "One-Class SVM"],
    "Handles High Dimensions": ["Yes", "No", "Sometimes"],
    "Learns From Unlabeled Data": ["Yes", "Yes",
                                   "No (novelty only)"],
    "Supports New Predictions": ["Yes", "No", "Yes"],
    "Scales to Large Data": ["Yes", "No", "No"],
    "Robust to Varying Densities": ["No", "Yes", "Partially"],
    "Main Strength": [
        "Fast, scalable, easy to use",
        "Detects local anomalies in varying densities",
        "Kernel-based boundary modeling"
    ]
}
summary_df = pd.DataFrame(data)
summary_df.set_index("Algorithm", inplace=True)
summary_df
```

Here's an easier-to-read version:

Algorithm	Handles High Dimensions	Learns From Unlabeled Data	Supports New Predictions	Scales to Large Data	Robust to Varying Densities	Main Strength
Isolation Forest	Yes	Yes	Yes	Yes	No	Fast, scalable, easy to use
Local Outlier Factor	No	Yes	No	No	Yes	Detects local anomalies in varying densities
One-Class SVM	Sometimes	No (novelty only)	Yes	No	Partially	Kernel-based boundary modeling

Figure 11.13 – Outlier comparison table

This comparison table highlights the core trade-offs across the three primary models used in this chapter.

How to do it...

We'll walk through example-driven decision criteria to choose the right method:

1. If your data is large and high-dimensional, consider the following:

```
# Isolation Forest is preferred
model = IsolationForest(contamination=0.1, random_state=2024)
```

2. If your data has clusters with varying densities, consider this:

```
# Local Outlier Factor is better suited
model = LocalOutlierFactor(n_neighbors=20, contamination=0.1)
```

3. If you want to train on only normal data and detect novel data points later, then consider this:

```
# One-Class SVM enables novelty detection
model = OneClassSVM(kernel='rbf', gamma='scale', nu=0.1)
```

Let's look at the pros and cons of each method now.

How it works...

Each algorithm has its strengths and limitations:

- **Isolation Forest**: Ideal for general-purpose outlier detection with large, high-dimensional datasets. It isolates anomalies quickly but may underperform with varying density regions.

- **LOF**: Detects local deviations, making it powerful in non-uniform data. However, it cannot make predictions on unseen data.

- **One-Class SVM**: Suited for novelty detection where only normal data is available during training. It can be computationally expensive on large datasets and is sensitive to feature scaling.

When in doubt, start with Isolation Forest for efficiency and iterate based on domain-specific needs.

There's more...

Consider these additional aspects when choosing the appropriate outlier/novelty detection approach:

- **Hybrid strategies**: Consider combining multiple techniques (e.g., LOF and Isolation Forest) to build ensemble models that capture both global and local anomalies

- **Explainability**: Isolation Forest provides feature importance via `feature_importances_()`, which can be helpful in interpreting results

- **Benchmarking**: Use precision-recall curves, ROC-AUC, or domain-specific success criteria to benchmark models against each other

Hands-on exercises

To illustrate these techniques, please reference the GitHub repository (`https://github.com/PacktPublishing/scikit-learn-Cookbook-Third-Edition`). You will engage in hands-on exercises that compare and contrast outlier detection techniques in scikit-learn. Although we've included the code examples, we encourage you to explore on your own and try using these tools with different arguments to see what results. The following steps outline a general workflow:

1. Create synthetic or load real-world datasets with known anomalies.
2. Fit `IsolationForest()`, `LocalOutlierFactor()`, and `OneClassSVM()` to the same dataset.
3. Record prediction labels and compare them to ground truth if available.
4. Evaluate each model using `confusion_matrix()`, ROC-AUC, or `classification_report()`.
5. Create a comparison DataFrame summarizing the strengths and trade-offs of each algorithm.
6. Visualize and interpret which technique performs best under different conditions.
7. Try ensemble strategies or voting mechanisms that combine multiple model outputs.
8. Consider operational requirements (e.g., speed and explainability) when selecting a final detection method.

Practical exercises in novelty and outlier detection

In this final section, we'll engage in practical exercises that involve detecting, evaluating, and handling anomalies in real-world datasets. These exercises are designed to reinforce the concepts introduced throughout the chapter, ranging from model selection to evaluation and strategy implementation. By the end of this section, you'll have direct experience working with a variety of detection methods and be better equipped to select and fine-tune them based on your data and goals.

Exercise 1: Applying Isolation Forest to a real-world dataset

In this exercise, we simulate a real-world anomaly detection scenario using synthetic data. The dataset consists of a dense cluster of normally distributed points and a smaller group of uniformly distributed outliers. You'll scale the data, apply the Isolation Forest algorithm, generate predictions, and evaluate the model's ability to identify anomalies.

These are the implementation steps:

1. Load the libraries.

2. Generate synthetic data with inliers and outliers.

3. Scale the data.

4. Apply Isolation Forest.

5. Evaluate the results.

6. Print a classification report as a styled DataFrame.

Exercise 2: Using LOF on a network intrusion dataset

In this task, we simulate an imbalanced network-like dataset with several clusters and injected noise. You'll apply the LOF algorithm to identify low-density regions where anomalous behavior might occur. Finally, you'll evaluate model performance using a confusion matrix and classification metrics.

These are the implementation steps:

1. Load the libraries.

2. Generate clustered data with synthetic noise.

3. Scale the data.

4. Apply LOF.

5. Evaluate the predictions.

Exercise 3: One-Class SVM for manufacturing sensor data

This exercise demonstrates novelty detection in a simulated manufacturing environment. You'll train a model only on normal operational data, then use it to detect novel observations from a mix of normal and abnormal test data. Finally, you'll visualize the inliers and detected novelties in 2D feature space.

These are the implementation steps:

1. Load the libraries.

2. Generate normal and novel data.

3. Fit One-Class SVM on normal data.

4. Visualize predictions.

Get This Book's PDF Version and Exclusive Extras

UNLOCK NOW

Scan the QR code (or go to packtpub.com/unlock). Search for this book by name, confirm the edition, and then follow the steps on the page.

Note: Keep your invoice handy. Purchases made directly from Packt don't require an invoice.

12

Cross-Validation and Model Evaluation Techniques

A well-known British statistician, George Box, is famous for saying that "All [statistical] models are wrong, but some are useful." As **machine learning** (**ML**) practitioners, this is valuable to keep in mind because it reminds us that no matter how much we train a model or fine-tune its hyperparameters, no matter how good it seems to perform when making predictions in production, there will always be instances where it makes a wrong prediction, the underlying data distribution changes, or any number of potential events that can make our model work less effectively. This is why, during training, we implement techniques to roughly simulate how our model will perform in a variety of situations.

This chapter explores advanced cross-validation methods, model evaluation metrics, and techniques for selecting the best models. Exercises focus on applying cross-validation and evaluation techniques to improve model selection. By the chapter's end, you will have an applicable understanding of utilizing cross-validation techniques for improving model performance evaluation.

In this chapter, we're going to cover the following recipes:

- Introduction to cross-validation
- Advanced cross-validation methods
- Model evaluation metrics overview
- Implementing cross-validation in scikit-learn
- Model selection techniques
- Evaluating model generalizability

Technical requirements

It is advisable to create a Python environment to safely isolate your work from other Python installations/libraries. See the GitHub repository for more details (`https://github.com/PacktPublishing/scikit-learn-Cookbook-Third-Edition`).

- Git >=2.46.x

- Python >=3.9.x

- Cloned GitHub repository and Python environment built from the `requirements.txt` file

Introduction to cross-validation

Cross-validation is a cornerstone technique for assessing how an ML model will perform on unseen data. Instead of relying on a *single* train-test split, we divide the dataset into *multiple* subsets, training and validating the model several times to get a better estimate of its generalization ability. In this recipe, we'll explore different types of cross-validation, including k-fold and stratified k-fold cross-validation, and walk through how to implement them using scikit-learn.

> k-folds
>
> The *k* in *k-fold* indicates the number of *folds* or subsets we'll split our dataset into. The term *k* is used similarly in K-means clustering we saw in the previous chapter.

Getting ready

We begin by loading the libraries and dataset we'll use to demonstrate cross-validation strategies. We'll use a classification dataset generated by `make_classification`.

1. Load the libraries:

```
import numpy as np
from sklearn.datasets import make_classification
from sklearn.model_selection import KFold, StratifiedKFold
from sklearn.linear_model import LogisticRegression
from sklearn.metrics import accuracy_score
```

2. Load the dataset:

```
X, y = make_classification(
    n_samples=500, n_features=10, n_informative=8,
    n_redundant=2, n_classes=2, random_state=2024
)
```

Using 500 samples in our synthetic dataset should provide an ample amount of records to demonstrate k-folds.

How to do it...

We'll apply k-fold and stratified k-fold cross-validation to evaluate a logistic regression model.

1. Initialize the k-fold cross-validator:

```
kf = KFold(n_splits=5, shuffle=True, random_state=2024)
```

2. Iterate through the folds and evaluate:

```
accuracies = []
for train_index, test_index in kf.split(X):
    X_train, X_test = X[train_index], X[test_index]
    y_train, y_test = y[train_index], y[test_index]
    model = LogisticRegression()
    model.fit(X_train, y_train)
    y_pred = model.predict(X_test)
    accuracies.append(accuracy_score(y_test, y_pred))
print(f"Average accuracy (KFold): "
    f"{np.mean(accuracies):.3f}")

# Output:
Average accuracy (KFold): 0.756
```

3. Use stratified k-fold for balanced class splits:

```
strat_kf = StratifiedKFold(
    n_splits=5, shuffle=True, random_state=2024)
strat_accuracies = []
for train_index, test_index in strat_kf.split(X, y):
    X_train, X_test = X[train_index], X[test_index]
    y_train, y_test = y[train_index], y[test_index]
    model = LogisticRegression()
    model.fit(X_train, y_train)
    y_pred = model.predict(X_test)
    strat_accuracies.append(accuracy_score(y_test, y_pred))
print(f"Average accuracy (StratifiedKFold): "
    f"{np.mean(strat_accuracies):.3f}")

# Output:
Average accuracy (StratifiedKFold): 0.766
```

Using stratified k-folds actually elicits a slightly higher accuracy, which is good news since the methodology is designed to make each fold more representative of real-world conditions than the totally randomized nature of k-fold alone.

How it works...

Standard k-fold cross-validation splits the data into k equally sized parts (or as close to equal as we can given the number of samples in the training dataset), trains the model on k-1 parts, and tests it on the remaining part – repeating this process k times. However, in classification problems, especially with imbalanced classes, this might lead to folds that do not represent the overall class distribution.

Stratified k-fold solves this by preserving the percentage of samples for each class in each fold. This provides a more reliable estimate of the model's performance across imbalanced classes.

The output prints the average classification accuracy across folds for both approaches. In most imbalanced cases, stratified k-fold yields more stable and fair evaluation results.

Hands-on exercises

To illustrate these techniques, please reference the GitHub repository (`https://github.com/PacktPublishing/scikit-learn-Cookbook-Third-Edition`). You will engage in hands-on exercises on classification model evaluation using cross-validation. Although we've included the preceding code examples, we encourage you to explore on your own and try using these tools with different arguments to see what results. The following steps outline a general workflow:

1. Clone the GitHub repository and ensure all necessary libraries are installed.
2. Choose or generate a classification dataset from scikit-learn.
3. Explore the distribution of classes to check for balance or imbalance.
4. Apply `Kfold()` and `StratifiedKFold()` using `sklearn.model_selection`.
5. Train a simple classification model, such as `LogisticRegression()`, in each fold.
6. Evaluate performance using `accuracy_score` or another classification metric.
7. Compare the consistency and reliability of both cross-validation strategies.

Advanced cross-validation methods

When we're working with complex models or small datasets, basic cross-validation strategies such as k-fold might not provide the control or precision we need. In this recipe, we'll explore two advanced techniques: **leave-one-out cross-validation (LOOCV)** and nested cross-validation. LOOCV is useful when we want to make the most out of limited data, while nested cross-validation helps us tune hyperparameters without data leakage between model selection and evaluation.

Getting ready

To begin, we'll load a small dataset and set up the libraries needed for LOOCV and nested cross-validation. We'll use ridge regression for demonstration, which benefits from regularization tuning.

1. Load the libraries:

```
import numpy as np
from sklearn.datasets import load_diabetes
from sklearn.model_selection import (
    LeaveOneOut, GridSearchCV, cross_val_score)
from sklearn.linear_model import Ridge
```

2. Load the dataset:

```
data = load_diabetes()
X = data.data
y = data.target
```

For this example, we will use the built-in diabetes dataset, which contains 10 features and a qualitative target variable representing disease progression.

How to do it...

We'll walk through both leave-one-out and nested cross-validation with scikit-learn.

1. Apply LOOCV:

```
loo = LeaveOneOut()
model = Ridge(alpha=1.0)
scores = cross_val_score(
    model, X, y, cv=loo,
    scoring="neg_mean_squared_error"
)
print(f"LOOCV mean MSE: {-np.mean(scores):.3f}")
```

2. Define a grid for hyperparameter tuning:

```
param_grid = {"alpha": [0.01, 0.1, 1, 10, 100]}
```

3. Apply nested cross-validation using GridSearchCV():

```
nested_scores = cross_val_score(
    GridSearchCV(Ridge(), param_grid, cv=5),
    X, y, cv=5
)
print(f"Nested CV mean score: {np.mean(nested_scores):.3f}")
```

```
# Output:
LOOCV mean MSE: 3327.655
Nested CV mean score: 0.480
```

Using a randomized search instead of a grid search would be another alternative for hyperparameter tuning since our final 0.593 MSE is not much better than guessing.

How it works...

LOOCV performs model evaluation by training on all data points except one, using the held-out point for testing. It repeats this for every data point, providing nearly unbiased estimates but at a higher computational cost.

Nested cross-validation is useful when tuning hyperparameters. An *inner* loop performs model selection (e.g., grid search) while the outer loop evaluates model performance. This prevents overfitting to the test set during hyperparameter tuning, yielding a more honest estimate of generalization performance.

The printed results will include the mean scores from both LOOCV and nested CV evaluations. Because nested CV handles tuning and evaluation in isolated folds, it's often preferred in model development pipelines.

Hands-on exercises

To illustrate these techniques, please reference the GitHub repository (https://github.com/PacktPublishing/scikit-learn-Cookbook-Third-Edition). You will explore leave-one-out and nested cross-validation approaches for both model validation and hyperparameter selection. The following steps outline a general workflow:

1. Clone the GitHub repository and ensure all necessary libraries are installed.

2. Choose a regression dataset from scikit-learn, such as `load_diabetes`.

3. Apply `LeaveOneOut()` cross-validation to evaluate baseline model performance.

4. Set up a hyperparameter grid for a regularized model such as Ridge.

5. Use `GridSearchCV()` to perform tuning.

6. Apply `cross_val_score()` with the `GridSearchCV()` estimator nested inside to evaluate generalization.

7. Compare LOOCV and nested CV scores to understand trade-offs in performance and computational cost.

Implementing cross-validation in scikit-learn

Once we understand the theory and importance of cross-validation, the next step is to put it into practice. scikit-learn offers streamlined tools to implement different cross-validation workflows. In this recipe, we'll walk through setting up basic and advanced cross-validation loops using `cross_val_score()`, `cross_validate()`, and `GridSearchCV()` to assess and compare model performance.

Getting ready

We'll use a classification problem as our basis and load the necessary tools from scikit-learn to apply cross-validation.

1. Load the libraries:

    ```
    import numpy as np
    from sklearn.datasets import make_classification
    from sklearn.linear_model import LogisticRegression
    from sklearn.model_selection import (
        cross_val_score, cross_validate, GridSearchCV)
    ```

2. Load and prepare the dataset:

    ```
    X, y = make_classification(
        n_samples=500, n_features=10,
        weights=[0.7, 0.3], random_state=2024
    )
    ```

We will use 500 samples again. This time, we will arbitrarily weight the distribution of classes so that the first class comprises 70% of the total dataset.

How to do it...

We'll demonstrate three ways to perform cross-validation using scikit-learn's high-level API.

1. Use `cross_val_score()` to compute average accuracy:

    ```
    model = LogisticRegression()
    scores = cross_val_score(model, X, y, cv=5, scoring='accuracy')
    print(f"Mean accuracy: {np.mean(scores):.3f}")

    # Output:
    Mean accuracy: 0.910
    ```

2. Use `cross_validate()` to compute multiple metrics:

```
results = cross_validate(
    model, X, y, cv=5,
    scoring=['accuracy', 'precision', 'recall', 'f1']
)
print(f"Mean precision: "
        f"{np.mean(results['test_precision']):.3f}")
print(f"Mean recall: "
        f"{np.mean(results['test_recall']):.3f}")
print(f"Mean F1: {np.mean(results['test_f1']):.3f}")

# Output:
Mean precision: 0.875
Mean recall: 0.820
Mean F1: 0.845
```

3. Use `GridSearchCV()` for hyperparameter tuning with cross-validation:

```
param_grid = {"C": [0.01, 0.1, 1, 10]}
grid = GridSearchCV(
    LogisticRegression(),
    param_grid, cv=5,
    scoring='accuracy'
)
grid.fit(X, y)
print(f"Best hyperparameter (C): {grid.best_params_['C']}")
print(f"Best accuracy: {grid.best_score_:.3f}")

# Output:
Best hyperparameter (C): 0.1
Best accuracy: 0.918
```

Although accuracy is the highest performing metric, remember that it isn't always the best performance metric to use all the time. Like before, we could have used a stratification approach to our cross-validation, but since we didn't and our dataset is imbalanced, it would be better to use precision, recall, or F1, depending on the use case.

How it works...

`cross_val_score()` provides a quick way to evaluate a model with a single metric using cross-validation. `cross_validate()` is more flexible, allowing multiple metrics to be captured simultaneously.

`GridSearchCV()` integrates cross-validation with hyperparameter search. It performs model training and evaluation on every combination of specified hyperparameters and selects the best based on the scoring metric.

This approach helps reduce overfitting and improves generalization by providing a more robust view of how a model will perform across different subsets of the data.

Hands-on exercises

To illustrate these techniques, please reference the GitHub repository (`https://github.com/PacktPublishing/scikit-learn-Cookbook-Third-Edition`). You will implement cross-validation techniques to evaluate and optimize classification models. The following steps outline a general workflow:

1. Clone the GitHub repository and ensure all necessary libraries are installed.
2. Generate a classification dataset using scikit-learn.
3. Initialize a baseline model such as LogisticRegression.
4. Use `cross_val_score()` to compute average accuracy across folds.
5. Use `cross_validate()` to collect multiple performance metrics.
6. Set up a parameter grid and use `GridSearchCV()` to tune a model.
7. Analyze the results and interpret performance trends based on different metrics and configurations.

Model selection techniques

Once we've evaluated our models using cross-validation, the next step is selecting the best one for deployment. Model selection techniques help us compare different algorithms and configurations in a statistically robust way. Although we won't cover it here because, frankly, it would be quite difficult to do so with all the different permutations of factors that exist, in the real world, we'd also have a variety of business rules that would impact our decision. These are typically tied to monetary metrics around costs and savings incurred by utilizing a model versus using another technique. In this recipe, we'll use grid search and randomized search to perform hyperparameter tuning and select the optimal model based on cross-validation scores.

Getting ready

We'll use a classification task and compare different regularization strengths for logistic regression using both exhaustive and randomized search strategies.

1. Load the libraries:

    ```
    import numpy as np
    from sklearn.datasets import make_classification
    from sklearn.linear_model import LogisticRegression
    from sklearn.model_selection import (
        GridSearchCV, RandomizedSearchCV, train_test_split)
    from sklearn.metrics import accuracy_score
    ```

2. Load and split the dataset:

    ```
    X, y = make_classification(
        n_samples=500, n_features=10,
        weights=[0.7, 0.3], random_state=2024
    )
    X_train, X_test, y_train, y_test = train_test_split(
        X, y, test_size=0.3,
        random_state=2024
    )
    ```

Now, let's apply both `GridSearch()` and `RandomizedSearch()` to find the optimal value for C.

How to do it...

We'll set up and compare both `GridSearchCV()` and `RandomizedSearchCV()` to find the best regularization strength for logistic regression.

1. Use `GridSearchCV()` to evaluate all combinations in the parameter grid:

    ```
    param_grid = {"C": [0.001, 0.01, 0.1, 1, 10, 100]}
    grid = GridSearchCV(
        LogisticRegression(), param_grid, cv=5,
        scoring='accuracy'
    )
    grid.fit(X_train, y_train)
    print(f"GridSearchCV best C: {grid.best_params_['C']}")

    # Output:
    GridSearchCV best C: 0.1
    ```

2. Use `RandomizedSearchCV()` to evaluate a random sample of parameters:

```python
from scipy.stats import loguniform
param_dist = {"C": loguniform(1e-3, 1e2)}
random_search = RandomizedSearchCV(
    LogisticRegression(),
    param_distributions=param_dist,
    n_iter=10, cv=5, scoring='accuracy',
    random_state=2024
)
random_search.fit(X_train, y_train)
print(f"RandomizedSearchCV best C: "
    f"{random_search.best_params_['C']:.4f}")

# Output:
RandomizedSearchCV best C: 0.1744
```

3. Evaluate the final model performance:

```python
final_model = random_search.best_estimator_
y_pred = final_model.predict(X_test)
print(f"Final accuracy on test set: "
    f"{accuracy_score(y_test, y_pred):.3f}")

# Output:
Final accuracy on test set: 0.940
```

Finding the correct hyperparameters for our model is a necessary step to guarantee our due diligence in finding the best model.

How it works...

`GridSearchCV()` performs an exhaustive search across the specified hyperparameter grid. While comprehensive, it can become computationally expensive as the number of parameters grows.

`RandomizedSearchCV()` samples a fixed number of parameter combinations from distributions we specify. It's often more efficient and yields comparable results with fewer evaluations.

We use these tools to identify the model configuration that yields the best performance during cross-validation and then validate it on unseen test data.

Hands-on exercises

To illustrate these techniques, please reference the GitHub repository (`https://github.com/PacktPublishing/scikit-learn-Cookbook-Third-Edition`). You will experiment with grid and randomized search to identify optimal hyperparameters. The following steps outline a general workflow:

1. Clone the GitHub repository and ensure all necessary libraries are installed.
2. Generate a classification dataset using scikit-learn.
3. Split the dataset into training and testing subsets.
4. Set up a parameter grid for logistic regression and apply `GridSearchCV()`.
5. Use `RandomizedSearchCV()` with a continuous distribution for sampling.
6. Evaluate and compare the test performance of both tuned models.
7. Reflect on time and accuracy trade-offs between the two search strategies.

Evaluating model generalizability

A well-performing model on training and validation sets doesn't always generalize well to unseen data, and even when it does, when initially put into production, data changes over time, so today's well-performing model is tomorrow's failed predictor. Due to this inevitable degradation of model performance over time, **machine learning operations**, or **MLOps**, was created for continuously evaluating model performance over time and, when that performance decreases beyond an acceptable level, the model is retrained.

This recipe focuses on techniques to assess and ensure the generalization capability of machine learning models. We'll explore learning curves, validation curves, and cross-validation strategies that help prevent overfitting and support robust model development.

Getting ready

We'll use a synthetic classification dataset and logistic regression to demonstrate how model performance changes with different amounts of training data and varying model complexity.

1. Load the libraries:

```
import numpy as np
import matplotlib.pyplot as plt
from sklearn.datasets import make_classification
from sklearn.linear_model import LogisticRegression
from sklearn.model_selection import (
    learning_curve, validation_ curve)
```

2. Load the dataset:

```
X, y = make_classification(
    n_samples=1000, n_features=20,
    weights=[0.7, 0.3], random_state=2024
)
```

We will work with a slightly larger dataset this time, using 1,000 samples.

How to do it...

We'll start by plotting learning curves to understand how the model performs as the training size increases, and then plot a validation curve to evaluate model performance across different values of a key hyperparameter.

1. Plot a learning curve:

```
train_sizes, train_scores, test_scores = learning_curve(
    LogisticRegression(), X, y, cv=5,
    scoring='accuracy',
    train_sizes=np.linspace(0.1, 1.0, 5),
    random_state=2024
)
train_mean = np.mean(train_scores, axis=1)
test_mean = np.mean(test_scores, axis=1)
plt.plot(train_sizes, train_mean,
         label='Training score')
plt.plot(train_sizes, test_mean,
         label='Cross-validation score')
plt.xlabel('Training set size')
plt.ylabel('Accuracy')
plt.title('Learning Curve')
plt.legend()
plt.grid(True)
plt.show()
```

Let's quickly visualize our graph.

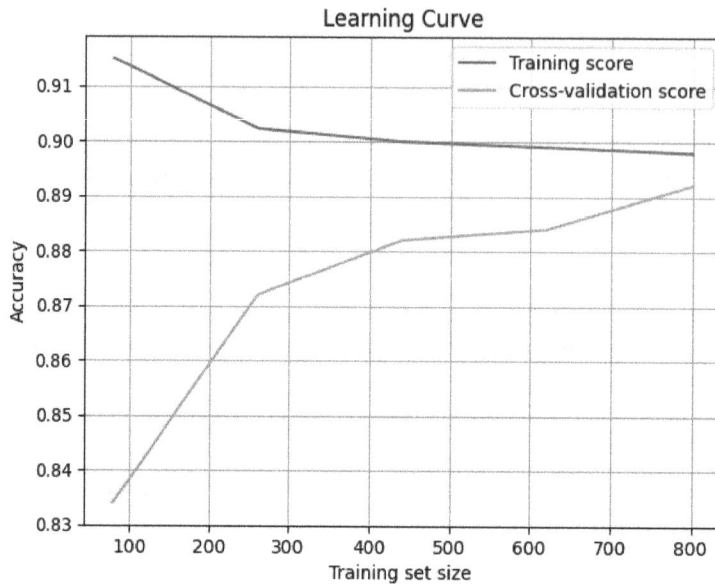

Figure 12.1 – Learning curve

The learning curve indicates how the model improves as we provide it with more training data to learn. The **Training score** indicates how well the model performs when we use it to predict the same labels it was used to train on. This score is almost always going to be high because our model has already *seen* this data and learned directly from it. The training score stays relatively flat even as the size of the dataset grows.

Alternatively, the **Cross-validation score** improves rapidly as the training dataset grows in size. This metric is calculated when passing data from the *test* set through the model, not the *training* set. In the real world, we'd be more interested in the performance of these metrics since the test set stands in as the *unseen* (i.e., not trained on) data our model will encounter in production.

Another note, you'll see both lines begin to converge around **800** samples. If we were to have a larger training set and extend this graph further to the right, we'd probably see both lines level off. This is because, after a while, no matter how much more training data we add to our model training process, the law of diminishing returns will mean we won't see any more dramatic improvements in performance.

2. Plot a validation curve:

```
param_range = np.logspace(-3, 2, 6)
train_scores, test_scores = validation_curve(
    LogisticRegression(), X, y, param_name="C",
    param_range=param_range, cv=5, scoring='accuracy'
)
train_mean = np.mean(train_scores, axis=1)
test_mean = np.mean(test_scores, axis=1)
plt.semilogx(param_range, train_mean,
             label='Training score')
plt.semilogx(param_range, test_mean,
             label='Cross-validation score')
plt.xlabel('C (Inverse Regularization Strength)')
plt.ylabel('Accuracy')
plt.title('Validation Curve')
plt.legend()
plt.grid(True)
plt.show()
```

Again, let's get a quick plot.

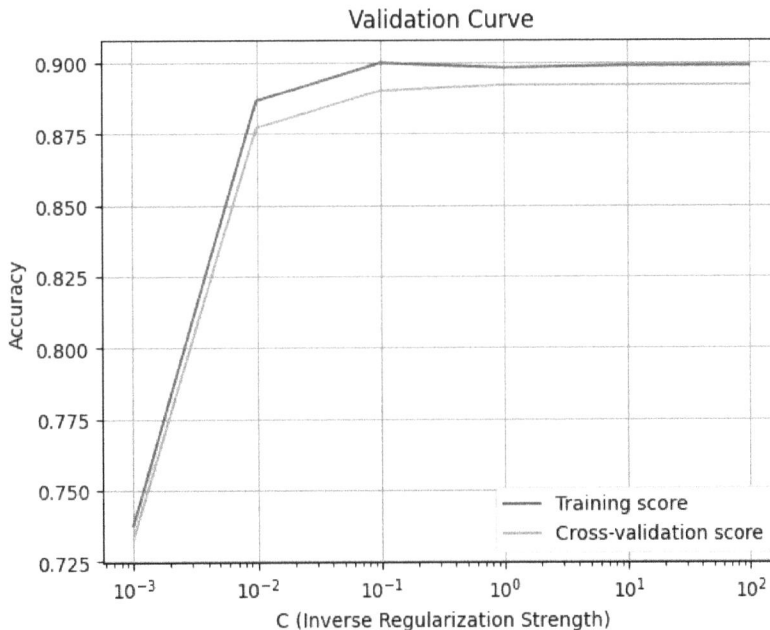

Figure 12.2 – Validation curve

The **Validation Curve** visualizes how different values for C impact model performance. Just like with the **Learning Curve**, we get diminishing returns at some point where further adjustment elicits no great improvement.

How it works...

The learning curve illustrates how training and validation accuracy evolve as more training data is used. A gap between the two lines often signals overfitting, while convergence suggests good generalization.

The validation curve helps identify whether the model is underfitting or overfitting at different levels of model complexity. For example, small values of C lead to strong regularization, potentially underfitting the data, while large values of C reduce regularization and may cause overfitting.

These diagnostics allow us to make data-driven decisions about model configuration and dataset sufficiency.

Hands-on exercises

To illustrate these techniques, please reference the GitHub repository (`https://github.com/PacktPublishing/scikit-learn-Cookbook-Third-Edition`). You will use learning and validation curves to evaluate and improve model generalization. The following steps outline a general workflow:

1. Clone the GitHub repository and ensure all necessary libraries are installed.
2. Generate a classification dataset using scikit-learn.
3. Use `learning_curve()` to plot training versus validation scores across increasing training sizes.
4. Use `validation_curve()` to examine model accuracy across different values of C.
5. Plot both curves using Matplotlib.
6. Interpret results to determine whether the model is overfitting, underfitting, or generalizing well.
7. Use these insights to guide further data collection or hyperparameter tuning.

Practical exercises in cross-validation and evaluation

In this final section, we'll engage in practical exercises that involve building, tuning, and evaluating models using cross-validation and performance metrics. These exercises are designed to reinforce the concepts explored throughout the chapter, including model selection, hyperparameter tuning, and generalization evaluation. By completing these exercises, we'll solidify our understanding of how to effectively assess model performance and select the best model for real-world applications.

Exercise 1: Cross-validating a logistic regression model

We'll evaluate a logistic regression classifier using k-fold cross-validation and report multiple metrics.

Here are the implementation steps:

1. Load the libraries.
2. Load the dataset.
3. Cross-validate and collect metrics.

Exercise 2: Tuning hyperparameters with grid search

We'll perform hyperparameter tuning using `GridSearchCV` and compare the results.

Here are the implementation steps:

1. Load the libraries.
2. Load and split the dataset.
3. Perform grid search.
4. Evaluate on the test set.

Exercise 3: Assessing model generalization with learning and validation curves

We'll use `learning_curve()` and `validation_curve()` to visualize how model performance varies with training size and model complexity.

Here are the implementation steps:

1. Load the libraries.
2. Plot the learning curve.
3. Plot the validation curve.

Get This Book's PDF Version and Exclusive Extras

UNLOCK NOW

Scan the QR code (or go to packtpub.com/unlock). Search for this book by name, confirm the edition, and then follow the steps on the page.

Note: Keep your invoice handy. Purchases made directly from Packt don't require an invoice.

13

Deploying scikit-learn Models in Production

As we reach the end of this cookbook, it's time to bring the reality of **machine learning** (ML) in production into the spotlight. Everything we've covered up to this point is of little use in the business world if it just sits on your laptop. Models must be deployed in compute environments that allow for scalability and high throughput while still maintaining predictive performance at or above the business rules that govern them. Although we are only devoting a single chapter to this topic, you should keep in mind that production ML deployment, monitoring, benchmarking, and the **continuous integration/continuous deployment or deployment/continuous training** (CI/CD/CT) cycle (among other topics) make up the lion's share of real-world challenges for utilizing ML in business. Many of the considerations are non-technical as well: how do I determine how well a model needs to perform in order to achieve a given ROI; how do I know when I need to retrain my model; do I need to use different models or approaches for different customer categories or even geographic regions I operate in? Answers to these types of questions would require yet another textbook, if not several! So, for our purposes, we'll keep things simple with the hope that you continue your journey beyond this cookbook.

This final chapter covers the best practices for deploying scikit-learn models in production environments, including model serialization, scaling, and monitoring. The exercises involve setting up deployment pipelines and managing the model life cycle.

In this chapter, we're going to cover the following recipes:

- Overview of model deployment
- Serialization and persistence techniques
- Scaling models for production
- Monitoring and updating deployed models
- Managing the model life cycle
- Setting up deployment pipelines

Technical requirements

It is advisable to create a Python environment to safely isolate your work from other Python installations/libraries. See the GitHub repository for more details (`https://github.com/PacktPublishing/scikit-learn-Cookbook-Third-Edition`).

- Git >=2.46.x

- Python >=3.9.x

- Cloned the GitHub repository and Python environment built from the `requirements.txt` file

Overview of model deployment

Deploying a model means moving it from your development environment into production, so that real users or systems can access its predictions. Deployment involves preparing a reliable **artifact**, or model metadata, serving it with appropriate latency and throughput, and ensuring that it continues to perform well as the data evolves. In this recipe, we'll walk through the typical steps of packaging, exposing, and verifying a trained scikit-learn model in production-like conditions.

Getting ready

Before deployment, ensure you have a trained scikit-learn model and the necessary libraries installed:

1. Load the libraries:

```
import numpy as np
from sklearn.linear_model import LogisticRegression
from sklearn.datasets import make_classification
from joblib import dump, load
```

2. Create and train a simple model:

```
X, y = make_classification(
    n_samples=1000, n_features=20, random_state=2024)
clf = LogisticRegression()
clf.fit(X, y)
```

With our simple model trained, let's see how to save it for future use.

How to do it...

We'll persist the model to disk and simulate loading it in a new environment (*persist* is just a way of saying we'll save the ML model in an appropriate format for future use in a prediction setting):

1. Save the trained model using `joblib`:

   ```
   dump(clf, "model.joblib")
   ```

2. Load the model back:

   ```
   clf_loaded = load("model.joblib")
   ```

3. Make a prediction with the loaded model:

   ```
   incoming = np.random.rand(1, 20)
   print(clf_loaded.predict(incoming))
   ```

With only four lines of code, we are able to save, load, and test an ML model using Python's built-in functions.

How it works...

The `joblib` module is the recommended way to persist scikit-learn models; it handles NumPy arrays efficiently compared to standard `pickle`. Once exported to `.joblib`, the model can be uploaded to a production server and loaded by the same library versions. After loading, the model behaves identically to the original, allowing your client systems to fetch predictions reliably.

There's more...

Deploying a model often means serving it via REST APIs, batch pipelines, or even serverless functions. In high-throughput contexts, bulk prediction (i.e., predicting many samples at once and/or for many users at once) is far more efficient than one-at-a-time calls due to linear algebra optimizations in NumPy and scikit-learn.

Hands-on exercises

To illustrate these techniques, please reference the GitHub repository (`https://github.com/PacktPublishing/scikit-learn-Cookbook-Third-Edition`). You will engage in hands-on exercises on model deployment/serializing a model, loading it in a fresh environment, simulating a prediction endpoint, and comparing latency when serving single versus batch requests.

The following steps outline a general workflow:

1. Clone the GitHub repository and ensure all of the required libraries are installed.
2. Train and export a logistic regression model using `joblib`.
3. Simulate a client process that loads the model and requests predictions.
4. Measure prediction time for a single instance and for a batch.
5. Examine throughput and latency to assess serving performance.

Serialization and persistence techniques

Saving and reloading models is essential for production workflows—training usually happens once in a given CI/CD/CT cycle, but prediction must happen repeatedly. In this recipe, we'll demonstrate how to serialize models with both `pickle` and `joblib`, discuss security and versioning considerations, and show how third party formats such as **Open Neural Network Exchange** (**ONNX**) may be used for Python free environments.

Getting ready

You'll need libraries to train a model and tools to persist it in multiple formats:

1. Load the libraries:

```
import numpy as np
from sklearn.ensemble import RandomForestClassifier
from sklearn.datasets import make_classification
import pickle
from joblib import dump, load
```

2. Train a classifier:

```
X, y = make_classification(
    n_samples=500, n_features=15, random_state=2024)
rf = RandomForestClassifier(
    n_estimators=10, random_state=2024)
rf.fit(X, y)
```

Let's apply both serialization techniques to convert our models into Python arrays.

How to do it...

Applying serialization with both `pickle` and `joblib` is straightforward:

1. Serialize using `pickle`:

    ```
    with open("rf.pkl", "wb") as f:
        pickle.dump(rf, f)
    ```

2. Serialize using `joblib`:

    ```
    dump(rf, "rf.joblib")
    ```

3. Load the `pickle` model:

    ```
    with open("rf.pkl", "rb") as f:
        rf1 = pickle.load(f)
    ```

4. Load the `joblib` model:

    ```
    rf2 = load("rf.joblib")
    ```

5. Ensure identical behavior after loading:

    ```
    assert np.array_equal(rf.predict(X[:5]),
                          rf1.predict(X[:5]))
    assert np.array_equal(rf.predict(X[:5]),
                          rf2.predict(X[:5]))
    ```

The resulting output of each technique for serialization should produce the same model we stored earlier.

How it works...

Python's `pickle` library works for serializing objects but can struggle with large NumPy arrays inside estimators. `joblib.dump` and `joblib.load` are optimized for such cases and are the recommended serialization methods for scikit-learn models. Note, however, that trust is required when *unpickling*—never use untrusted files—and that models saved with one version of scikit-learn may break if loaded with a different version. For contexts where Python is *not* available, converters to ONNX or **Predictive Model Markup Language** (**PMML**) may be used, although these formats may not support all scikit-learn estimators.

> **Serialization**
>
> Once a model is trained and ready for persistence, serialization is a common technique for model storage that transforms your model into a byte stream—think of this as a series of binary values (i.e., "1s" and "0s") that represent your trained model in a decomposed data format readable by most computer systems regardless of their hardware, software, and so on. Serialization not only helps compress and store ML models, but also allows for their mobility, meaning you can deploy them in a variety of systems without having to worry about those systems having the same requirements as the one you trained it on.

There's more...

Model persistence best practices include snapshotting the code, library versions, training data, and validation outputs so you can evaluate consistency across scikit-learn upgrades or agreements from the original training environment. You may also use `cloudpickle` (`https://pypi.org/project/cloudpickle/1.1.1/`) when standard `pickle`/`joblib` serialization fails (e.g., with custom or dynamically generated estimators).

Hands-on exercises

To illustrate these techniques, please reference the GitHub repository (`https://github.com/PacktPublishing/scikit-learn-Cookbook-Third-Edition`). You will serialize models with both `pickle` and `joblib`, attempt restoring them in isolation, compare outputs, and explore exporting to ONNX with the skl2onnx package. The following steps outline a general workflow:

1. Clone the GitHub repository. Install dependencies.
2. Train a scikit-learn classifier.
3. Save copies in `.pkl` and `.joblib` formats.
4. Load them in separate Python sessions.
5. Verify predictive consistency.
6. Explore ONNX export and runtime prediction (if desired).

Scaling models for production

When deploying models in real-world environments, you may encounter large datasets, distributed infrastructure, or high inference demand. In this recipe, we'll explore techniques to scale model training and prediction, including leveraging `n_jobs`, `joblib` parallelism, connecting to external backends such as Dask (`https://www.dask.org/`), and designing for batch serving.

Getting ready

You'll need tools to run parallel inference and synthetic data to benchmark performance:

1. Load the libraries:

    ```
    import numpy as np
    from sklearn.datasets import make_classification
    from sklearn.ensemble import RandomForestClassifier
    from sklearn.model_selection import cross_val_score
    import time
    ```

2. Train a forest model on synthetic data:

    ```
    X, y = make_classification(
        n_samples=2000, n_features=50, random_state=2024)
    clf = RandomForestClassifier(
        n_estimators=100, n_jobs=-1, random_state=2024)
    clf.fit(X, y)
    ```

Next, let's try predicting on a random batch size of text data.

How to do it...

Next, let's test the model:

1. Measure single-batch latency:

    ```
    batch = np.random.rand(1000, 50)
    start = time.time()
    clf.predict(batch)
    print("Time:", time.time() - start)
    ```

2. Train with parallel cross-validation:

    ```
    scores = cross_val_score(
        RandomForestClassifier(n_estimators=50),
        X, y, cv=3, n_jobs=-1
    )
    print("CV Accuracy:", np.mean(scores))
    ```

3. (*Optional*) Use Dask as a joblib backend if available:

    ```
    # from dask.distributed import Client
    # from dask_ml.model_selection import GridSearchCV as daskGSCV
    ```

Dask is a powerful library for Python distributed computation, although newer versions of Python do allow parallelism.

How it works...

Many scikit-learn estimators support the n_jobs parameter for parallelization via joblib. For distributed environments, Dask can serve as an alternate joblib backend or support parallel *meta-estimators* for large workloads (basically, think of cloning your model several times across several compute/storage devices—like building an army of models). Batch serving—predicting large collections of inputs at once (i.e., in *batches*)—offers significantly better throughput than serving individual requests due to lower overhead and better CPU utilization.

There's more...

You may also use streaming or incremental training for models such as SGDClassifier using partial_fit when data arrives over time. In production, containerization (Docker), autoscaling, and GPU-backed feature serving (with cuML or PyTorch wrappers) can further enhance scalability. These are beyond the scope of this book, however, since GPUs can require significant configuration upfront for use in ML pipelines.

Hands-on exercises

To illustrate these techniques, please reference the GitHub repository (https://github.com/PacktPublishing/scikit-learn-Cookbook-Third-Edition). You will train models with different n_jobs values, benchmark batch versus single-instance predictions, and (optionally) explore using Dask as a backend. The following steps outline a general workflow:

1. Clone the GitHub repository and install any required dependencies.
2. Train and deploy a random forest with n_jobs=1, then with n_jobs=-1. Compare the latency.
3. Evaluate cross-validation runtime differences with these settings.
4. (*Optional*) Set up a Dask client and re-run a grid search or batch prediction.

Monitoring and updating deployed models

Once your model is live, its performance *will* degrade over time due to changes in input data distributions (*drift*) or external conditions. This is basically a given in any scenario where an ML model is used and is not unexpected. This is where the **CT** in **CI/CD/CT** comes into play. You may be familiar with the term **CI/CD or deployment**, which is a software engineering paradigm for building and releasing software. However, in an ML deployment, we must also consider **CT** for monitoring and managing models as they degrade. This recipe guides you through strategies to monitor deployed models, detect drift, and update (retrain or adjust) models to maintain reliability.

Getting ready

You'll simulate incoming batches of data and require incremental-capable models to experiment with:

1. Load the libraries:

    ```
    import numpy as np
    import matplotlib.pyplot as plt
    from sklearn.linear_model import SGDClassifier
    from sklearn.datasets import make_classification
    ```

2. Simulate initial training and streaming data:

    ```
    X_train, y_train = make_classification(
        n_samples=500, n_features=10, random_state=2024)
    X_pub, y_pub = make_classification(
        n_samples=200, n_features=10, random_state=2025)
    stream_batches = np.array_split(X_pub, 4)
    stream_labels = np.array_split(y_pub, 4)
    ```

In order to simulate streaming data, we will take our original arrays and split them using the NumPy library.

How to do it...

Next, let's train our model in batches to simulate data evolution:

1. Train an incremental `SGDClassifier` on initial data:

    ```
    clf = SGDClassifier(
        loss="log_loss", random_state=2024, warm_start=True)
    clf.partial_fit(
        X_train, y_train, classes=np.unique(y_train))
    ```

2. Monitor each incoming batch:

    ```
    batch_scores = []
    for xb, yb in zip(stream_batches, stream_labels):
        yf = clf.predict(xb)
        batch_scores.append(np.mean(yf == yb))
    ```

3. Trigger retraining when accuracy drops below the threshold (e.g., < 0.8):

    ```
    if min(batch_scores) < 0.8:
        clf.partial_fit(X_pub, y_pub)
    ```

4. Plot batch-by-batch accuracy:

```
plt.plot(batch_scores, marker="o")
plt.title("Batch Accuracy Over Time")
plt.xlabel("Batch Number")
plt.ylabel("Accuracy")
plt.grid(True)
plt.show()
```

Although there is a dip initially with accuracy in the first batch, it's to be expected that this could go either way. We'd expect the accuracy to increase over each consecutive batch, which appears to be the case.

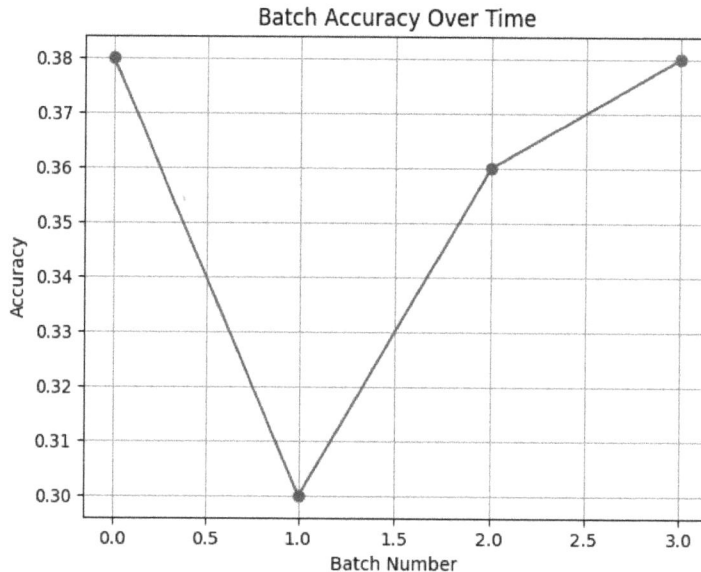

Figure 13.1 – Batch accuracy over time

Although we are only simulating three batches, we can see that the general trend is going up.

How it works...

For models that support `partial_fit` and `warm_start`, such as `SGDClassifier`, you can continue training as new data arrives. Monitoring batch accuracy provides a simple drift detector. If performance drops below a defined threshold, retraining the model—or updating it with streaming data—can restore accuracy. Visualizing accuracy trends enables easy interpretation of degradation.

There's more...

More sophisticated drift detection methods include monitoring distribution statistics or embedding inputs to calculate the **KL divergence** or statistical tests. Batch-level retraining may also be automated using control systems with alerting and rollback capabilities.

Hands-on exercises

To illustrate these techniques, please reference the GitHub repository (`https://github.com/PacktPublishing/scikit-learn-Cookbook-Third-Edition`). You will simulate streaming batches, train an incremental model, monitor its performance over time, and automate retraining when accuracy degrades. The following steps outline a general workflow:

1. Clone the GitHub repository and install the required environment.

2. Use an incremental model (e.g., `SGDClassifier`) and train on historical data.

3. Feed synthetic or real validation batches over time.

4. Track batch-by-batch performance and visualize trends.

5. Automate retraining when accuracy falls below your chosen threshold.

Managing the model life cycle

Managing a model's life cycle ensures it remains reliable, reproducible, and maintainable over time. Building ML models is never a *set it and forget it* procedure. All models deteriorate over time and become less effective at making predictions for a variety of reasons (i.e., data changes, prediction targets change, etc.). In this recipe, we cover versioning, reproducibility measures, document control, and ensuring consistency across training and serving environments.

Getting ready

You'll prepare a model-saving script and tools to snapshot metadata and validation outputs:

1. Load the libraries:

```
import numpy as np
from sklearn.ensemble import RandomForestClassifier
from sklearn.datasets import make_classification
from sklearn.datasets import load_iris
from sklearn.metrics import accuracy_score
from joblib import dump
import json
```

2. Train a model and simulate the versioning environment:

```
X, y = make_classification(
    n_samples=800, n_features=20, random_state=2024)
clf = RandomForestClassifier(
    n_estimators=50, random_state=2024)
clf.fit(X, y)
```

Now let's embed additional metadata when we save our model.

How to do it...

Saving model artifacts is necessary for model governance over time and helps us understand the *why* and the *what* behind its performance over time. Do the following:

1. Save the model artifact with the versioned filename:

```
version = "v1.0"
dump(clf, f"rf_{version}.joblib")
```

2. Save metadata about the training environment:

```
meta = {"version": version,"sklearn": "1.3.2",
        "numpy": str(np.__version__)}
with open(f"rf_{version}_metadata.json", "w") as f:
    json.dump(meta, f)
```

3. Capture the validation set performance snapshot:

```
Xv, yv = load_iris(return_X_y=True)
yv_pred = clf.predict(Xv)
val_acc = accuracy_score(yv, yv_pred)
with open(f"rf_{version}_val.txt", "w") as f:
    f.write(f"{val_acc:.4f}")
```

While this is a very simplified version of metadata's use case, there are many MLOps tools in existence that aid in creating far more robust documentation of models and their performance over time.

How it works...

The scikit-learn roadmap recommends snapshotting not only the model but also the code, library versions, and a small validation set with its predicted outputs, to ensure the model can be validated after future upgrades or porting. Storing metadata with each artifact helps trace back issues, roll back to previous versions, and ensure reproducibility.

There's more...

Model registries such as MLflow (`https://mlflow.org/`) and BentoML (`https://www.bentoml.com/`) offer automation for artifact storage, metadata tracking, and rollback capabilities. Even if you use such tools, snapshotting your dependencies and validation outputs remains a best practice.

Hands-on exercises

To illustrate these techniques, please reference the GitHub repository (`https://github.com/PacktPublishing/scikit-learn-Cookbook-Third-Edition`). You will version the saved model as an artifact, document its metadata, run validation checks post-deployment, and plan for rollbacks. The following steps outline a general workflow:

1. Clone the GitHub repository and set up your environment.

2. Train a model and assign a semantic version.

3. Save the model, metadata, and validation performance snapshot.

4. Simulate a scikit-learn upgrade or change, attempt to load the artifact, and validate predictions.

5. Record and compare results to detect consistency or deviation.

Setting up deployment pipelines

Deploying models reliably requires automation. As mentioned previously, since model performance can (and will) change over time, it's necessary to implement systems that can handle this without constant human intervention. In this recipe, we'll show how to integrate model serialization, validation checks, and serving logic into a CI/CD pipeline using scikit-learn constructs, enabling consistent transitions from development to production.

Getting ready

You'll need tools to train a pipeline, export it, and programmatically validate performance:

1. Load the libraries:

```
import numpy as np
from sklearn.datasets import make_classification
from sklearn.preprocessing import StandardScaler
from sklearn.linear_model import LogisticRegression
from sklearn.pipeline import Pipeline
from joblib import dump, load
from sklearn.metrics import accuracy_score
```

2. Create data and the pipeline:

```
X, y = make_classification(
    n_samples=500, n_features=10, random_state=2024)
pipe = Pipeline([
    ("scale", StandardScaler()),
    ("clf", LogisticRegression())
])
pipe.fit(X, y)
```

Python's `Pipeline` class is a very straightforward way to string together the necessary steps in data pipelines.

How to do it...

Let's add a conditional at the end of our pipeline to test an arbitrary threshold:

1. Export the entire pipeline:

```
dump(pipe, "pipeline.joblib")
```

2. Load the pipeline in the deployment environment:

```
prod_pipe = load("pipeline.joblib")
```

3. Simulate CI—validate accuracy on a test set:

```
Xt, yt = (
    np.random.rand(100, 10),
    np.random.randint(0, 2, 100)
)
acc = accuracy_score(yt, prod_pipe.predict(Xt))
print("Validation accuracy:", acc)
```

4. Conditionally deploy only if accuracy > threshold (e.g., > 0.8):

```
if acc > 0.8:
    print("Auto-deploy allowed")
else:
    print("Halt deployment and review")
```

Although we set an accuracy threshold of 80% here in the code, keep in mind that your thresholds will vary. There are countless factors to keep in mind when setting a standard threshold for determining whether or not a model needs to be retrained or replaced. Not all of these factors are purely from the ML realm either; in fact, most of them are dictated by business logic and rules.

How it works...

Using `Pipeline` ensures that preprocessing and prediction are tied together in a single object that can be validated as a unit and reused consistently across environments. This promotes repeatability and simplifies CI/CD/CT, because a single artifact includes the entire inference logic. Post-export, you can embed validation logic in your CI scripts to test the model against a small validation or canary set and only promote the model if it meets performance thresholds. This guards against *silent* regressions in deployed performance.

There's more...

CI/CD/CT workflows can be built using GitHub Actions, CircleCI (`https://circleci.com/`), or other tools, triggering retraining, serialization, validation, and deployment to cloud endpoints. Containerizing pipelines with Docker and versioning artifacts further increases reliability.

Hands-on exercises

To illustrate these techniques, please reference the GitHub repository (`https://github.com/PacktPublishing/scikit-learn-Cookbook-Third-Edition`). You'll create a preprocessing and model pipeline, save and load it as a single artifact, validate performance in simulated CI logic, and enforce deployment gating based on thresholds. The following steps outline a general workflow:

1. Clone the GitHub repository and install dependencies.
2. Build and train a scikit-learn pipeline with preprocessing and a classifier.
3. Serialize the pipeline into a single file.
4. Simulate a CI check by loading the pipeline and scoring it on a test dataset.
5. Enforce deployment conditions based on accuracy or other metric thresholds.

Practical exercises in model deployment

In this final section, we will engage in practical exercises that involve exporting and serving scikit-learn models, simulating live inference, and integrating monitoring and update strategies. These exercises are designed to consolidate our understanding of model deployment pipelines and demonstrate best practices for real-world ML operations. By the end of these exercises, we will have applied the full life cycle of model deployment using scikit-learn.

Exercise 1: Saving and reloading a model pipeline for deployment

In this exercise, we will serialize a trained model pipeline and reload it to simulate a production environment. This exercise ensures that preprocessing and inference logic are bundled together and reusable across environments.

The following are the implementation steps:

1. Load the libraries.
2. Create and train the pipeline.
3. Save and reload the pipeline.
4. Generate new predictions.

Exercise 2: Monitoring model accuracy over time

This exercise involves simulating streaming data and tracking a deployed model's performance on incoming batches to detect model degradation.

The following are the implementation steps:

1. Load the libraries.
2. Simulate the streaming setup.
3. Train and evaluate incrementally.
4. Plot batch accuracy.

Exercise 3: Automating deployment checks using validation thresholds

In this example, we'll simulate a CI/CD deployment check that evaluates whether a serialized model meets performance criteria before promoting it to production.

The following are the implementation steps:

1. Load the libraries.
2. Train and export the model.
3. Load and validate with test data.
4. Conditionally approve the deployment.

Get This Book's PDF Version and Exclusive Extras

UNLOCK NOW

Scan the QR code (or go to packtpub.com/unlock). Search for this book by name, confirm the edition, and then follow the steps on the page.

Note: Keep your invoice handy. Purchases made directly from Packt don't require an invoice.

14

Unlock Your Exclusive Benefits

Your copy of this book includes the following exclusive benefit:

- ☁ Next-gen Packt Reader
- 📄 DRM-free PDF/ePub downloads

Follow the guide below to unlock them. The process takes only a few minutes and needs to be completed once.

Unlock this Book's Free Benefits in 3 Easy Steps

Step 1

Keep your purchase invoice ready for *Step 3*. If you have a physical copy, scan it using your phone and save it as a PDF, JPG, or PNG.

For more help on finding your invoice, visit `https://www.packtpub.com/unlock-benefits/help`.

> **Note**
>
> If you bought this book directly from Packt, no invoice is required. After *Step 2*, you can access your exclusive content right away.

Step 2

Scan the QR code or go to `packtpub.com/unlock`.

On the page that opens (similar to *Figure 14.1* on desktop), search for this book by name and select the correct edition.

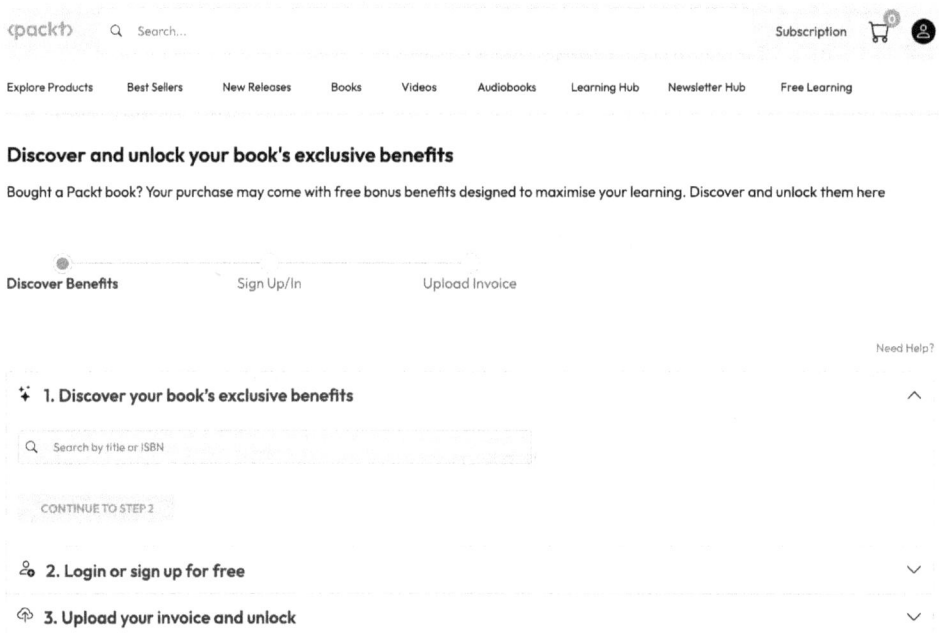

Figure 14.1 – Packt unlock landing page on desktop

Step 3

After selecting your book, sign in to your Packt account or create one for free. Then upload your invoice (PDF, PNG, or JPG, up to 10 MB). Follow the on-screen instructions to finish the process.

Need help?

If you get stuck and need help, visit
`https://www.packtpub.com/unlock-benefits/help`
for a detailed FAQ on how to find your invoices and more. This QR
code will take you to the help page.

Note

If you are still facing issues, reach out to `customercare@packt.com`.

Index

<packt>

packtpub.com

Subscribe to our online digital library for full access to over 7,000 books and videos, as well as industry leading tools to help you plan your personal development and advance your career. For more information, please visit our website.

Why subscribe?

- Spend less time learning and more time coding with practical eBooks and Videos from over 4,000 industry professionals

- Improve your learning with Skill Plans built especially for you

- Get a free eBook or video every month

- Fully searchable for easy access to vital information

- Copy and paste, print, and bookmark content

At www.packtpub.com, you can also read a collection of free technical articles, sign up for a range of free newsletters, and receive exclusive discounts and offers on Packt books and eBooks.

Other Books You May Enjoy

If you enjoyed this book, you may be interested in these other books by Packt:

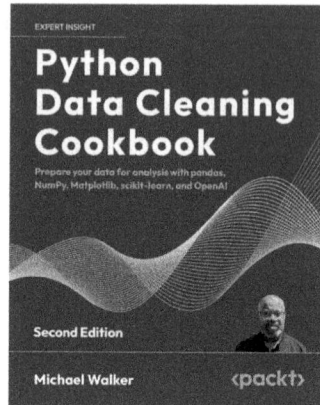

Python Data Cleaning Cookbook - Second Edition

Michael Walker

ISBN: 978-1-80323-987-3

- Using OpenAI tools for various data cleaning tasks
- Producing summaries of the attributes of datasets, columns, and rows
- Anticipating data-cleaning issues when importing tabular data into pandas
- Applying validation techniques for imported tabular data
- Improving your productivity in pandas by using method chaining
- Recognizing and resolving common issues like dates and IDs
- Setting up indexes to streamline data issue identification
- Using data cleaning to prepare your data for ML and AI models

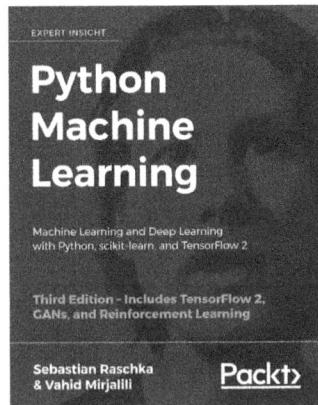

Python Machine Learning - Third Edition

Sebastian Raschka, Vahid Mirjalili

ISBN: 978-1-78995-575-0

- Master the frameworks, models, and techniques that enable machines to learn from data
- Use scikit-learn for machine learning and TensorFlow for deep learning
- Apply machine learning to image classification, sentiment analysis, intelligent web applications, and more
- Build and train neural networks, GANs, and other models
- Discover best practices for evaluating and tuning models
- Predict continuous target outcomes using regression analysis
- Dig deeper into textual and social media data using sentiment analysis

Packt is searching for authors like you

If you're interested in becoming an author for Packt, please visit `authors.packt.com` and apply today. We have worked with thousands of developers and tech professionals, just like you, to help them share their insight with the global tech community. You can make a general application, apply for a specific hot topic that we are recruiting an author for, or submit your own idea.

Share Your Thoughts

Now you've finished *scikit-learn Cookbook*, we'd love to hear your thoughts! Scan the QR code below to go straight to the Amazon review page for this book and share your feedback or leave a review on the site that you purchased it from.

`https://packt.link/r/1-836-64445-0`

Your review is important to us and the tech community and will help us make sure we're delivering excellent quality content.